OREGON FREE

A GUIDE TO THE BEST OF THE
STATE'S COST FREE ATTRACTIONS

Other books by KiKi Canniff

SAUVIE ISLAND
A Step Back in Time

WASHINGTON FREE
A Guide to the Best of the State's Cost Free Attractions

FREE CAMPGROUNDS OF WASHINGTON & OREGON

OREGON FREE

A GUIDE TO THE BEST OF THE
STATE'S COST FREE ATTRACTIONS

By KiKi Canniff

Illustrations by Janora Bayot.

Ki² Enterprises
P.O. Box 13322
Portland, Oregon 97213

Library of Congress Cataloging-in-Publication Data

Canniff, KiKi, 1948–
    Oregon free.

    Includes index.
    1. Oregon--Description and travel--1981-   Guide-
books. 1. Title.
F874.3.C35 1986   917.95'0443   85-14788
ISBN 0-9608744-5-3 (pbk.)

ISBN #0-9608744-5-3

Ki² Enterprises
P.O. Box 13322
Portland, Oregon 97213

TABLE OF CONTENTS

HOW TO USE THIS BOOK

This book is designed to be used in conjunction with an Oregon state highway map. For simplicity the state has been divided into five vertical sections, each with its own map. Attractions have then been grouped alphabetically by city. All of the cities shown offer nearby free attractions.

The following symbols have been used to categorize the attractions featured in this book. Each item falls into at least one category with many being marked by more than one symbol.

Natural and man-made attractions that are unique -- waterfalls, lava caves, hot springs, awesome views, gardens, wildlife areas, free ferry rides, clamming, parks and national forests.

Historical attractions -- old buildings, covered bridges, historical sites, pioneer and/or Native American exhibits and bygone towns are all covered by this symbol.

Stretch your legs! Hiking trails, exercise tracks, tennis courts, bicycle paths and other activity orientated places.

Museums

Tours . . . industrial - auto - walking

Of interest to rockhounds

Art galleries . . . exhibits . . . statues . . . sculpture . . . fountains

Annual event

INTRODUCTION

Oregon Free was written to aid you in viewing this beautiful state in its non-commercial state. So many of the state's treasures often go unnoticed because no dollar signs or neon lights mark their existence. Natural wonders, covered bridges, Oregon heritage, museums, gardens, art, nature, area festivities, tours and more lie awaiting your discovery across the state. All for free.

Many cost free sights are maintained by volunteer labor. This often comes in the form of just picking up after yourself and sometimes those who proceeded you. Museums require a regular staff and donations are heartily encouraged.

This book was first put together after months and months of active research. Many people across the state gave freely of their time and knowledge so that all might enjoy Oregon's free bounty. They're eager to help you too. Whenever you visit a new town stop in at the local Chamber of Commerce office and visit the Forest Service facilities for area information. (The section titled Important Addresses will enable you to write ahead for information.)

Although everything listed herein has been carefully verified time often brings changes. If you find any listed attraction charging a fee please drop a line to the publisher so that future printings can delete the attraction. If you chance on something that was missed let us know that too so we can check it out for future printings.

OREGON STATE MAP

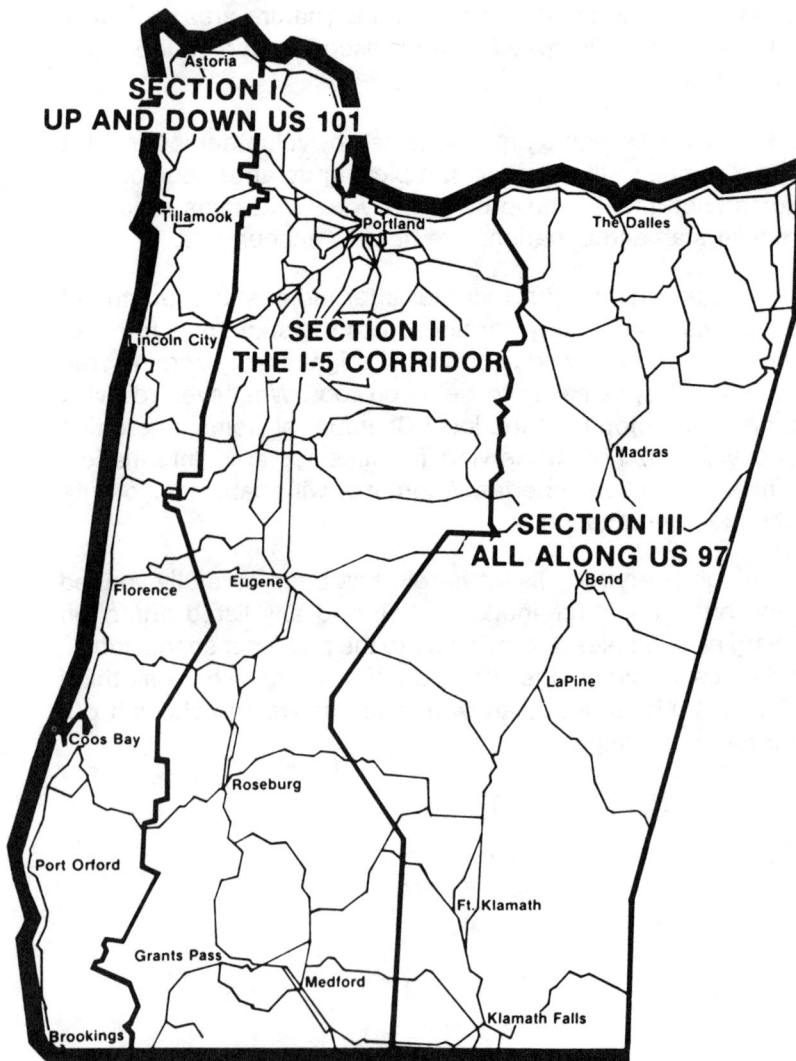

Astoria

SECTION I
UP AND DOWN US 101

Tillamook

Portland

The Dalles

Lincoln City

SECTION II
THE I-5 CORRIDOR

Madras

SECTION III
ALL ALONG US 97

Florence   Eugene   Bend

LaPine

Coos Bay

Roseburg

Port Orford

Ft. Klamath

Grants Pass

Medford

Klamath Falls

Brookings

Fine lines indicate major highways.

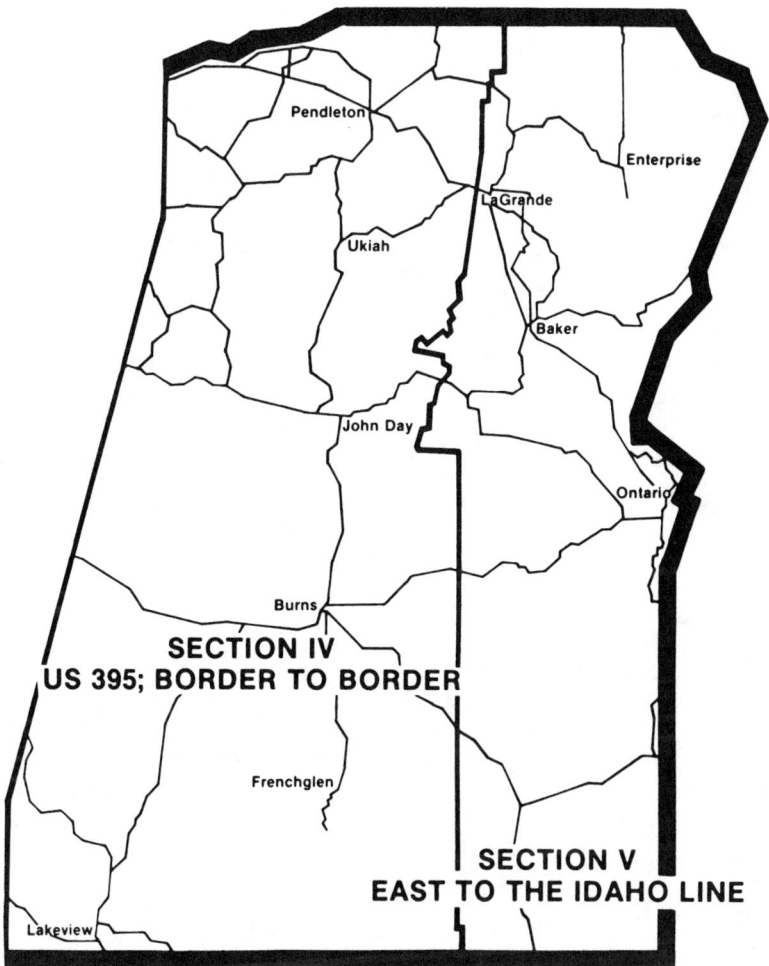

Pendleton

Enterprise

LaGrande

Ukiah

Baker

John Day

Ontario

Burns

SECTION IV
US 395; BORDER TO BORDER

Frenchglen

SECTION V
EAST TO THE IDAHO LINE

Lakeview

SECTION I
UP AND DOWN U.S. HIGHWAY 101

The Oregon Coast is a special place where the scenery is as varied as the grains of sand along the shore. Flat, open beaches rapidly change to abrupt stretches of rocky headlands and back again. The weather is as varied as the land. A heavy fog can move in at a moments notice, but often that curtain only extends inland a few miles and a jaunt into the countryside provides sunshine and smiles.

But sunny weather isn't always the best weather for the Oregon Coast. Storms send spray and foam furiously pummelling against land that has held its own for millions of years. Each new wave brings with it a part of the sea. Driftwood, glass floats, remains of sunken ships and untold curiosities are brought to shore during storms and heavy winds. The early beachcomber is often rewarded heavily.

Tidal pools offer a look at life beneath the water. Starfish, mussels, sea urchins and anemones can be easily discovered. These pools serve as nature's gardens. By law and common courtesy these pools must remain undisturbed but the exhileration of finding a window into the world beneath the sea is unbeatable.

Japanese glass net floats are probably the most highly prized find for beachcombers. These balls break loose from fishing nets and are carried along by the Japanese Current. They often travel the ocean for two to four years and cover thousands of miles before washing ashore. They vary in size from tiny to huge while colors range from sea green to blues or a deep wine red. The best time of year for hunting glass floats is between late fall and early spring when easterly winds and high tides bring them ashore. The competition is great so it is often a case of being there at just the right time.

Whale watching is another coastal pleasure. Migration of the California gray whale takes place from November to March. Traveling to lagoons along the Central and Southern Pacific Coastline of Baja, Mexico from the Arctic they carry on a tradition that goes back millions of years.

Coastal headlands that jut out into the ocean offer excellent vantage points for early morning vigils. Most often the first thing seen is the "blow" when a whale exhales water up to 12' into the air. By following a pattern of blows you may soon be rewarded with the sight of a whale's head and back or the raised tale flukes as it begins a deep dive. Whales generally travel in groups. Hours of scanning the horizon may reap all of its rewards in a short time as a group rises out of the water creating spectacular splashing and glimpses of their enormous bodies.

Just walking the coastal shore provides one of Oregon's greatest free treasures. Clamming is fun for everyone and minus tides are the best time for digging. Beaches from Tillamook Head to the Columbia River are generally open from September to mid-July. Surf fishing does not require a license either. In this section I have tried to supply a guide to the best coastal spots as well as areas where you can find inland activities when you're ready for a change.

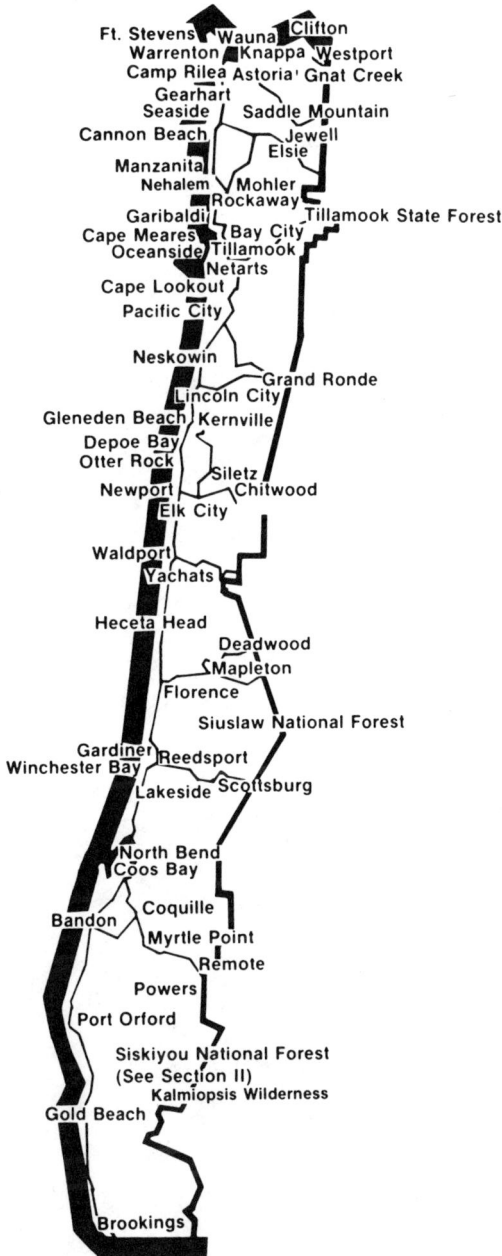

Ft. Stevens Wauna Clifton
Warrenton Knappa Westport
Camp Rilea Astoria Gnat Creek
Gearhart
Seaside Saddle Mountain
Cannon Beach Jewell
Elsie
Manzanita
Nehalem Mohler
Rockaway
Garibaldi Tillamook State Forest
Cape Meares Bay City
Oceanside Tillamook
Netarts
Cape Lookout
Pacific City

Neskowin
Grand Ronde
Lincoln City
Gleneden Beach Kernville
Depoe Bay
Otter Rock
Siletz
Newport Chitwood
Elk City

Waldport
Yachats

Heceta Head
Deadwood
Mapleton
Florence
Siuslaw National Forest
Gardiner Reedsport
Winchester Bay
Lakeside Scottsburg

North Bend
Coos Bay
Coquille
Bandon
Myrtle Point
Remote
Powers
Port Orford
Siskiyou National Forest
(See Section II)
Kalmiopsis Wilderness
Gold Beach

Brookings

17

ASTORIA

ART GALLERIES

Clatsop Community College, at the east end of Lexington Avenue, offers a chance to view local work in their Art Center Gallery. The Astoria phone book will reveal the locations of other small local galleries.

ASTORIA COLUMN

This 125' tower commands a sweeping view of both the Columbia River and the Pacific Ocean. It sits atop Coxcomb Hill with all of Astoria's waterfront spread out below. The exterior is decorated with a pictorial frieze. Inside, steps lead upward to the viewing platform at its top.

This historic monument was commissioned in 1926 by the Great Northern Railroad. To reach it you just follow Coxcomb Drive through Astoria to its top.

ASTORIA REGATTA

The Astoria Regatta is one of the longest-running community happenings in the Pacific Northwest. The festival dates back to 1894. Many related events are cost free. Festivities include three parades - children's, boat and grand floral, and races range from bathtub and tricycle to hydroplane and sailboat. These and other special events are topped off with a waterfront fireworks display.

BICYCLE ROUTES

To avid cyclists Astoria is known as the western terminus for the 4200 mile Bikecentennial Route. The less experienced rider will probably prefer the six miles of maintained bicycle trails located in Fort Stevens State Park.

COAST GUARD BUOY DEPOT

This Coast Guard installation was built in 1874 to provide service to navigational aids in both the Columbia River and along the coast. Several Coast Guard vessels are based here. The depot is located along Tongue Point.

HISTORIC HOMES

Within a 16 block area near downtown Astoria you can view over 3 dozen pre-1900 buildings. A tour between 8th and 17th Streets and Exchange and Grand will take you past 43 buildings of historical note. Except for the Flavel House all belong to private individuals and can only be viewed from the street.

441 Eighth Street (1883)
This is the Flavel House. For a small charge you can tour the inside as well. This building houses the Clatsop County Historical Museum and is considered to be one of the finest examples of Victorian architecture in Oregon.

765 Exchange Street (1863)
This home was built for the family of Captain Flavel's wife, Mary.

817 Exchange (1852)
This is one of the very oldest buildings in Astoria. It's basic structure is made of cedar.

788 Franklin (1884)

584 Eighth Street (1885)

818 Grand Avenue (1885)
Located one block up the hill.

828 Franklin Avenue (1885)
This was once a wing on the corner house.

960 Franklin Avenue (1888)

989 Franklin Avenue (1870)

656 Eleventh Street (1897)

674 Eleventh Street (1897)

690 Eleventh Street (1897)

1167 Grand Avenue (1885)

591 Twelfth Street (1895)

1229 Franklin Avenue (1870)

1243 Franklin Avenue (1875)

1278 Franklin Avenue (1898)
The addition was added in 1913.

1294 Franklin Avenue (1892)

1337 Franklin Avenue (1852)
This is the oldest house in Astoria and one of the oldest
homes in the state. It was originally built in East Astoria
and brought here by barge in 1862.

1370 Franklin Avenue (1892)

1388 Franklin Avenue (1867)

1393 Franklin Avenue (1879)

637 Fourteenth Street (1879)
This house was originally the south wing of the Franklin
Avenue home. It was detached in 1900 when the home
was remodeled.

1410 Franklin Avenue (1869)

636 Fourteenth Street (1895)

698 Fifteenth Street (1865)
This house has been moved. It originally stood on the
corner of Fourteenth and Franklin.

672 Fifteenth Street (1880)

1543 Exchange Street (1880)
This apartment complex is made up of parts from two of
Astoria's finest old homes.

1585 Exchange Street (1885)

637 Sixteenth Street (1883)
This was originally the rectory for the Grace Episcopal
Church.

1583 Franklin Avenue (1868)

1555 Franklin Avenue (1885)
Grace Episcopal Church is the oldest church building in
Astoria in continuous use.

1681 Franklin Avenue (1870)

690 Seventeenth Street (1893)

1711 Grand Avenue (1890)

1687 Grand Avenue (1880)

1661 Grand Avenue (1886)

1643 Grand Avenue (1893)

1607 Grand Avenue (1890)

1588 Grand Avenue (1897)

1574 Grand Avenue (1888)

1573 Grand Avenue (1885)

836 Fifteenth Street (1883)

THE WATERFRONT

There's a lot to see during a walk along the city's waterfront. A good place to start is at the Astoria Maritime Park
at the foot of 17th Street. Here you can see the Columbia
Lightship on display. (There is a charge to go inside the
Lightship).

At 9th and Exchange, a monument commemorates the two fires which brought near ruin to Astoria. The first was in 1883; the second in 1922. These two fires leveled 40 square downtown blocks.

The Astoria Bridge was built in 1966 to replace the ferry system, then operating between Oregon and Washington. It marked the completion of a continuous highway system running from Canada to Mexico. A toll bridge, it is the longest continuous truss bridge in the world. The West End Mooring Basin below is an excellent place for a close up look at both private and commercial fishing vessels.

In a city like Astoria, the waterfront is the very heartbeat of the city. The port docks were built in 1914 and handle commerce for all parts of the world. Logs and wheat are the principal exports.

At the waterfront's west end, you will find charred pilings left behind by the 1922 fire which brought total destruction to the city's commercial area.

US CUSTOMS HOUSE MARKER

Just east of Astoria on US 30, an official marker notes the location of the first customs office established west of the Rocky Mountains. Established in 1848 it was destroyed by fire 61 years later.

(East of the City)

LEWIS & CLARK NATIONAL WILDLIFE REFUGE

Five miles east of Astoria, 35,000 acres of tidelands, open water, sand bars and islands make up the Lewis & Clark National Wildlife Refuge. These islands are accessible only by boat but can viewed from US 30.

They provide wintering grounds for over 3,000 Whistling Swans, 2,000 Canada Geese and over 50,000 other waterfowl and shorebirds.

FORT CLATSOP
NATIONAL MEMORIAL

This is a reconstruction of Fort Clatsop. Here Captain William Clark of the Lewis & Clark expedition prepared many of the maps from their journeys. Stop at the exhibit room for an audio-visual presentation of the fort's history.

During the summer, members of the park staff hold demonstrations in period costume of frontier skills used at Fort Clatsop during the winter of 1805-1806. Take a stroll along the trails to the expedition's canoe landing and spring. Picnic tables are available just west of the parking areas.

Location: 6 miles southwest of Astoria off US 101.
Hours: Summer 8:00 a.m. to 8:00 p.m. daily.
Winter 8:00 a.m. to 5:00 p.m. daily.

LOGGING DRY SORT YARD
OBSERVATION TOWER

If you take the US 101 alternate route along the Lewis and Clark River, stop at the Crown Zellerbach dry sort yard. Here, they have erected an observation tower where visitors can see logs sorted for rafting to sawmills and to the Port of Astoria.

KLASKANINE PARK & FISH HATCHERY

Klaskanine Park is a lovely spot for a quiet picnic. It is located 12 miles southeast of Astoria on State 202. Nearby, you will find the Klaskanine Fish Hatchery where fall chinook and coho salmon are raised.

SIGFIDSON FARM

You can stop for a picnic 10 miles out of Astoria at this lovely spot. It is located adjacent to the Klaskanine River on State 202.

YOUNGS RIVER FALLS COUNTY PARK

Youngs River Falls Park is located 15 miles south of Astoria along Youngs River Loop Road. The river drops nearly 100 feet here into a cool shaded flatland open to the public for fishing, hiking and swimming. This has been a popular picnic spot since 1889 when it was the location of a pulp mill.

BANDON

ANNUAL CRANBERRY FESTIVAL

Bandon is the Cranberry Capital of Oregon and in late September, they celebrate the fact with their annual cranberry festival. It all begins on Saturday morning with a parade. Other public events include a fair, art show and races.

Another time to visit this area is during the cranberry harvest. Late each fall the bogs are flooded and the bright red berries shaken from the vines to float to the surface. The berries are then pushed with large rakes toward a submerged hopper and loaded by conveyors into trucks. With over 900 acres of cranberry bogs in the Bandon area, a visit at the right time of year can be both colorful and rewarding. Cranberries grown around Bandon are prized by commercial canners because of their deep red color.

BANDON BEACH LOOP ROAD

The Bandon Beach Loop Road provides a scenic drive along the beach area that includes both the North & South Jetty. At Face Rock Viewpoint you can view a rock formation which has been shaped by battering seas to resemble the head of a sleeping man. This road has many beach accesses and begins at US 101 and 11th Avenue.

BANDON HARBOR

The Bandon Harbor is a great place to watch lumber barges, dredges, tug boats, commercial fishing vessels, sail boats and other pleasure craft come and go. Walk down on a summer evening to Bandon Seafood Fisheries loading dock to see huge catches of salmon, bottom fish and shrimp unloaded. This area is known as Old Town. The waterfront retains the flavor of historic Bandon. A variety of tempting shops can be found here.

BANDON HISTORICAL SOCIETY
MUSEUM

The Bandon Historical Society Museum is located on 1st Street in Old Town. It offers a large collection of memorabilia representing early shipping, logging, pioneer and Indian life in the area. A large photograph collection is also housed there plus a slide/tape program on shipbuilding. The main exhibit changes quarterly.

COQUILLE VALLEY DAIRY COOP

At the Coquille Valley Dairy Coop the annual cheese production is over 2 million pounds. Cheese making in the Coquille Valley began around 1880. In 1939 the local dairymen formed the Coquille Valley Dairy Cooperative and today their plant is considered to be one of the finest small cheese plants on the west coast. They maintain traditional vat-type production using hand processing.

Stop for a visit and watch as the cheese is made. A color slide presentation fills in with all the facts. They are open to the public year round Monday thru Saturday, 1:00 p.m. to 4:00 p.m. During the summer they open up at 10:00 a.m. To find the Coop simply head north on US 101.

RIVERS END ART GALLERY

The Rivers End Art Gallery has a large exhibit of sea related paintings. It is located at Michigan Avenue and US 101.

TENNIS COURTS

You will find public tennis courts in back of the high school gym on Ninth Street.

(North of the City)

BULLARDS BEACH
STATE PARK

The entrance to Bullards Beach State Park is just half mile north of the Coquille River Bridge on US 101. Trails, picnic facilities, jetty and surf fishing and beachcombing are just a few of the attractions offered here. The 1200 acre park is bordered on the south by the Coquille River. This was considered prime gold country in 1853 when hordes of gold seekers swarmed all over the area.

The Coquille River Lighthouse lends atmosphere to the area. It has become one of the coast's most photographed sites. Built in 1896, it was recently restored and is open to the public during the day.

SEVEN DEVILS ROAD

Seven Devils Road winds through the rural countryside between Bandon and Charleston, as it makes it's way between US 101 and the ocean shore. At the water's edge, you will be brought to Whiskey Run and **Merchant's Beach, also known as Seven Devils Wayside, where rockhounds delight in finding agatized myrtle and other woods, banded agates and flower jaspers. Agate Beach is another great rockhounding area.**

You can pick up the loop road just north of Bandon. After about 10 miles, you'll find yourself just outside Charleston.

BANDON FISH HATCHERY

One mile east of Bandon you can visit the Bandon State Fish Hatchery. You can tour the hatchery where thousands of fish from teeny minnows to huge salmon, steelhead and trout can be viewed.

BANDON BEACH

Bandon Beach, at 11th Avenue and US 101, is quite picturesque and makes an ideal place to capture a sunset. Smooth white surf, jetties, sea gulls, spouting whales, darting seals, sea parrots and pelicans all add to its beauty.

OREGON MYRTLEWOOD FACTORY

Visitors can watch skilled craftsmen at work at the Oregon Myrtlewood Factory 6 miles south of Bandon on US 101. Call 347-2500 to arrange for a tour.

PACIFIC MYRTLEWOOD

Viewing stations allow the public to watch as myrtlewood is turned into Oregon treasures. Pacific Myrtlewood is located 7 miles south of Bandon on US 101. Tours can be arranged by calling 347-2200.

BAY CITY

ART & DICK'S SAUSAGE

Public tours are available at Art & Dick's Sausage daily from 9:00 a.m. to 7:00 p.m. except Sunday when they open at 10:00 a.m. Here you will have the opportunity to see how sausage, jerky, smoked meats and pepper bacon are processed.

BROOKINGS

ANNUAL AZALEA FESTIVAL

Each year Brookings holds their annual Azalea Festival over the Memorial Day weekend. Events include a parade, quilt display, flower show, arts & crafts fair, old time fiddlers contest, boat parade and more!

AZALEA STATE PARK

This park is in full bloom from April through June with azaleas of all sizes. Some of the plants found here are over 300 years old. Located just outside the city limits, the park also offers trails, picnic tables and running water.

CHETCO VALLEY HISTORICAL
SOCIETY MUSEUM

The Chetco Valley Historical Society Museum is housed in an old stagecoach way station/trading post. This is the oldest standing house in the Brookings area and is filled with pioneer relics. One room contains cases of cameras and WWI keepsakes, another a patchwork quilt dated 1844 and still another has indian baskets and arrowheads.

Location: 15461 Museum Road

Hours: Summer - Wednesday through Sunday, Noon to 5:00 p.m.
Winter - Friday, Saturday and Sunday, 9:00 a.m. to 5:00 p.m.

Donations accepted.

NATIONAL CHAMPION CYPRESS TREE

Right next to the Chetco Valley Historical Society Museum, take the short flight of stairs leading up from the highway for a chance to view the world's largest cypress tree. The trunk of this tree is more than 27 feet around.

PELICAN BAY ARTS ASSOCIATION GALLERY

The Pelican Bay Arts Association offer four season shows from spring to autumn. The artists here are also the staff members so it provides you with a chance to talk with the creators. The gallery is located at US 101 and Hoffeldt in the Harbor area.

(North of the City)

S.H. BOARDMAN STATE PARK

This 11 mile long stretch of land lies along US 101 just north of Brookings. The park has 3 main areas with parking, picnic facilities, drinking water, restrooms and lots of beautiful coastal hiking.

There are several short trails including one at Indian Beach that winds through wind dwarfed spruce to reveal a sand dune protected by steep rocky cliffs. This was once a popular place where Indians came to catch shell-fish and make arrowheads.

At Whale's Head Cove, you'll find a large sea stack which gets it's name because it spouts like a surfacing whale. Lone Ranch Creek and Arch Rock are two other popular places to stop.

HARRIS BEACH STATE PARK

Harris Beach State Park is 2 miles north of Brookings. From here you can watch birds, as they gather around Goat Island, a popular rookery located about a half mile offshore.

LOEB STATE PARK

Ten miles northeast of Brookings, you'll find Loeb State Park along the Chetco River. This 320 acre park contains a grove of redwoods considered to be the most northerly stand in the U.S. It also contains a large grove of myrtlewood trees which serves as the park's picnic area. Running water and swimming facilities make this a great place to stop, especially when the coast is blanketed with fog.

PALMER BUTTE RECREATION SITE

Just northeast of Brookings the Palmer Butte Recreation Site offers a spectacular view and a few quiet picnic sites.

(South of the City)

STRAHM'S LILIES

For over 20 years, Strahm's Lily Farm has cultivated the commercial lily just south of Brookings. They are in full bloom from late May all the way through August. The fields are tinted in colors ranging from white, yellow, brown and pink to deep red. The blooms are often from 6 to 12 inches across. Strahm's is at 15723 Oceanview Drive in Harbor.

Other lily farms are located in the area and a drive through the countryside during the summer will yield colorful views.

WINCHUCK RECREATION AREA

Winchuck Recreation Area is operated by the U.S. Forest Service. It is located 10 miles southeast of Brookings and offers a few picnic tables in a primitive setting.

CAMP RILEA

CLATSOP PLAINS PIONEER
PRESBYTERIAN CHURCH

At the Camp Rilea cutoff from US 101, you will find the Clatsop Plains Pioneer Presbyterian Church. This is the oldest continuous Presbyterian Church west of the Rocky Mountains.

The original church building was finished in 1851. Strong winds brought it down in 1872. A replica of this pioneer building can be seen in the Fellowship room of the new church. The model was made before the turn of the century, from the four posts on which the 1851 church stood. The new church was built over 50 years ago and also houses the original pulpit which was made from a cedar log that washed up on the beach at Clatsop Plains in 1850. For over 40 years a 40 foot Daffodil Cross has been planted each spring on the slope in front of the church to celebrate the coming of Easter. It makes an awesome sight.

The cemetery behind the church received it's first burial in 1849. It holds the graves of many local pioneers.

CANNON BEACH

ARTSGIVING

Twice each year Cannon Beach hosts Artsgiving. This showing of local arts and crafts happens in November and April. Contact the Cannon Beach Chamber of Commerce for the exact date.

CANNON BEACH ART GALLERIES

Cannon Beach has more art galleries than almost any other Oregon Coastal town. At last count there were over a dozen, each with it's own slant on displaying work done by local artists and crafters.

CANNON BEACH CITY PARK

Away from the ocean this small park has tennis courts, picnic tables and a ball field.

CANNON BEACH SAND SCULPTURE CONTEST

The date of this annual event is dictated by the tides. Entrants are given three hours to create their own sandcastle. The masterpieces take a variety of shapes. Judging and viewing hours are from 10:00 a.m. to 1:00 p.m. when the grand finale begins, as the rising tide eats away at the days endeavors, eventually to wash them away until they will be rebuilt again next year. Contact the Cannon Beach Chamber of Commerce for the exact date of this early summer contest.

DICKENS FESTIVAL

Each December the Dickens Festival adds a festive touch to the town's activities. Almost everyone dresses for the occasion and a local lamplighter makes his rounds each evening to light the kerosene street lights.

ECOLA STATE PARK

The Tillamook Rock Lighthouse and Haystack Rock are both in full view at Ecola State Park. The park can be reached by following the signs just off US 101 at Cannon Beach's north entrance. There is a minimum charge on weekends and holidays.

The park runs from Tillamook Head, just south of Seaside, to Chapman Point, near Cannon Beach. It includes 6 miles of ocean beaches and over 1,100 acres. Popular spots include Indian Beach, a great surfing beach; and the sea lion rookery just offshore. When the sea is calm, you can hear them quite plainly. Wildlife is plentiful. Deer and elk seem almost tame and squirrels and chipmunks are always in evidence.

A six-mile trail traverses Tillamook Head from Indian Beach to Seaside. From here you can get a good view of the 1879 lighthouse. This building has been continually hammered by pounding seas and violent storms. Large rocks have been tossed through lights and walls. The lighthouse was decommissioned in 1957.

ECOLA CREEK

According to the journals of Lewis and Clark, it was here that Captain William Clark brought Sacajawea to view a beached whale. The explorers purchased a portion of the blubber for their expedition. Clark named the creek Ecola which means big fish.

Located near the north end of town, Ecola Creek runs into the ocean creating a great playground for children or anyone tired of the ocean's beat.

HAYSTACK ROCK

Haystack Rock is the world's third largest monolith. This 235 foot rock is under constant change as the sea pounds and swirls around it's base. It is a National Bird Sanctuary. The rocky crags provide shelter and a nesting ground for gulls and sea birds. During low tide, it is accessible to man and the surrounding tidal pools can be found alive with starfish, small crabs, fish, sea anemones and an occasional baby octopus or jelly fish. It is a sanctuary and the removal of living creatures, other than mussels, from these pools is prohibited.

(North of the City)

CLARK'S VIEWPOINT

This viewpoint towers 1138 feet above the sea and was mentioned in the journals of Lewis and Clark. It is located along the hiking trail running between Indian Beach and Seaside, directly east of Tillamook Rock.

(South of the City)

ARCADIA BEACH WAYSIDE

Arcadia Beach Wayside is located 1.5 miles south of Cannon Beach. Picnic facilities, restrooms and beach access make it a popular coastal stop.

ARCH CAPE CREEK

Two miles past Hug Point State Park, just before the tunnel through the mountains, you'll find Arch Cape Creek. This beach offers an excellent spot for the gathering of driftwood. Turn right on Leech Street for parking near the beach.

CANNON BEACH CANNON

This rusty relic washed ashore in 1846 when the U.S. Schooner Shark sank offshore. It brought with it a name for the town. You can view the cannon 5 miles south of Cannon Beach, near Arch Cape.

HUG POINT STATE PARK

When early pioneers used the beach here as their road it was passable only at low tide. Travelers were forced to hug the cliffs in order to keep their wagons from ending up in the sea, henceforth the name. Roads over the hills did not appear until the late 1930's.

This small state park is located on US 101, four miles south of Cannon Beach. A walk around the area can reveal one or more of the natural caves found here. Picnic facilities and public restrooms make it a convenient place to stop and stretch your legs.

OSWALD WEST STATE PARK

Ten miles south of Cannon Beach, you can visit a park made up of virgin forests and long reaches of rocky headlands pierced with sea caves and teeming with marine life.

Several trails lead from the parking areas along US 101. The trail to the top of the cape begins at the view area and winds it's way through a lush rain forest. At the end of your hike, you will be treated to a view of a spouting horn.

Short Sands Bay has a lovely beach and is reputed to have been a popular haven for buccaneers. Often referred to as Smuggler's and Pirate's Cove, rumors say the crew of one wrecked Spanish Galleon came ashore to hide their treasures on the slopes of nearby Neahkahnie Mountain.

SILVER POINT VIEWPOINT

This viewpoint is located at the south end of Cannon Beach and provides an excellent place to enjoy the ocean's beauty.

TOLOVANA PARK WAYSIDE

Near the south end of Cannon Beach, on alternate US 101, the Tolovana Beach Wayside offers easy access to the beach for swimming, fishing or beachcombing. Restrooms, drinking water and even a few picnic tables are located here.

CAPE LOOKOUT

This year round park has everything, trails, bathhouse, outside theatre, fishing, rockhounding, swimming and picnic facilities. There is a minimum charge on weekends and holidays.

Located just off US 101, it is 12 miles southwest of Tillamook. It's 1500 acres contain nearly every geological feature found along the entire Oregon coast. Over 150 species of birds are found here.

A 2½ mile trail takes you from the parking area to the south side of the cape for a view of Cascade head. At the trail's end, you reach the tip of the cape and one of the most spectacular spots along the Oregon coast. At it's base, the ocean has carved a large cave into the cape.

A shorter, self-guided nature trail begins near the registration booth and walk the ¼ mile trail. It will guide you through an area of typical coastal rain forest vegetation.

CAPE MEARES

ANDERSON'S VIEWPOINT

Located just south of Cape Meares State Park, you can get a panoramic view of Netarts Bay and Cape Meares from Anderson's Viewpoint.

CAPE MEARES STATE PARK

This is a great place to stretch your legs. Take the trail leading to the Octopus Tree. This tree was once featured in **Ripley's Believe It or Not** as "Seven Trees in One". It is located just a short distance from the parking lot.

A short hike in the opposite direction will take you to the Cape Meares Lighthouse. The original site was to be at Cape Lookout, 10 miles farther south; but materials were wrongfully delivered here in the roadless wilderness of 1890 and the installation site had to be changed by Congress.

Sea Lions can often be seen frolicking on the rocks below. Viewpoints offer an opportunity for photographing them, and the jagged sea cliffs dotted with caves.

South along the coast lies Short Beach, Lost Boy Cave, Agate Beach and a tunnel carved by the tides. To the north is a Migratory Bird Sanctuary and Bayocean. Bayocean was once a booming resort town. It featured an elaborate natatorium containing 50'x160' pool with an imitation waterfall at one end and a 40 room hotel. The town was founded in 1907. By 1917, the wealthy lot owners had begun to notice the shoreline was receding a foot each year. Little remains today. The ocean has long ago undercut the land, sending the elaborate homes crashing into the ocean.

CHITWOOD

CHITWOOD COVERED BRIDGE

The Chitwood Covered Bridge is 17 miles east of Newport on US 20. The bridge spans the Yaquina River with it's 96' length. It was built in 1930 and is one of only four such bridges still standing in Lincoln County.

This entire area is of historic interest. Chitwood is a station on the Southern Pacific line. This railroad was built between 1881 and 1885. A pioneer quarry can be found south of town toward Elk City. It was put into use in 1868. Sandstone from here once made it's way into buildings in San Francisco and Corvallis. It was also quite commonly used for pioneer grave headstones.

CLIFTON/BRADWOOD

Just east of milepost marker 76 on US 30 is the road north to two barely inhabited towns. To the right you'll encounter a weather worn wooden bridge leading to the town of Bradwood. Once a company town, built by Bradley-Woodard Lumber Co., it is now just a sleepy collection of old homes.

If you turn left, you'll travel along the railroad tracks running beside the river to Clifton. Remains include a long abandoned cannery and several old buildings. The Clifton post office was officially opened in 1874. That was long before the railroad tracks were laid. Two pioneer salmon packers operated a cannery here.

COOS BAY

BAYVIEW MYRTLEWOOD MANUFACTURING COMPANY

At the Bayview Myrtlewood Manufacturing Company you can tour the facilities and watch as craftspeople work the native wood. They are open daily from 8:00 a.m. to 4:30 p.m. during the summer months but closed weekends during the rest of the year. To find them take US 101 north 5 miles past the North Bend Bridge.

CIRCLE THE BAY ROAD RUN

This annual 18 mile run is held each summer. It starts at the Coos Bay Mall at 8:00 a.m. and is almost as much as fun for spectators as it is for contestants. Contact the Coos Bay Chamber of Commerce for the exact date.

COAST GUARD CUTTER CITRUS

You will find the Coast Guard Cutter Citrus docked at the Port Dock in Coos Bay. It is open daily for tours. Weekdays, you can climb aboard from 1:00 p.m. to 3:00 p.m. and on weekends and holidays from 1:00 p.m. to 7:00 p.m.

COOS ART MUSEUM

Built in 1914, this building was originally a Carnegie Library. Today it holds a permanent collection of work done by contemporary artists. They feature a changing exhibit with a new collection being put on display each month. The museum is located at 515 Market Street and can be visited Tuesday through Sunday between 1:00 p.m. and 4:00 p.m.

COOS BAY HISTORICAL TOUR

The streets of Coos Bay offer many turn of the century homes. Although these homes are not open to the public, a walking tour of the streets offers an interesting opportunity to view period architecture.

The first group of buildings are clustered near Second and Birch. At First and Fir is the Sun Building. The city's first newspaper was published here in 1891. This two story building was once a hubbub of activity.

491 North Second (1898)

202 North Second (1893)

276 Birch (1893)

682 North Third (1902)

697 North Third (1873)
This house was built by a crew of shipwrights.

A second group of historical buildings center around Fifth and Hall.

480 Hall (1906)

7th & Ingersoll
IOOF Cemetery established in 1888

893 South Fifth (1908)

955 South Fifth (1911)

965 South Fifth (1907)

1007 South Second (1900)
This house was moved to it's present location in 1923.

HOUSE OF MYRTLEWOOD

The House of Myrtlewood at 1125 South First offers tours of their facilities 7 days a week.

MARSHFIELD SUN PRINTING MUSEUM & WORKING PRINT SHOP

The town of Coos Bay was originally known as Marsh-field, and this museum is a tribute to the local paper established in 1891. The 4 page weekly was set and printed by hand until 1944. The museum is located along US 101 and open by appointment only - 269-1363.

MINGUS PARK

Mingus Park is located at 10th and Commercial in Coos Bay. It features a lovely rhododendron garden, tennis courts and picnic tables. Here you can stretch your legs on the hiking trail, feed the ducks or just plain play.

NATIVE AMERICAN RESEARCH CENTER

The Native American Research Center in plainer words is an Indian museum. Located at Wallace and Michigan Avenues, it is open daily, summers only, from 10:00 a.m. to 4:00 p.m.

PREFONTAINE MEMORIAL RUN

This was Steve Prefontaine's home, so every year, Coos Bay sponsors a 10,000 meter run along the athlete's favorite training route. The run begins at 4th and Anderson and concludes at the Marshfield High track where his running career began. This exciting event is held in September. There's no charge to watch and spectators are encouraged to come and cheer the runners along.

WEYERHAEUSER LUMBER MILL

The Weyerhaeuser Lumber Mill is located on US 101 between Coos Bay and North Bend. From mid-June to early September tours are offered weekdays at 1:30 p.m. The balance of the year tours are given on Fridays only at 1:30 p.m.

(East of the City)

GOLDEN FALLS/SILVER FALLS

Northeast of Coos Bay, past Allegeny, you can hike in a short distance for a pleasing view of both Golden and Silver Falls.

ROOKE-HIGGINS COUNTY PARK

This county park is 10 miles east of Coos Bay on a branch of Coos River known as the Millicoma. It provides restrooms, picnic facilities and a boat ramp.

(South of the City)

BASTENDORF BEACH COUNTY PARK

Bastendorf Beach is protected by the bar's south jetty. The park offers picnicking, hiking trails and a bathhouse. It is 11 miles southwest of Coos Bay off US 101.

CAPE ARAGO STATE PARK

At Cape Arago State Park, you can find Eocene marine fossils in the sea cliffs. This spot has been carved out over a period of 50 million years as the tide has rushed against the shoreline. The south cove has some unique cliff rock formations making it one of Oregon's most spectacular state parks.

Located 14 miles southwest of Coos Bay, it is a great place for whale watching, and it's surf often holds frolicking seals and sea lions.

ESTUARINE SANCTUARY

The University of Oregon's Marine Biology Institute maintains this sanctuary for the preservation of coastal wildlife. It's 6,600 acres provides a natural habitat for birds, small marsh animals, deer, elk and marine wildlife.

The sanctuary is located at the southern tip of Coos Bay. Visitors are welcomed as part of their extensive wildlife education program.

SHORE ACRES STATE PARK

Shore Acres State Park was once owned by Lewis J. Simpson, a shipping magnate. The lovely family mansion once was situated here among acres of formal gardens guarded by monolithic cliffs. The gardens, cliffs and view remain.

Here, protected from the sea by towering cliffs, you can see the beautiful Oriental garden. It surrounds a sunken pool adorned by bronze herons. This area is also abundant in white rhododendrons and features a formal English Garden. A self-guided brochure is available.

The 1,000 acre park also contains some wildly beautiful coastal land. It is located 13 miles southwest of Coos Bay off US 101. There is a minimal charge on weekends and holidays throughout the summer.

SUNSET BAY STATE PARK

A visit to this state park at sunset will reveal how the area received it's name. The cliff sheltered beach hides a narrow sea channel and is one of the calmest beaches along the coast.

Tide pools are filled with anemones, star fish, mollusks, darting fish and crabs. Low minus tides reveal a wealth of marine life. The park is located 12 miles southwest of Coos Bay.

JANORA BAYOT

CHARLESTON FISHERY TOURS

Two Charleston fisheries offer tours of their facilities. If your timing is good you may even get a chance to meet the commercial fishing fleet as they pull in to sell the day's catch. Tap Fisheries is located at the east end of Charleston Bridge. Tours are available weekdays between 8:00 a.m. and 5:00 p.m. At Hallmark Fisheries, 540 Bayview, tours are given between 9:00 a.m.and 5:00 p.m.

COAST GUARD LIFEBOAT STATION

The Coast Guard Lifeboat Station in Charleston offers free boat tours from 1:00 p.m. to 3:00 p.m. weekdays. Weekends and holidays you can see the boat between 1:00 p.m. and 4:00 p.m.

COQUILLE

COQUILLE VALLEY ART CENTER

The Coquille Valley Art Center is two miles east of Coquille on State 42. The gallery is open Wednesday through Sunday from 1:00 p.m. to 4:00 p.m. Exhibits include both local and guest artists.

TENNIS COURTS

Public tennis courts can be found at the Fifth Street Park, Sanford Heights Park and Fortier Field.

LAVERNE COUNTY PARK

The LaVerne County Park is located 12 miles northeast of Coquille off State 42. The park is situated along the quiet Coquille River shaded by maple, oak and myrtle trees. Lots of picnic tables and restroom facilities make this a pleasant place to spend a hot afternoon.

DEADWOOD

DEADWOOD CREEK COVERED BRIDGE

From Florence, take State 126 east to State 36 out of Mapleton. Turn left at Deadwood Creek Road. The 105' covered bridge is 5 miles down this road. The wooden structure was built in 1932.

DEPOE BAY

ART GALLERIES

There are currently five art galleries along US 101 in Depoe Bay:

Crickett Hollow (outside gallery - wood sculptures)
Gaslight Gallery
Sea Cove Gallery
Shannon Gallery
Richard Hazelton Gallery

DEPOE BAY FIRE HALL MUSEUM

At the Depoe Bay Fire Hall they have put together a small museum filled with firefighting memorabilia. Children and adults alike will love this opportunity to see toy firetrucks and horse drawn hook and ladder rigs.

FLEET OF FLOWERS CEREMONY

Each Memorial Day, on Monday, Depoe Bay hosts a ceremony dedicated to all who have lost their lives at sea. Fishing boats laden with floral wreaths made by the community, make their way from the bay and through the narrow rocky channel to cast their flowers like a blanket on the sea. This silent tribute can be watched from the sea wall and provides a warm and colorful experience.

OBSERVATION DECKS

On the north end of the Depoe Bay bridge, you will find an observation deck. It provides a great viewpoint from which to watch the activity in the boat basin below. If your timing is right, you can see the charter boats unloading the day's catch.

The Depoe Bay State Park Building also has an observation deck where you can watch the fleet, as it passes between the high rock walls of the narrow channel.

SPOUTING HORNS

Depoe Bay is famous for it's spouting horns which burst over the high seawall to spray cold water all over watching tourists. From December through May, you might get a chance to watch as gray whales make their yearly journey from the Bering Sea to Mexico. The seawall is one of the best viewing areas along with the two state parks on either side of Depoe Bay.

THUNDERING SEAS

Thundering Seas is a school for gold and silversmiths. Visitors are welcome in both the school workshop and the mineral display room. Here you will have the opportunity to observe students as they work, creating jewelry from precious metals.

The Thundering Seas Museum is only open from 4:30 p.m. to 5:15 p.m. Films, exhibits and lectures are also held from time to time.

They are located one mile south of town on a 200' stretch of rocky land overlooking the Pacific. Closed Wednesdays and Sundays.

(South of the City)

ROCKY CREEK STATE PARK

Two miles south of Depoe Bay, the Rocky Creek State Park offers another good area for whale watching. The trail north of the park drops to secluded Whale Cove. It was so named in 1903 because of the 89' whale that washed ashore.

The bridge was named for pioneer lawyer, Ben F. Jones. He is considered the "Father of the Roosevelt Coast Highway", better known as US 101.

ELK CITY

TOWN PROPER

Elk City is one of the oldest settlements in Lincoln County. It looks much like it did in 1866. This picturesque community has less than 100 residents and sits at the junction of the Yaquina River and Big Elk Creek. A county park on the Yaquina River marks the site of the Franklin Marion Carter homesite.

ELSIE

SPRUCE RUN COUNTY PARK

This 52 acre county park is located 6 miles southwest of Elsie, off US 26. Hiking trails, swimming and picnicking are fun here along the banks of the lower Nehalem River. Restrooms and a pump make it convenient.

FLORENCE

FLORENCE PARK

This park is right in Florence. Trails, picnic tables, drinking water, swimming and a bathhouse all make it an excellent place to spend the day.

HONEYMAN STATE PARK

At Honeyman State Park you will find sand dunes, lakes and wild rhododendrons. Nothing can surpass the beauty of these flowers. Here, the favorable climate brings out colors ranging from pale pink to a deep red. The warm air brought in by the Japanese current gives them a long flowering season.

The park also offers hiking trails and a bathhouse.

MAPLETON LOOP DRIVE

This is a beautiful 35 mile drive. The Loop starts along the North Fork of the Siuslaw River, crosses a covered bridge and heads up over Neely Mountain before arriving in Mapleton. The return route takes you along the Siuslaw River past mills and marinas on an excellent paved road.

MUNSEL LAKE

Munsel Lake is a great place to take the kids fishing. It is located just a little northeast of Florence and is considered to be one of the best spots in the area for bank fishing.

NORTH FORK BRIDGE

This is a great spot for digging bay clams. Any low or minus tide will provide diggers and onlookers alike with a lot of activity. No license is required and each person in possession of a shovel and pail may keep the first 36 clams they dig. These clams are found between 6 and 16 inches below the surface.

OLD TOWN

Old Town Florence is the Bay Street area and was the original river town of Florence. A close look will reveal an interesting, fun and exciting area. It is a town within a city and offers unique shops and recreational areas for tourists.

Across from Fisherman's Wharf is a small Gazebo overlooking the river. This is a pleasant place to sit and watch the river pass by.

The area is also a favorite of local artists.

OREGON DUNES NATIONAL
RECREATION AREA

A 40 mile stretch of Oregon coast referred to as the Oregon Dunes begins just south of the bridge at Florence and extends to Coos Bay. This is one of the largest coastal dune areas in the world. Many state, forestry and private parks line the area. Most offer picnic facilities, restrooms and beach access.

The Umpqua Dunes Scenic Area is closed to motor vehicles and makes an excellent place for hiking. This 3,000 plus acre area is home to many kinds of wildlife. Deer, raccoon, beaver and various waterfowl can often be seen here in the early morning.

South of the Siuslaw River bridge, take the South Jetty Road to the right for a look at some real dune buggies in action. These are some of the most challenging dunes in the West and many designers bring their buggies here for testing.

RHODODENDRON FESTIVAL

The Rhododendron Festival is held each year, late in May, and features a Grand Parade. Florence has been sponsoring this spectacular event for over three-fourths of a century.

The Siuslaw Gallery of Local Arts holds it's "Spring Fever" exhibit in conjunction with the annual Rhododendron Festival. The Florence Chamber of Commerce can supply you with the date and location.

RHODODENDRON LOOP DRIVE

Take Rhododendron Drive west for a nine mile loop that takes you past the Coast Guard Station along roads lined with wild rhododendrons. They are most beautiful from May through mid-June.

At Harbor Vista Park you will want to stop at the viewpoint. There, you can see the forming of breakers as the Siuslaw River flows into the ocean. At the north end of the park is the jetty.

Continue north to Heceta Beach Road before turning east for the trip back to Florence. You will rejoin US 101, four miles north of town.

SIUSLAW PIONEER MUSEUM
& ART GALLERY

The Siuslaw Pioneer Museum & Art Gallery is just south of Florence on US 101. Located in a former church, exhibits include pictures, clothing, tools and a complete pioneer kitchen as well as Indian crafts. An art gallery lets you view the work of local artists.

Hours: Summer - 1:00 p.m. till dusk, Tuesday through Saturday.

Winter - Tuesday, Wednesday & Friday after-noons.

WHALE MEMORIAL

This carved memorial was made by Gorge von der Linden to commemorate the spot where 41 sperm whales beached themselves in June of 1979. It can be seen at the end of the South Jetty Road and marks an excellent place for whale watching.

(North of the City)

DARLINGTONIA BOTANICAL WAYSIDE

Five miles north of Florence is the Darlingtonia Botanical Wayside where exotic Cobra Lilies can be seen. These carnivorous plants trap and eat live insects. Raised walkways keep your feet dry and give you an opportunity to view these giant plants during daylight hours.

Restrooms and picnic tables are also provided.

DEVIL'S ELBOW
STATE PARK

Thirteen miles north of Florence is Devil's Elbow State Park. From here you will be treated to a view of the Heceta Head Lighthouse built in 1894. Supplies for building were first shipped from San Francisco and then hauled by wagon along the beach and over the mountain. The 1,5000,000 candlepower beam stands 205' above the sea. This is probably one of America's most photographed lighthouses.

Rockhounds will love the beach as outgoing tides often reveal translucent agates. Picnic tables, restrooms, drinking water and hiking trails make this an ideal place to stop.

SUTTON LAKE

This U.S. Forest Service park is 6 miles north of Florence. There are actually three areas here; Sutton Lake, Sutton

Beach and Sutton Creek. Picnic facilities, restrooms, drinking water, hiking trails and a boat ramp all have been provided.

FT. STEVENS

BATTERY RUSSELL

Battery Russell was built in 1904. It is the only fortification in the continental United States to have been fired on by an enemy since the War of 1812. This was the target of Japanese offshore shelling during WWII. It was designed to protect the mouth of the Columbia River and held two 10" rifles.

FIRE CONTROL TOWER

East of US 101, this tower was built to direct the fire of the big guns at Battery Russell.

FORT STEVENS
HISTORICAL AREA

The original construction of Fort Stevens was begun in 1863. It's purpose was to defend the mouth of the Columbia River from a Confederate invasion. Military operations were based here from 1865 until 1947.

A walking tour begins at the War Games Building where a visitor's center and historical office is located. Pick up a brochure here that will lead you through the remains of buildings and batteries constructed at the fort. The tour highlights 32 individual locations including the original earthwork of 1865, the 1900 torpedo loading room, the mine loading building and 8 concrete gun batteries.

FORT STEVENS
STATE PARK

This park is definitely for those who enjoy the outdoors. There is a minimum charge on weekends and holidays but no charge the rest of the year. For the bicyclist, there is a seven mile paved trail winding its way through the park past Battery Russell and the rusting skeleton of the Peter Iredale.

A 2½ mile hiking trail circles Coffenbury Lake where fishermen reel in bass, perch and trout. This lake also offers swimming areas and a boat ramp. The Pioneer Nature Trail makes a half mile loop past a variety of plants, identified for nature lovers. Yet another trail leads from parking area C along Clatsop Spit to the South Jetty. This massive stone barrier was begun in 1885 to channel the Columbia River. It was not completed until over 30 years later. The South Jetty is also the start of the famed Oregon Coast Trail.

The beach from Fort Stevens State Park south to Gearhart is open to automobile traffic when the tide is low. The speed limit is 25 miles per hour. It's an exciting drive for those who have never experienced it. Stay out of the soft sand and away from wet looking spots.

OREGON COAST TRAIL

The Oregon Coast Trail begins beside the South Jetty, along the mouth of the Columbia River. The first 15 miles travel along the beach to Gearhart. Here, the trail turns inland to make it's way around the Necanicum River Estuary to Seaside.

Back at the beach, the trail ascends Tillamook Head in Ecola State Park. This is the same trail taken by the Lewis & Clark Expedition in 1806 when they journeyed here to view the beached whale. Twenty-six miles down the trail, you arrive at Indian Beach where mounds of shells attest to it's long Indian occupancy. Be sure to hit Arch Cape at low tide or you won't be able to get around Silver,

Humbug and Hug Points. These areas are impassable at high tide. Once you reach Arch Cape, the trail turns inland again until it reaches Arch Cape Creek and Oswald West State Park.

For the next 5 miles, you will traverse the old coastal rain forest to Cape Falcon, Smuggler Cove and Short Sand Beach. At 44 miles the trail takes the route of an old Indian trail up the hill to Neahkahnie Punchbowl where buried pirate's treasure is said to lay hidden. You then descend the mountain back to US 101 to Nehalem Road where you once again follow the beach to Manzanita.

The next 7 miles around the estuary will take you through the towns of Nehalem, Wheeler and Brighton. From here, you return to the beach and travel past Manhattan Beach and Rockaway to Barview County Park.

The entire trail is 62 miles long. A detailed map is put out by the State Park Department located in Salem.

SUBMARINE MONUMENT

A stone marker points out the spot where a Japanese shell exploded here on June 21, 1942. The Japanese submarine fired 17 rounds of shells. Soldiers were sent from Fort Stevens in anticipation of an enemy landing craft operation but this was the only sign of war and it ended almost as soon as it began.

WRECK OF THE PETER IREDALE

You can take Peter Iredale Road out to the site of the 1906 wreck of the British Peter Iredale. Grounded under full sail the skeletal remains can still be seen.

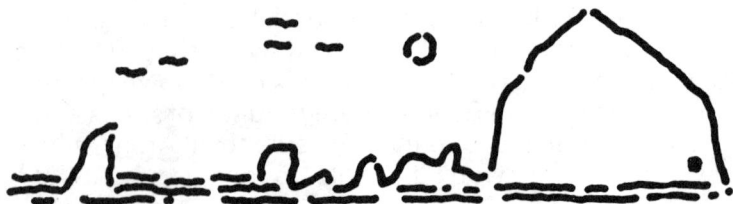

GARDINER

GARDINER PIONEER CHURCH

On the bluff, overlooking the town of Gardiner stands the oldest mission still in operation on the Northwest coast. To reach St. Mary's Episcopal Church simply follow North Second Street. The cemetery beyond, is full of elaborate headstones bearing dates from the 1860's. This town was named for the Boston merchant whose ship was wrecked here at the Umpqua River's mouth in 1850. Most of the goods found their way to shore.

INTERNATIONAL PAPER COMPANY

International Paper Company is the largest paper company in the world. Here at Gardiner, they have both paper and lumber mills. Tours of the paper mill are given on Tuesday and Thursday at 12:45 p.m. from early June through the end of August. They ask that no children under twelve be brought along.

SOUTHSIDE COUNTY PARK

This secluded little park can be found at the base of a bluff, along the Smith River five miles east of Gardiner along L. Smith River Road.

VINCENT CREEK RECREATION SITE

The Bureau of Land Management has a small park at Vincent Creek. Head northeast, out of Gardiner, past Sulphur Springs and Smith River Falls. Swimming, picnicking and nature study are just three great things to do here.

GARIBALDI

BARVIEW COUNTY PARK

Just north of Garibaldi is one of the northernmost opportunities to see the famed Oregon sand dunes. Picnic tables and restrooms are available.

BAY FRONT BAKERY

Tillamook County lists this bakery on their cheese and wine tour. Opening at 7:00 a.m. every day but Tuesday, they make fresh pastries and bread daily.

GARIBALDI DAYS

This annual celebration is held the last weekend in July. Write to the local Chamber of Commerce for this year's date and a list of free events.

MEMORIAL LUMBERMAN'S PARK

The Memorial Lumberman's Park has a steam locomotive as well as logging and railroad equipment from the early 1900's on display.

OLSON OYSTER COMPANY

At the Olson Oyster Company, you can watch as oysters are prepared for marketing. Visitors are welcome from April through mid-September, 9:00 a.m. to 5:00 p.m. They are located on Fisherman's Wharf.

PHIL & JOE'S CRAB COMPANY

Phil & Joe's Crab Company is open to visitors year round. Seafood and crab are processed here while you watch. Summer hours are 9:00 a.m. to 8:00 p.m. but they close up at 5:00 p.m. during the winter.

SMITH'S PACIFIC SHRIMP COMPANY

You can visit Smith's from April 1 to October 15 for a look at how shrimp is canned. Large viewing windows give you the opportunity to see them as they pick, clean, cook and can the tiny pink delicacies. Open 9:00 a.m. to 5:00 p.m.

GEARHART

CRANBERRY BOGS

Just north of Gearhart and east of US 101, the land is covered with cranberry bogs. The cranberries are harvested in late fall and makes a colorful sight.

GLENEDEN BEACH

ART GALLERIES

The area currently has three art galleries where the public can view the work of Northwest artists.

Lawrence Gallery
@ Salishan on US 101

Mossy Creek Pottery
Immonen Road

The Gallery Room
@ Salishan on US 101

BEACH ACCESS

Gleneden Beach is for the picnicker. Seven miles south of Lincoln City, this beach has tables, drinking water and restrooms near the ocean.

GNAT CREEK

GNAT CREEK PARK & FISH HATCHERY

Gnat Creek Park is just off US 30, east of Astoria and offers shaded spots to picnic and wade in the creek. The fish hatchery is just south of the highway with a gravel road 1 mile west leading north to the creek. The road isn't marked and the spot is relatively unused. Take Shingle Mill Road and head south off US 30 to Gnat Creek Falls, a primitive falls area.

At the hatchery, they have been raising steelhead since 1960. Over 585,000 a year.

GOLD BEACH

CURRY COUNTY MUSEUM

The Curry County Museum, on Ellensburg Avenue, houses a nice collection of artifacts, photographs, interpretive exhibits and an interesting group of petroglyphs. They are closed Monday but open the balance of the week from 11:00 a.m. to 5:00 p.m.

The Curry County Historical Society is currently sponsoring the restoration of the vessel, Mary D. Hume at the north end of the Port of Gold Beach. Built here in Gold Beach in 1881, she has been registered with the National Trust for Historic Preservation and can be viewed at her moorage.

GOLD BEACH CITY PARK

Tennis courts and playground equipment are the enticements offered at this park.

LOBSTER CREEK

Lobster Creek is located in the Siskiyou National Forest, 10 miles east of Gold Beach. This Forest Service Park has swimming, picnic tables, running water and a boat ramp.

ROCKHOUNDING

Oregon jade and serpentine are found in the gravel bars of both the Rogue and Illinois Rivers as well as the beaches near Gold Beach.

ROGUE RIVER

In 1968, Congress declared 84 miles of the Rogue River to be classified as a Wild and Scenic River. This area is generally inaccessible except by trail or boat and runs from the mouth of the Applegate River downstream to Lobster Creek. Maps showing the trails through this area are available at the US Forest Service Office in Gold Beach.

Gold was first discovered here in 1859 and the place was soon crawling with prospectors. Evidence of mining can still be seen. Piles of stones along streambeds, gouges left by hydraulic mining, shafts and abandoned equipment are easily sighted.

THOMAS CREEK BRIDGE

North of Gold Beach, you can cross over the highest bridge in the entire state. Rising 350' above the ground, the Thomas Creek Bridge is higher than the Golden Gate Bridge.

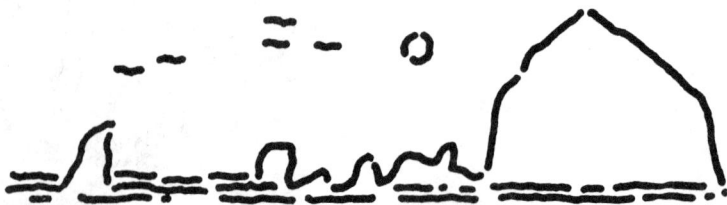

GRAND RONDE

VAN DUZIER CORRIDOR

Coming into Lincoln County along State 18, you will pass through the Van Duzier Corridor where some of Oregon's biggest trees are growing.

Ten miles west of Grand Ronde on State 22, is the H.D. VanDuzen State Park. Located amongst these magnificent trees, it sits on the Yamhill River. This is a great place for a picnic.

HECETA HEAD

MURIEL O. PONSLER WAYSIDE

This tiny park offers a quiet place for a break. It was donated by Jack Ponsler as a memorial to his wife. An ornamental drinking fountain, old-fashioned violets, wild strawberries and daisies make this a quaint little spot.

ROCKHOUNDING

Beaches stretching from Heceta Head to Yachats are prime hunting grounds for sagenitic agates, bloodstones, jasper and agates.

C.G. WASHBURNE MEMORIAL
STATE PARK

Early morning at the C.G. Washburne Memorial Park is a great time to watch elk in the nearby meadows and campgrounds. Trails, picnic tables, restrooms and a bathhouse add to the park's niceties.

JEWELL

JEWELL MEADOWS WILDLIFE AREA

The Jewell Meadows Wildlife Area provides food for the wintering Roosevelt elk and other native wildlife. The public is welcome to view the animals here in their natural surroundings. Two great times to make the trip are in mid-June when the calves begin coming out into the open or early October when the bull elks are at their rowdiest.

Just off State 202, elk can often be seen in great numbers from November through April. Songbirds, jays, crows, red-tailed hawks and an occasional eagle are also around.

Take the Beneke Creek-Crawford Ridge Loop to circle the area. This route will show you the Cascade Mountains to the East and Saddle and Nicolai mountains to the West and North. You will also be treated to a panoramic view of Clatsop County's extensive forest.

LEE WOODEN COUNTY PARK

Three miles west of Jewell Meadows Wildlife Area, Fishhawk Creek Falls make their 100' drop into the Nehalem Valley. This is a lovely spot for an intimate picnic.

WICKIUP LOOKOUT

About halfway between Olney and Jewell, off State 202, is the Wickiup Lookout. A former forest fire lookout, it sits atop a 2,522' peak and affords a panoramic view of the surrounding area.

KALMIOPSIS WILDERNESS

This 180,000 acre wilderness was named for a small shrub found growing here which is a relic of the pre-ice age. This area has a large number of plant species, including many rare and some extremely rare ones.

The wilderness consists of some of the most rugged and inaccessible country in the Siskiyou National Forest, made up of rocky, bushy, low elevation canyons.

A map of the area is available through most US Forest Service offices which will show you where the trailheads and water sources are located. This is not for the inexperienced but an adventure into solitude for those who know how to deal with it and the environment.

KERNVILLE

OLD KERNVILLE

Located about 2 miles above the present site of Kernville, on State 229, Old Kernville was built in 1896. This became the site of Lincoln County's first industry when the Kern brothers built their salmon cannery here. It was along the north bank, accessible only by water. The sawmill, post office and original community were on the southwest bank.

Nearby, on the Siletz River, there is a large rock given the name of Coyote Rock. According to Indian legend, Coyote attempted to dam the Siletz River here to insure himself of a constant supply of salmon. The tale says it is due to his partial success that large Chinook wait here each fall for the first rains before they can finish their ascent to up-river spawning beds.

KNAPPA

BIG CREEK PARK

Big Creek Park offers picnic tables along the banks of one of the more popular fishing creeks. It is located 15 miles east of Astoria on US 30.

BRADLEY PARK

This park was donated to the state in 1921. It is located 22 miles east of Astoria on US 30 and affords a spectacular view of the Columbia River and Puget Island. Picnic sites, drinking water and toilet facilities make it a comfortable rest stop.

NICOLAI MOUNTAIN

The top of this 3,020' peak was once the site of a forest fire lookout station and the center of much logging activity. Today it is deserted but provides a magnificent view of the surrounding area.

LAKESIDE

TENMILE LAKE

Tenmile Lake is the fourth largest lake in Oregon. It is located adjacent to the city of Lakeside. This is a popular spot for small sailboats. It offers a boat ramp.

LINCOLN CITY

ALDER HOUSE II

Alder House II is the oldest glassblowing studio in Oregon. It is located just south of Lincoln City, on Immonen Road. Here you can wander back to the geodesic dome where you can witness this ancient art. You will see molten glass drawn from the furnace and shaped into the artist's personal creation. Step by step, the craftsman explains the entire process.

They are closed during the months of December, January and February. Open from 10:00 a.m. to 5:00 p.m. every day but Monday, the balance of the year.

ART GALLERIES

Lincoln City had 12 galleries at last count. A tour of the area, reveals lots of local talent and Northwest artists.

Cascade Artists Gallery
2945 NW Jetty Avenue

Demori Designs
1621 NW Highway 101

Frame Cellar & Gallery
2150 NW Mast

Iron Gate Gallery
North Logan Road

Lincoln Art Gallery
620 NE Highway 101

Lincoln City Art Guild
1106 SW 51st Street

Nichols Frameshop & Gallery
1166 SW 50th Street

Oceanside Gallery
North of Lincoln City on US 101

Seagull Gallery
US 101

Seaport Square

Stephens Gallery
1640 NE US 101

Thelma Pearson Gallery
446 South US 101

ARTS & CRAFTS FAIR

Each year, in mid-June, there is a big arts and crafts fair held at Nelscott Strip. Over 100 artists exhibit their wares here. The Lincoln City Chamber of Commerce can supply you with the date.

CITY PARKS

Lincoln City operates 7 city parks. They also provide 22 beach accesses. Holmes Road Park, Regatta Grounds Park and View Point Park are 3 of the biggest.

DEVIL'S LAKE

According to Indian legend, this lake was once inhabited by a Lochness type monster. The lake is connected to the Pacific Ocean by the world's shortest river. The "D" River is 440' long.

This 2½ mile long fresh water lake is often host to hydroplane racers. Many speed records have been set here. The lake is considered to be one of the fastest racing lakes in the world.

"D" River State Park is also located here and offers the public an excellent swimming area. This is also the location of Holmes Road City Park and Regatta Grounds Park with it's half-mile jogging trail.

FIREWORKS DISPLAY

Every Fourth of July, the Taft-Nelscott-Delake Fire Departments put on a spectacular fireworks display at Taft Dock. The day long celebration includes a parade and festivities.

68

ROADS END WAYSIDE

This is a photographers haven with it's rock formations and tide pools. Located just north of the city, it provides rockhounds with an opportunity to search and gather jasper, agates, Oregon jade and petrified wood.

SEA COAST HARVEST FAIR

Each year the Lincoln City Chamber of Commerce along with the Oregon Coast Council for the Arts, host the annual Sea Coast Harvest Fair.

Besides numerous art shows and musical entertainment, the fair includes kite flying, crafts and a sandcastle building contest. Sailboat racing, a children's festival, windsurfing on Devil's Lake and outdoor musical performances at the Regatta Grounds have all been features of previous years' celebrations. Contact the Lincoln City Chamber of Commerce for this year's date and a list of free events.

SILETZ BAY

Just west of Schooner Creek Bridge at Siletz Bay, you can watch as children and adults dig for sand shrimp during low tide.

TIDAL TREASURE DAYS

During the first two weekends in May, hordes of people search local beaches from Neskowin to Otter Crest for plastic floats cast to sea by local area merchants. These contain gift certificates and are a part of the celebration of Tidal Treasure Days.

CASCADE HEAD

Cascade Head is located approximately 6 miles north of Lincoln City on US 101. This area is unique in that it is not densely covered with trees or underbrush. This is mostly due to it's extreme vulnerability to storms raging out of the southwest.

The Nature Conservancy Trail can be found just off Three Rocks Road. It is well marked, two miles long, and requires about two hours round trip. The trail leads you past some fabulous views of the coastline that include a birdseye view of the Salmon River Estuary and a look at the snow covered mountains of the Coast Range.

The hike to Hart's Cove is more demanding. To reach this trail take US 101 to Forest Service Road 1861. Turn left and follow it for 4 miles. This trail takes you into some of the best of the giant spruce forest. Here, Sitka spruce hundreds of years old rival those famous redwoods found several hundred miles south. You'll also be treated to a look at Chitwood Creek as it plunges 300' into the ocean below.

CASCADE HEAD EXPERIMENTAL
FOREST AUTO TOUR

This 10 mile drive takes US 101 north out of Lincoln City toward Neskowin. After crossing the Salmon River, take the first right on Three Rocks Road. In the spring, this area is covered in lush forest growth, highlighted by a profusion of wildflowers. Sitka spruce, western hemlock, shrubs, mosses, lichens, salal, evergreens, huckleberries and sword fern are all there. Black tailed deer often cross the highway, especially in the early morning or at dusk.

You will find several nice picnic spots at Neskowin Creek Campground and lots of room to stretch your legs. The Siuslaw National Forest has provided several signs in this area explaining the coastal forest and it's growth.

SALMON RIVER FISH HATCHERY

Six miles east of Lincoln City, turn right over the bridge and take the north bank road to see the Salmon River Fish Hatchery. Coho, fall and spring chinook salmon can be seen. Over 750,000 eggs are brought here each year.

(South of the City)

UPPER DRIFT CREEK COVERED BRIDGE

To reach the Upper Drift Creek Covered Bridge, take Drift Creek Road, 3 miles south of Lincoln City. Head east for 1½ miles and then turn right. One half mile down this road, you will find the 66' bridge. It was built in 1914 and has been restricted to foot traffic.

MANZANITA

JULY 4TH CELEBRATION

Every year Manzanita goes all out to celebrate the Fourth of July. Events include a parade, turkey shoot and fireworks. All for free.

NEAHKANIE MOUNTAIN TRAIL

This mountain's 1600' peak overlooks northern Tillamook County and it's coastline. To reach the 1.5 mile trail, take US 101 south to a point 2.6 miles south of the Short Sands parking area. Signs point the way to the trail.

The trail makes it's way to the summit ridge. Another path found there can be taken over three of the mountain's humps.

MAPLETON

LAKE CREEK COVERED BRIDGE

Lake Creek Covered Bridge is located northeast of Mapleton. Follow State 36, 17 miles to Nelson Mountain Road. You will find the bridge .5 mile down this road over Lake Creek. It is 105' long and was built in 1928.

LAKE CREEK RECREATION SITE

This nearby BLM park has picnic tables, drinking water, swimming and restrooms.

WHITTAKER CREEK

Whittaker Creek is a BLM park near Wildcat Creek Covered Bridge. Take State 126, 14 miles southeast of Mapleton where you will find access to the Siuslaw River. Boat ramp, hiking trails and picnic facilities are here.

WILDCAT COVERED BRIDGE

Southeast of Mapleton turn left on Stagecoach Road to find the Wildcat Covered Bridge. This 1925 bridge is 75' long.

MOHLER

NEHALEM FALLS

This is another State Forestry Park. Located 10 miles east of Mohler, it provides you with the opportunity to view Nehalem Falls.

ROY CREEK COUNTY PARK

This 12 acre park is southeast of Mohler. Restrooms, picnic tables and a swimming beach are all features in this lovely setting.

MYRTLE POINT

COQUILLE MYRTLE GROVE STATE PARK

Facilities are primitive here, but the surroundings are great! This picnic park is located 14 miles south of Myrtle Point.

FRONA COUNTY PARK

A county park, Frona is located 18 miles northeast of Myrtle Point. It offers hiking trails and picnic sites, ideal for family outings.

MARIA C. JACKSON STATE PARK

The Maria C. Jackson State Park is 22 miles northeast of Myrtle Point off State 42. Here, along Brummit Creek, you can view virgin myrtle. Hike around and take a close look at this special Oregon tree.

NEHALEM

NEHALEM ARTS FESTIVAL

The Nehalem Bay Arts Festival is held each July in Nehalem's Waterfront Park. Artists and craftsmen exhibit their work on the town's streets during this event.

NEHALEM BAY STATE PARK

Three miles south of the Manzanita Junction off US 101 is the Nehalem Bay State Park. Here you will find ocean access, restrooms, picnic tables and drinking water.

NEHALEM FISH HATCHERY

The Nehalem Fish Hatchery is located 12 miles east of the city on State 58. Fall chinooks, cohos and winter steelhead can be viewed at this location.

NEHALEM RIVER CANOE RACE

The Nehalem River Canoe Race is held each March. Spectators are welcome. Contact the local Chamber of Commerce for details.

NESKOWIN

HAWK CREEK GALLERY

Hawk Creek Gallery is located on US 101 in Neskowin.

NETARTS

INDIAN VILLAGE

Between Netarts Bay and the Pacific Ocean is a long, sandy peninsula. This is the former site of a long deserted Indian village where archaeologists have found many artifacts.

NEWPORT

AGATE BEACH

There is still lots of good agate hunting here on this wide, sandy beach. Surfing, sun-bathing and beachcombing are other popular pastimes here.

Agate Beach is one mile north of Newport and just below Yaquina Head Lighthouse. Picnic tables and restrooms can be found here.

BLESSING OF THE FLEET

Each year, early in March, Newport holds their annual Blessing of the Fleet, in memory of all those who have been lost at sea. Yaquina Bay offers many viewpoints from which to watch this colorful event.

BURROWS HOUSE MUSEUM

This house was built in 1895 at a cost of $1400. It's original purpose was a boarding house. In later years, it was operated as a funeral home. Located next to the Log Cabin Museum, it has some outstanding exhibits. One of my favorites illustrates Newport as a seaside resort town in the 1860's, when it took over 2 days to get there from Salem. Other displays include an early Hotpoint electric stove that would dwarf most modern-day kitchens and an interesting display on our ancestor's pets.

Hours: Summer - 10:00 a.m. to 5:00 p.m.
          Winter - Closed Mondays - 11:00 a.m. to 4:00 p.m.

Donations welcome.

CITY PARKS

Newport has eight city parks. At Big Creek you will find walking trails in a small park near the city reservoir. Frank

V. Wade Memorial Park offers tennis courts. Mombetsu Sister City Park, is a small Japanese Park and at Nye Creek Canyon, you can take a walking trail into a natural canyon.

COLUMBUS DAY REGATTA

This annual boating event can be enjoyed from the banks of the bay.

FOURTH OF JULY EXTRAVAGANZA

Be at the bay at dusk for a spectacular fireworks display on the Fourth of July.

LOG CABIN MUSEUM

This log cabin museum was built mostly with donated materials and volunteer labor in the early 1960's. You can find a few outstanding items there, like the 200 plus year old captain's desk, an early jigsaw, a collection of beaded Indian skirts and a scaled down model of a covered bridge.

Hours: Summer - 10:00 a.m. to 5:00 p.m.
Winter - 11:00 a.m. to 4:00 p.m. - Closed Mondays
Donations welcome.

LOYALTY DAYS & SEA FAIR FESTIVAL

This event is held on the weekend nearest May 1st. Numerous events, including a parade are open to the public. A Coast Guard ship is also on hand for guided tours.

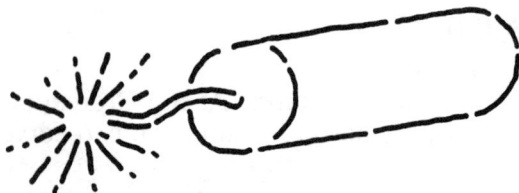

JANORA BAYOT

OREGON STATE UNIVERSITY MARINE SCIENCE CENTER

At Oregon State University's Marine Science Center, you can see displays and exhibits of Oregon's marine fishes and invertebrates. These impressive exhibits include; films, mounted birds, aquarium and marine specimens and a touching pool where visitors can handle intertidal life, including an octopus.

Hallways around the center courtyard are often used to display the work of Oregon artists and photographers, whose works center around coastal themes.

During the summer, the center offers the Seatauqua Summer Program which includes many free activities. This all happens between June and mid-September.

Summer hours are 10:00 a.m. to 6:00 p.m. During the winter, they close up at 4:00 p.m. They are open daily.

US COAST GUARD STATION

The U.S. Coast Guard Station at Yaquina Bay, welcomes visitors for tours between 9:00 a.m. and 4:00 p.m. This station answers distress calls from both commercial and sport fishing boats as well as pleasure craft.

There is a memorial park here in front of the station. It contains a 36 foot motor lifeboat which has been retired after scores of rescue journeys from Yaquina Bay.

YAQUINA BAY STATE PARK

The Yaquina Bay State Park provides lots of picnic space. It also offers a view of an 1871 lighthouse that is said to be tenanted by spirits. This Light Station was supposed to be erected at Otter Crest but a shipment error brought the materials here. The original lenses, made in Paris in 1868, are still in use.

BEVERLY BEACH STATE PARK

This is a lovely driftwood scattered beach, seven miles north of Newport. Miocene marine fossils, including shells and the bones of whales and sea lions, have been found in the cliffs here. This is a large park with excellent facilities.

DEVIL'S PUNCHBOWL STATE PARK

The Devil's Punchbowl is a rock formation resembling a huge bowl where waves continuously churn. It is located 8½ miles north of Newport, off US 101.

The state park provides an opportunity for swimming, picnicking and hiking.

(South of the City)

LOST CREEK

Take US 101 seven miles south of Newport to this quiet picnic spot.

ONA BEACH STATE PARK

Eight miles south of Newport, where Beaver Creek flows into the Pacific, is Ona Beach State Park. Ona is Indian jargon for razor clams. The state provides a bathhouse and picnic tables here.

SOUTH BEACH STATE PARK

Just two miles south of Newport South Beach State Park provides another opportunity to explore the beach.

NORTH BEND

COOS-CURRY HISTORICAL MUSEUM

Inside this museum, you'll find a wide variety of exhibits. Some outstanding collections include spinning wheels, flags, Indian artifacts, walking sticks, sling shots and music boxes. Something for everyone. The museum is closed on Mondays with summer hours being from 11:00 a.m. to 5:00 p.m., and winter hours 1:00 p.m. to 5:00 p.m.

The museum is located at Simpson Park where rhododendron bushes are as big as trees and logging equipment and an old time steam locomotive, provide excitement for the children.

OCEANSIDE

AGATE BEACHES

Each winter, the sandy beach near Oceanside is carried away to expose a gravelly layer containing numerous agates. Even a quick hike is bound to turn up some gems. At the north end of the beach, pounding seas have carved through the rocky point to provide access to a quiet beach which would otherwise remain inaccessible, except at low tide.

THREE ARCH ROCKS NATIONAL BIRD & SEA LION REFUGE

This nationally famous refuge, is offshore near Oceanside. It is the permanent home of a large herd of Northern Sea Lions and the nesting place of countless Murres. The sea lion pups are born mainly in May and June and can be seen playing in the surf along the beach year round.

OTTER ROCK

OTTER CREST LOOKOUT
MARINE MUSEUM

Four miles south of Depoe Bay, at the Otter Crest Lookout museum, you can see a display of artifacts taken from ships wrecked in nearby waters.

From here, you can see Cape Foulweather. This was Captain Cook's first look at the Pacific Northwest coast. His published logs aroused world interest in the area and soon brought the attention of the fur trade industry.

OTTER CREST LOOP

This loop runs from Otter Rock to Whale Cove, making it's way along the lower cliffs where you can see the pounding surf and sand beaches surrounded by lush vegetation. The road allows for viewpoints at several spots.

Along this road, you will find the State of Oregon observation area atop Cape Foulweather. This cape received it's name in 1778 because of the dense fog which swirls abruptly to obscure everything from sight.

PACIFIC CITY

CAPE KIWANDA

One mile north of Pacific City, you can stand on the beach and watch as local dory fishermen launch their boats into the surf and land again as breakers bring them to a skidding stop on the sandy beach. You will also be treated to a view of Cape Lookout and Cascade Head.

PACIFIC CITY DORY DERBY

The Pacific City Dory Derby is held each year in June and marks the beginning of the commercial fishing season. Saturday is the day for the parade and kite flying contest with Sunday being reserved for the dory events, when you can see the races and rowing exhibitions.

SAND BEACH FOREST SERVICE PARK

This forest service park offers another opportunity to enjoy the Oregon sand dunes. It is located nine miles north of Pacific City off US 101. Picnic tables and restrooms make this a popular place to stop.

WEBB PARK

Webb Park can be found north of Pacific City off US 101. Picnic, hike or just relax.

WHALEN ISLAND COUNTY PARK

Located on Sand Lake, this six acre park is five miles north of Pacific City. It sits on the opposite side of the lake from Sand Beach Park and offers swimming and picnic facilities.

WOODS COUNTY PARK

This lovely two acre park northeast of Pacific City is a great spot for a quiet picnic.

PORT ORFORD

ART GALLERIES

At the Port Orford Art Center and the Pacific Fine Art Cooperative, you can view the works of local artists and craftspeople. Both are located on Jackson Street. Quarles Gallery is located at 515 West 10th.

PORT ORFORD HEADS WAYSIDE

This viewpoint along US 101 at Port Orford is an excellent spot for whale viewing. They're most likely to be seen in early fall and can be spotted when they blow small umbrellas of water against the sky. Sometimes they can be seen leaping from the water, briefly silhouetting against the horizon. Picnic tables are available.

WOODEN NICKEL

The Wooden Nickel is a myrtlewood shop where visitors are welcome to watch as the craftspeople work.

(North of the City)

CAPE BLANCO
LIGHTHOUSE & STATE PARK

The Cape Blanco Lighthouse is the oldest lighthouse in the state of Oregon. It has been aiding ships since 1870, along this hazardous stretch of coastline.

The Lighthouse is off limits to visitors but can be viewed from Cape Blanco State Park. The state park is located nine miles north of Port Orford off US 101. It has a nice picnic area, trails, running water and restrooms.

At Cape Blanco, you will find black sand beaches and the restored Hughes House. This was the former home of Patrick and Jane Hughes, two pioneers of the Cape Blanco area. It was built in 1891. The two story house is surrounded by 1880 acres of former ranch property now belonging to the state.

This home has been entered in the National Register of Historic Places. It is a well preserved example of one form of architecture popular in the late 1880's.

Another feature of the area is the Pliocene-Pleistocene fossils found in the cliffs just south of the lighthouse.

83

BATTLE ROCK

In 1851 Captain William Tichenor brought the 400 ton steamship Sea Gull into what is now the Port Orford harbor. He had great visions of wealth to be gained here in terms of gold and timber. He planned to establish the first settlement on the Southern Oregon Coast.

With promises to return in 2 weeks, he left a small group of settlers on what would soon be known as Battle Rock. The men were attacked almost immediately by the Indians and again fifteen days later, when their ship did not return, as they had told the Indians it would. At last, with ammunition and food running low, they escaped under cover of darkenss and headed for Scottsburgh on the Umpqua River.

A well defined trail leads to the top of Battle Rock where you can enjoy the fantastic view and imagine what it must have been like to sit here and wait for the Indians to make their attack.

BUFFINGTON PARK

This 20 acre city park borders Garrison Lake, the second largest natural lake in Curry County. Here you will find a swimming dock, picnic tables, Swiss paracourse for exercise buffs, jogging trail, tennis, basketball and baseball areas as well as a large play area for small children. There are also hiking trails here in this natural setting. To reach the park turn west on 14th Street from downtown Port Orford.

JUBILEE CELEBRATION

Port Orford holds it's annual Jubilee Celebration around the 4th of July. This is an old fashioned celebration for all ages. One highlight of the event is the re-enactment of the Battle Rock conflict at the original site.

Climaxing the Jubilee is a gigantic fireworks exhibition fired from the beach and atop Battle Rock. Viewers can scatter themselves across the hillside adjacent to the site for a spectacular sight. Contact the Port Orford Chamber of Commerce for details.

OCEAN FISHING

No license is necessary to fish for perch, sea trout, ling cod or snapper in the breakwater at Port Orford. You can find many hours of enjoyment and maybe even catch something for dinner. At low tide, you can uncover mussels attached to rocks along the beach, they make great bait.

PORT ORFORD HARBOR

This harbor is popular with divers because of it's abundance of sea life and clear waters.

SALMON HATCHERY

Follow the wide paved road found three miles north of Port Orford west eight miles to the Elk River Salmon Hatchery. This is a beautiful drive bordered on one side by the Elk River and on the other by mountains shrouded in Douglas Fir.

(South of the City)

HUMBUG MOUNTAIN

Six miles south of Port Orford is one of the largest state parks in southwest Oregon. Here you will find a three mile trail to the top of Humbug Mountain. It gives the hardy hiker some pretty spectacular views of the coastline.

This coastal mountain rises 1756' above sea level. At the top there is a lovely tree encircled plateau with a view to the south of Cape Sebastian.

Brush Creek winds it's way through the park along one side of the picnic area. Tables, fireplaces, electric stoves, sink and running water are located here.

POWERS

POWERS PARK

This park is located in the city of Powers on the South Fork Coquille River. Picnic tables, running water and a great swimming hole make this a nice stop.

SOUTH FORK COQUILLE FOREST
SERVICE PARK

South of Powers, you will find this Forest Service park. There are six areas along the river to choose from. They range from four to twenty three miles south of the city. Some provide picnic tables and primitive facilities.

REEDSPORT

DEAN CREEK ELK HERD

You can often see elk grazing in the pasture lands south of State 38, six to seven miles east of Reedsport. The wild elk are most easily spotted in early morning during the fall and winter. The herd gets it's name from Dean Creek which runs nearby.

OREGON DUNES NATIONAL
RECREATION AREA

At the Oregon Dunes National Recreational Area office, 855 Highway Avenue, in Reedsport you can learn how the dunes were formed and obtain information and maps of the area. This 40 mile stretch of the Oregon coast is one of the largest coastal dune areas in the world.

UMPQUA RIVER LIGHTHOUSE
STATE PARK

The Umpqua River Lighthouse was built in 1894 and is the second lighthouse here at Umpqua River. The white tower stands 165' above the sea where it has a flashing red/white signal. Douglas County operates a Visitors Center at the lighthouse. Summer hours (May thru September) are Wednesday thru Saturday from 10:00 a.m. to 5:00 p.m., Sunday 1:00 p.m. to 5:00 p.m. The balance of the year they are open weekends only.

ZIOLKOUSKI BEACH

Ziolkouski Beach is seven miles south of Reedsport. This is an excellent place to park the car and take advantage of Douglas County's beautiful scenery. Hike the sand dunes or walk the beach.

REMOTE

SANDY CREEK COVERED BRIDGE

This covered bridge was built in 1921. It sits adjacent to State 42 near Remote. The 60' bridge spans Sandy Creek.

ROCKAWAY

ROCKAWAY WAYSIDE

Near the city of Rockaway, this wayside has two picnic tables and offers a panoramic view of the Pacific Ocean. Restrooms and beach access are available.

SADDLE MOUNTAIN

SADDLE MOUNTAIN STATE PARK

Saddle Mountain is located 8 miles northeast of the Necanicum Junction on US 26. A trail to the top of the mountain takes you up 2½ miles for a spectacular view of the area. At 3,283', this is the highest peak in Clatsop County and a former forest fire lookout. Picnic tables, toilet facilities and drinking water are available.

SCOTTSBURG

SCOTTSBURG COUNTY PARK

This beautiful little park is adjacent to the Scottsburg Bridge and right on the Umpqua River. What a great place for a picnic!

LOON LAKE

This is one of the most popular recreation sites in the dune area. It offers boating, fishing, swimming, hiking and picnic facilities. The land is part of the Bureau of Land Management's acreage. To reach it head east of Reedsport 13 miles then west 7 miles.

SEASIDE

ART GALLERIES

A look at the local telephone directory will reveal many area art galleries. Each August Seaside puts on a large arts and crafts festival. This provides an excellent opportunity to become acquainted with the area craftspeople.

BEACHCOMBER FESTIVAL

This annual event happens during the first part of April and includes a parade. Contact the Seaside Chamber of Commerce for the exact date and details of free events.

BEE GEE, INC.

At Bee Gee, Inc., 1005 Broadway, you can tour the facilities and see how they take ash and clay and transform it into natural pieces of extreme beauty. Tours are offered daily, June 1st thru mid-September, between 10:00 a.m. and 5:00 p.m. The balance of the year tours are given Tuesday thru Sunday between 10:00 a.m. and 6:00 p.m.

CULLABY LAKE COUNTY PARK

This very popular park is just off US 101 between Seaside and Astoria. It is a favorite spot for fishing, boating, water skiing and picnicking. Located 6 miles north of Seaside it offers you a chance to study nature, hike or just relax.

The park covers 180 acres on the west side of Cullaby Lake and offers 4 boat ramps. This is also the site of the historic Lindgren House.

KLOOTCHY CREEK PARK

This is the site of the world's largest Sitka spruce. Located 6 miles south of Seaside on US 26, this tree is 195' tall, measures 16' in diameter and is over 500 years in age. It's worth a stop if only to see the tree, but you can also explore the area and visit the creek. If it's a hot summer day this is a great place to cool off. Drinking water is piped in and pit toilets are available.

LEWIS & CLARK SALT CAIRN

At Seaside you can see a replica of the salt cairn where a small detachment of men from the Lewis & Clark Expedition spent two months making salt during the winter of 1806. It was constructed to specifications found in diaries of the journey. The low rock cairn has been flattened on top to hold small kettles. The 1806 crew produced 3-4 quarts of salt each day of their stay. This salt was used on the expedition's return journey.

LEWIS & CLARK TURNAROUND

This turnaround officially marks the end of the Lewis and Clark Trail and is the official/unofficial gathering point for all who visit this resort town. A marker commemorates the spot. To get there take Avenue U west to Beach Drive. Head north on Beach Drive 3 blocks to Lewis and Clark Way.

MARKER - UNKNOWN SAILORS GRAVES

In 1895, four unknown Portuguese sailors washed up here on the beach. A simple stone marker commemorates the graves just north of Tillamook Head. In 1965, this area was turned into a shrine.

MISS OREGON PAGEANT

Each year, Seaside is the site of the Miss Oregon Pageant. Activities include a parade and a free picture taking session. It all happens the first weekend after July 4th.

SEASIDE PROMENADE

Seaside is often referred to as Oregon's leading resort city by the sea. It's title as the "Coastal Capital of Oregon" is reflected by the promenade built in 1920. It runs 8,000' along the city's ocean frontage property.

Here the casual stroller has a majestic view south of Tillamook Head, east to Saddle Mountain and west across the Pacific Ocean.

TENNIS COURTS

Public tennis courts are located at Broadway School and Seaside High School.

TRAILS END MARATHON

On the last Saturday in February, Seaside is host to a 26 mile race which is the West Coast version of the Boston Marathon. Although originally organized only to bring tourists to town during the off-season, it has succeeded beyond those goals. The race begins at the Turnaround overlooking the beach, where more than 2000 entrants line up for a real feat of endurance. Spectators line the course to cheer them on.

Seaside is also host to the Seaside Beach Run held each August. This 7 mile course is also interesting for spectators. There is a charge to compete in both races but it's always free to watch and provide encouragement for the participants.

SILETZ

COUNTY PARKS

Lincoln County operates many parks in and around Siletz. Hee-Hee-Ilahee Park, on Highway 229, has a boat ramp and picnic tables. Twin Bridges Park can be visited 5 miles upstream from Siletz. There you will find fishing, swimming, boat ramp, restrooms and picnic facilities. Follow County Road 307 out of nearby Logsden to reach Moonshine Park. This riverside park offers fishing and swimming. Downstream from Siletz you can visit Crawford, Johnson, Morgan and Strome Parks. Morgan and Strome both have boat ramps and picnic facilities.

SILETZ BAY PUBLIC FISHING DOCK

This rugged bit of wharf gives you a chance to fish a little deeper into the ocean without getting your feet wet.

SILETZ FISH HATCHERY

Nine miles from Logsden, on State 209, is the Siletz Fish Hatchery. They raise coho salmon and provide an interesting stop.

SILETZ RIVER STUDIO

Here's your chance to visit a private working studio, meet the artist and experience the natural setting she uses in her work. Take the Kernville-Siletz River Road off US 101 for 5.2 miles to reach the studio. It is open Saturday and Sunday only from 1:00 p.m. to 5:00 p.m.

SIUSLAW NATIONAL FOREST

The Siuslaw National Forest is the only national forest within the first 48 states with any appreciable amount of ocean shoreline. It extends roughly from Tillamook to Coos Bay along the coast and encompasses 624,883 acres in all. The climate of this forest is mild and wet from late fall through early spring. Rainfall is frequent. Summer months are mild.

You can obtain information on public trails and facilities from offices located in Corvallis, Alsea, Reedsport, Hebo, Mapleton and Waldport. The staff can help you to choose hiking trails and, direct you to some of the outstanding scenic wonders located here.

JANORA BAYOT

TILLAMOOK

BLIMP HANGARS

Just south of Tillamook, off US 101, you will see some of the largest wooden structures in the world. This was once a U.S. air base but now houses an industrial area. The hangars are 1,080' long, 300' wide and 195' high. Although you cannot tour the buildings you may drive right up to the hangars and it is interesting to know that they were once used as blimp hangars.

BLUE HERON FRENCH CHEESE FACTORY

Here at Blue Heron you can watch through windows looking into the factory as fine French style cheese is processed. Open from 9:00 a.m. to 6:00 p.m. daily they are ¼ mile north of downtown Tillamook on US 101. Cheese and wine tasting are available.

CLAMMING

The ocean beaches and bays of this area have the largest area of clam beds of any Oregon county. This exciting sport provides excellent food any month of the year. Both razor clams and bay clams can be found. Be ready to dig one hour before low tide and plan on getting wet. You will have to check the current regulations for limits.

The county's four bays also provide excellent sport crabbing most months of the year. No license is needed for either sport.

KILCHIS COUNTY PARK

Off US 101, eight miles north of Tillamook, is Kilchis County Park. A 2½ mile trail, stream, picnic tables, water and restrooms are available in this 2,000 acre recreational spot.

KINGS MOUNTAIN TRAIL

This trail is 2½ miles each way and reaches a high point of 3226'. It is usually closed from December to March because of snow. To reach the trail, take the Wilson River Highway east to Lees Camp Junction and an unmarked logging road on the north side of the highway.

LUCIA WILEY MURAL

Across the street from the Tillamook County Pioneer Museum, in the south lobby of the Tillamook County Courthouse, is a fresco done by Lucia Wiley. The title is "Building of the Morning Star" and it depicts just that. It's worth a stop.

MARINE PARK

Marine Park has picnic tables and a boat ramp. You can find it on Hoquarton Slough and US 101.

MUNSON CREEK FALLS COUNTY PARK

This county operated park contains a 266' waterfall, the highest waterfall in the Coast Range. Located seven miles from Tillamook you can hike amongst old growth firs, maples, alders, cedars, spruce and hemlock. Picnic facilities are available.

TILLAMOOK CHEESE FACTORY

Just north of Tillamook, on US 101, the Tillamook County Creamery is open for self-guided tours from 9:00 a.m. to 5:00 p.m. daily. Large, clean viewing windows allow you to watch as they work the product to its finished state. They process 21 million pounds of cheese here each year and it is the west's largest cheese plant. You will also have the opportunity to sample the finished produce.

Outside is a full-scale, seaworthy, replica of the Morning Star. The original pioneer sailing craft was constructed in 1854 by settlers of the isolated Tillamook Bay area to provide a means of marketing their products.

TILLAMOOK COUNTY PIONEER MUSEUM

This museum is located in the old courthouse and contains three floors of exhibits that include a replica of the interior of a pioneer home, an extensive mounted wildlife collection, military room, rock and mineral collections, natural history exhibits, old automobiles, Indian artifacts, logging artifacts and one of the largest mounted bird collections in the area.

This is a place the whole family will enjoy. Each can view at his own pace wandering about freely. The people on duty are always friendly and ready to give out information on the displays found here. Donations are welcome. The museum is open 8:30 a.m. to 5:00 p.m. weekdays and Saturday, 1:00 p.m. to 5:00 p.m. Sunday. Closed Mondays from October 1st to May 1st.

TILLAMOOK RIVER WAYSIDE

This five acre park is located off US 101, south of Tillamook. It offers a quiet place for a family picnic.

TRASK RIVER FISH HATCHERY

Two fish hatcheries can be visited east of Tillamook. They raise fall and spring chinook as well as coho salmon at both. The first is 7.5 miles east on Chance Road, the second 16 miles east on Trask River Road.

TRASK RIVER RAFT RACES

Each March the Trask River Raft Races are held. Contact the Tillamook Chamber of Commerce for time and location. These races make a great spectator sport.

TILLAMOOK STATE FOREST

The Tillamook State Forest is located in northwestern Oregon. This area was once known as the "Tillamook Burn". Four devastating fires ravaged the area between 1933 and 1951 before a massive rehabilitation/reforestation program was implemented.

In 1973, the land officially became a state forest. It provides a 23 mile network of scenic and historical trails offering a variety of challenge. Shorter hikes, horse and motorcycle trails are available. Contact the Oregon State Department of Forestry for a brochure and trail map.

WALDPORT

BEACHCOMBER DAYS

This festival has been an annual event for over 25 years and is held in July. Prize floats donated by area merchants are dropped by plane on incoming tides. Highlights of the celebration have included a grand parade, sand castle contest, water skiing on the bayfront and dog sled races on the beach. The Newport Chamber of Commerce can provide you with the date and listing of this year's events.

FISHER SCHOOL COVERED BRIDGE

From Waldport, head east on State 34. After 20 miles, take a right on Five Rivers Road. At Siletz Road bear left. Go past Buck Creek Road. One mile on the right you will see the Fisher School Covered Bridge. Crossing over Five Rivers it is now closed to all but foot traffic. Built in 1919 it is 72' long.

GOVERNOR PATTERSON PARK

Barely south of Waldport is another quiet place for a picnic. A hiking trail gives you the opportunity to stretch your legs and view the area.

JAILHOUSE

In Waldport's Old Town you will find a reminder that it wasn't so very long ago that the West was still plenty wild. This sturdy one-room jailhouse doesn't look like a very pleasant place to be locked up.

W. B. NELSON STATE WAYSIDE

Two miles east of town at the W. B. Nelson State Wayside, you will find a nice freshwater swimming dock.

SEAL ROCK

Located three miles north of Waldport is one of Oregon's most delightful beaches. Seal Rock was at the west end of Oregon's first road linking the interior valleys with the coast. The beach here is protected by cliffs and monoliths. These large rocks were created by an underground lava flow 14 million years ago. Early visitors found them covered with large sea lions.

Picnic tables and trails to the beach make this one of the prettiest spots for a picnic on a bright sunny day.

SEAL ROCK ART COOPERATIVE

This art gallery has changing monthly shows devoted to Oregon artists. Located near Seal Rock State Park, they are closed on Mondays and Tuesdays but open from 11:00 a.m. to 5:00 p.m. during the balance of the week.

THE POTWORKS

At The Potworks, visitors are welcome to watch as potter Jim Gore creates stoneware. His studio is located in downtown Waldport.

WARRENTON

WARRENTON CITY PARK

Located near 5th and Main, this quiet little park offers tennis courts, basketball court, baseball field and picnic tables. Parts of this town were settled in 1848.

WARRENTON DEEP SEA, INC.

If you can get there in the early morning, you can see this small cannery in action. The people are friendly and will take you out where the boats pull up to hoist their catch up to the facilities. Watch as it is sorted, weighed, processed, cooked and put into cans. This is a small operation, friendly and particularly appealing to children.

WAUNA

CROWN ZELLERBACH TOUR

Here at Wauna, Crown Zellerbach offers a tour of their wood fiber manufacturing complex. These tours are available on Tuesdays and Thursdays at 2:30 p.m.

WESTPORT

WESTPORT TUNNEL

Westport was settled in 1850. It was named for John West who ran a sawmill here. The Westport tunnel was made by early settlers who saw it as the best way to get their logs down to the river. It is totally unmarked and generally unnoticed except by area residents.

Heading into Westport, from the east, on US 30 you will see a sign directing you to the Westport Toll Ferry. This is on the right. You will turn left and the road immediately Y's. Bear left and look to your right about 1/10 of a mile to see this crude tunnel carved through the hillside.

WINCHESTER BAY

SALMON HARBOR

This has to be one of the best spots along the Oregon Coast to watch commercial fishing boats as they come and go. It is located 4 miles south of Reedsport. This harbor contains around 300 commercial berths and 600 pleasure berths.

UMPQUA RIVER COAST GUARD STATION

Just northwest of Salmon Harbor, in the old Boat Basin, is the Umpqua River Coast Guard Station. They are open to the public daily from 1:00 p.m. to 4:00 p.m.

WINDY COVE PARK

Next to the Salmon Harbor port complex, is Windy Cove Park. It offers hiking, picnic tables, restrooms and a children's playground that includes an old red and white wooden boat. Moored in a sea of sand, children of all ages find it inviting.

YACHATS

ARTS & CRAFTS FAIR

This annual event is a showcase where many local artists display their creations. It is held in March. Contact the Newport Chamber of Commerce for the exact date.

CAPE PERPETUA

The first stop to make here is at the Cape Perpetua Visitor Center. It's theme "Forces of Nature" tells the story of how the area came to be and the changes that have taken place over the past 40 million years. It is open all summer from 9:00 a.m. to 6:00 p.m.

Long before explorers visited the area, Indian villages dotted its land. Today those spots are marked by huge mounds of shells. Trails provide access to tidepools and panoramic vistas. The Riggin' Slinger Trail makes a 6 mile loop. At the visitors center, you can obtain an informational guide for this hike.

Take the Trail of the Restless Waters for a look at Devil's Churn. This foam covered chasm is especially spectacular during coastal storms. The Captain Cook Trail shows off spouting horns and shell mounds. Other trails include Cape Cove, Saint Perpetua and Cape Creek.

A self conducted auto tour starts at the Devil's Churn and winds 22 miles through forested hills and valleys before returning to US 101 at Yachats. A special leaflet is available marking off 19 stops along the route.

As the Oregon coast's highest promontory, Cape Perpetua offers excellent viewpoints for sighting gray whales in the fall.

KITE FESTIVAL

Held on the beach at Yachats early in October, this festival draws kite lovers from all over the country. The exact date varies each year.

LITTLE LOG CHURCH-BY-THE-SEA

This church was built with donated logs, shingles and labor in 1932. Located at 2nd and Pontiac Streets they are open from June through September on Friday, Saturday and Sunday from noon to 4:00 p.m. Local artifacts are on display.

NEPTUNE STATE PARK

Three miles south of Yachats you will find picnic tables, drinking water and restrooms along the coast. This area has an especially scenic rocky shoreline.

NORTH FORK OF THE
YACHATS COVERED BRIDGE

Built in 1938, the North Fork of the Yachats Covered Bridge is just 42' long. From Yachats head east on Yachats River Road for 7 miles. Turn left just beyond the cement bridge. You will travel another 2 miles before coming to this historic bridge.

OF SHIPS & SEAS NAUTICAL MUSEUM

Located on US 101, this museum features nautical antiques and marine decor. They are open daily.

PREHISTORIC LIFE MUSEUM

The Prehistoric Life Museum is located 6½ miles south of Yachats. It includes fossils of a dinosaur egg and bones and teeth of animals that existed eons ago. You will also see fossils of fish, shells and a dragonfly. It's like taking a short journey through 600 million years of time. Children will enjoy this hands on exhibit.

Pictorial dioramas of past geological ages, educational exhibits, a slide program and a 3-D map of Oregon showing rock and fossil collecting areas are a few of the attractions.

They are open daily from May 15 through September.

ROCK CREEK PARK

This Forest Service Park is located ten miles south of Yachats on US 101. Hiking trails and restrooms can be found here.

SMELT BEACH PARK WAYSIDE

Smelt Beach Park Wayside is a well known length of beach where netters come by the thousands each year to harvest the silver smelt that come to shore here between May and September.

YACHATS SILVER SMELT FRY

Yachats is one of the few places in the world where the sea-run smelt come to shore. Early each July the annual run is celebrated with a community Smelt Fry. Many free events accompany this event. The date varies each year.

SECTION II
THE I-5 CORRIDOR

The I-5 corridor includes the fertile Willamette Valley, luscious green forests and outrageous mountains. Portland, Oregon's largest city, and Salem, the capitol, are both here along with hundreds of other cities and towns. Each has its own appeal.

This section offers outstanding views, architectural tours, covered bridges, festivals, winery and industrial tours, museums and art.

Far too many times travelers cover this stretch of road at maximum highway speeds exiting only for a quick meal or gasoline. Yet a look at the following map will show that many other fine roads travel the countryside offering a glimpse of life going on all around the freeway.

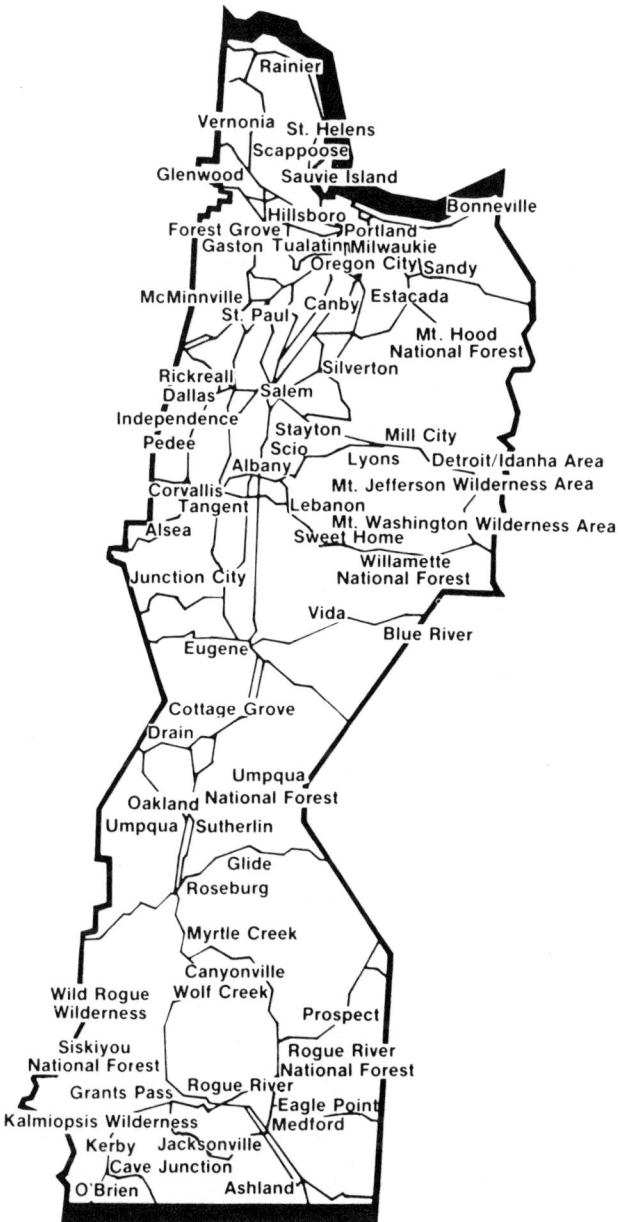

Rainier

Vernonia St. Helens
Scappoose
Glenwood Sauvie Island
Bonneville
Hillsboro
Forest Grove Portland
Gaston Tualatin Milwaukie
Oregon City Sandy
McMinnville Canby Estacada
St. Paul
Mt. Hood
National Forest
Silverton
Rickreall
Dallas Salem
Independence
Pedee Stayton Mill City
Scio
Albany Lyons Detroit/Idanha Area
Corvallis Mt. Jefferson Wilderness Area
Tangent Lebanon
Alsea Mt. Washington Wilderness Area
Sweet Home
Junction City Willamette
National Forest
Vida
Eugene Blue River
Cottage Grove
Drain
Umpqua
Oakland National Forest
Umpqua Sutherlin
Glide
Roseburg
Myrtle Creek
Canyonville
Wild Rogue Wolf Creek
Wilderness Prospect
Siskiyou
National Forest Rogue River
Grants Pass Rogue River National Forest
Kalmiopsis Wilderness Eagle Point
Kerby Jacksonville Medford
Cave Junction
O'Brien Ashland

ALBANY

ARCHITECTURAL TOUR

Albany, Oregon is unique architecturally. It is credited by historians and architects with having the most varied collection of historic buildings in the entire state. No other city can boast of more vintage homes.

Visitors to Albany will discover some 350 buildings of historic value. Many are listed in the National Register of Historic Places. Most are either well preserved or have been faithfully restored to their original condition. Virtually all of these historic homes are private residences. Although they are not open for tours, they offer an unequalled opportunity to view, from the street, homes constructed in nine major styles popular between 1848 and 1930. Architectural styles include Federal, Classic Revival, Gothic Revival, Italianate, French Second Empire Baroque and Colonial Revival. Included are several architecturally elaborate churches and a number of commercial buildings.

The first settlers to the Albany area were farmers who came in the 1840's. In 1848 Walter and Thomas Monteith purchased a plot of land and laid out town lots on the east bank of the Willamette River, just below the mouth of the Calapooia River. Their city was named after Albany, New York. In 1849 the Monteiths built their first frame house. It still stands at 518 Second Avenue SW.

In 1849 Abram Hackleman had the foresight to purchase 70 acres on the east side of Albany for future development.

It isn't any wonder then that two of Albany's three historical areas are named Monteith amd Hackleman. The third is the Downtown District. All three Albany Historical Districts are listed in the National Register of Historic Places.

Below you will find a listing of some of the more spectacular vintage buildings. For an in depth tour maps and brochures can be obtained at the Albany Chamber of Commerce or viewed at the Gazebo located at Eighth Avenue and Ellsworth Street.

Downtown Historic District
213 Water Street (1866)
First & Second Avenue - The 200, 300 and 400 blocks of First & Second Avenues are lined with historic brick buildings. They date from 1866 to 1912. Note the cast iron pilasters and arch windows on some. Since this is an active business district many of these buildings can be viewed from the inside.

Monteith Historic District
Second Avenue - 518 (1849), 528 (1865), 538 (1865)
Fifth Avenue - 510 (1891), 520 (1910), 539 (1888), 630 (1875), 637 (1909), 726 (1900), 802 (1897), 806 (1878), 839 (1885), 914 (1860's), 955 (1889)
Sixth Avenue - 316 (1892), 319 (1910), 320 (1892), 538 (1883), 540 (1898), 705 (1895), 725 (1878), 728 (1892)
Seventh Avenue - 220 (1904), 522 (1900), 532 (1913), 540 (1901)
Eighth Avenue - 339 (1930), 817 (1885)
Eleventh Avenue - 318 (1897)
Twelveth Avenue - 414 (1859)
Broadalbin Street - 624 (1900), 627 (1898), 717 (1885), 724 (1885), 731 (1910), 732 (1886), 804 (1887)
Calapooia Street - 323 (1896), 334 (1889), 432 (1885), 505 (1910), 523 (1898), 606 (1893), 722 (1915), 808 (1860's), 828 (1928)
Ellsworth Street - 704 (1886)
Elm Street - 514 (1889), 516 (1868)
Ferry Street - 506 (1868), 532 (1900), 928 (1897), 940 (1885), 952 (1910), 964 (1910), 1106 (1885)
Maple Street - 906 (1920's), 916 (1920's), 924 (1920's), 934 (1920's)
Walnut Street - 732 (1898)

Washingon Street - 632 (1891), 718 (1905), 730 (1906),
   922 (1885), 1001 (1908), 1004 (1902), 1014 (1892), 1134
   (1912)

Hackleman Historic District
Second Avenue - 522 (1893), 606 (1885), 608 (1885)
Third Avenue - 238 (1875), 529 (1893), 605 (1880), 606
   (1909), 704 (1899), 712 (1899), 718 (1899)
Fourth Avenue - 222 (1898), 240 (1865), 416 (1895), 718
   (1895)
Fifth Avenue - 118 (1868), 128 (1910), 140 (1880), 238
   (1895), 420 (1895), 508 (1878), 527 (1895), 606 (1875),
   627 (1890), 638 (1875)
Sixth Avenue - 208 (1880), 237 (1889), 306 (1906)
Seventh Avenue - 208 (1884), 319 (1886)
Baker Street - 532 (1893), 606 (1875), 632 (1889)
Jefferson Street - 405 (1878)
Lyon Street - 733 (1892), 810 (1889)
Montgomery Street - 331 (1893), 630 (1903)

FREEWAY LAKES

Located southeast of Albany is a delightful spot called
Freeway Lakes. To reach it simply take Three Lakes
Road five miles. Swimming, picnic facilities and a boat
launch are all to be found here. No motors are allowed on
the lake.

PETERSON BUTTE

For an overall view of the city, take a drive to the top of
Peterson Butte, southeast of the city. Leave I-5 on exit 34
toward Lebanon. Turn left on Steckley Road to Sand
Ridge Road. This will take you to the butte.

SPRING ARTS FESTIVAL

Each April, historical homes, museums, galleries and local businesses work together on the Spring Arts Festival. There are many free exhibits held in conjuction with this event. Contact the Creative Arts Guild (928-2999) for details.

TIMBER-LINN MEMORIAL PARK

Timber-Linn Memorial Park is located next to the airport. It offers picnic facilities, playground equipment, softball fields and tennis courts. It also provides an excellent spot from which to watch small aircraft.

VETERAN'S DAY CELEBRATION

This is said to be the world's largest Veteran's Day Celebration. Contact the Albany Chamber of Commerce for a listing of events.

WATERFRONT

Albany's waterfront area represents the restored locale of earlier days when the water was traveled by steamboat.

ALSEA

ALSEA FALLS

Alsea Falls is actually a series of small waterfalls and pools. These pools provide an excellent place for swimming and wading. Here you will also find a small picnic area with trails running beside the river.

To reach the falls turn right just past the bridge, west of Alsea, off State 34. At Alsea Falls Road you will turn left for another nine miles.

HAYDEN COVERED BRIDGE

The Hayden Covered Bridge spans Alsea River two miles west of Alsea. Built in 1918, it is one of the oldest covered bridges in the state. To find this 91' bridge take State 34 west of Alsea to Hayden Road. Turn left to bridge.

MISSOURI BEND PARK

Twelve miles southwest of Alsea, just off State 34, is Missouri Bend Park. This park provides access to the Alsea River. Facilities include picnic tables and a boat ramp.

ASHLAND

EMIGRANT LAKE

At Emigrant Lake you will find boating, water skiing, a swimming area, playground equipment, picnic tables, barbecues and shade trees. Take State 66, five miles south of Ashland. There is a minimal charge on weekends and holidays.

HISTORIC HOMES

Ashland has many late 19th century homes which can be easily viewed from the street. For a minimal charge a brochure mapping out a self-guided walking tour is available at the Ashland Chamber of Commerce. Another area worth viewing is the historic railroad district.

HOLLENBECK ENVIRONMENTAL
STUDY AREA

Just out of Ashland, turn left off State 66 onto Dead Indian Road. After about 15 miles you will reach the

Hollenbeck Environmental Study Area near Conde Creek Road. The rocky slopes of this area harbor a naturally-produced flower garden of continually changing colors.

At milepost marker 26 you will find a short trail leading into a forest thick with glossy evergreens, tall ferns and patches of wildflowers.

HOWARD PRAIRIE LAKE

Dead Indian Road also leads to Howard Prairie Lake. This recreation area is just one in a series of small mountain lakes. Facilities here include a boat ramp.

LITHIA PARK

This is the setting for Ashland's world famous Shakespearean Festival. The 99 acre park is located along Ashland Creek and includes self guided nature walks. These walks are suitable for unsighted visitors.

Children will enjoy the large playground and fountains supplied with Lithia Spring Water. The pipes for this water system were laid in the 1920's and lead from a spring bubbling up on the Cascade foothills. Summer brings band concerts to the park.

OLD FASHIONED
FOURTH OF JULY CELEBRATION

This annual event includes a parade, old time fiddlers contest, baby contest, craft exhibits and a six mile fun run. Fireworks conclude the day's activities.

OREGON COLLEGE OF ART

The Oregon College of Art has a foyer gallery at 30 South First Street. They are open Monday thru Friday from 9:00 a.m. to 1:00 p.m. with later hours during the school year.

SOUTHERN OREGON STATE COLLEGE

Next to the Life Science's greenhouse on the Southern Oregon State College campus is a 30' Dawn Redwood. This tree is from a species common to Oregon millions of years ago and for a long time thought to be extinct.

The Stevenson Union Gallery changes its art exhibits every 3-4 weeks. They are open from 8:00 a.m. till 5:00 p.m. Monday thru Friday staying open until 8:00 p.m. on Mondays.

The Museum of Vertebrate Natural History can also be found on campus. It contains zoological exhibits. Vertebrate specimens, birds, mammals, fish, reptiles and amphibians are all represented.

BLUE RIVER

COUGAR RESERVOIR HOT SPRINGS

Five miles east of Blue River, take Cougar Dam Road off State 126. At the dam stay right, following the road around the west side of the reservoir. You will be on the opposite side from the boat ramp. A half mile trail leads to the springs which are located along a quiet creek. There are three pools.

BONNEVILLE

BONNEVILLE FISH HATCHERY

The Bonneville Fish Hatchery has been in continuous operation since 1909. Within the hatchery complex are 58 rearing ponds, 5 adult holding ponds and a fish ladder. The incubation building has room for 720 hatching baskets. They produce more fish here than in any other hatchery in Oregon.

115

CANBY

CANBY FERRY

Located three miles northwest of Canby, the Canby Ferry is one of the last to operate on the Willamette. Operated by Clackamas County it provides free crossing to cars from 10:00 a.m. to 7:00 p.m. daily. This ferry is cable drawn.

CHAMPOEG STATE PARK

Located twelve miles west of Canby, Champoeg State Park sits on the bank of the Willamette River where an Indian settlement was once situated. The park offers picnic areas, footpaths and a bicycle trail. This is also the location of an informal arboretum. The bicycle path begins at the main parking lot of Riverside Picnic Area and continues for 4 miles. The route passes through large, open plains of former Champoeg townsite and the historic town of Butteville. The park has a minimal charge on weekends and holidays.

At the Visitor's Center, on the bluff overlooking the old Champoeg townsite, you can see an interesting interpretive display about the Indians, fur trade, Oregon Provisional Government and Champoeg townsite.

Two other sites of historic interest are also located here. The Robert Newell Residence and Pioneer Mother's Home. There is a slight admission charge to both.

CLACKAMAS RIVER FISH HATCHERY

The Clackamas River Fish Hatchery was built in 1876. This historic facility is located just off State 212 in McIver State Park.

HEBB PARK

Operated by Clackamas County, this small park includes a picnic area, ball grounds and a boat launch on the Willamette River. It's located just downriver from the Canby Ferry on the north side, off Hoffman and Pete's Mountain Roads.

MAPLE STREET PARK

In Canby, the Maple Street Park provides tennis courts, ball fields, playground and picnic facilities.

MOLALLA RIVER STATE PARK

The Molalla River State Park is a natural habitat that includes a Great Blue Heron rookery and wildlife area. The land borders the Willamette, Molalla and Pudding Rivers. To reach the park follow 99E to the east end of Canby. From there you will take Territorial Road to Holly Street, turn right and continue north three miles to the park.

(Southwest of the City)

AURORA BANK OF OREGON

Southwest of Canby, in the town of Aurora, you can visit the historic Bank of Oregon. Open Monday thru Thursday from 1:00 p.m. to 5:00 p.m. and Fridays from 1:00 p.m. to 6:00 p.m. it is an interesting combination of the old and the new. Rocking chairs, ancient typewriters, bank memorabilia and restrooms complete with old fashioned pull chain toilets are some of the highlights of this living, functioning museum.

CANYONVILLE

CANYONVILLE COUNTY PARK

One mile east of Canyonville, on the banks of the South Umpqua River, this park offers picnic tables and limited hiking. Take the Tiller-Trail Road out of Canyonville.

CHARLES V. STANTON COUNTY PARK

Just north of Canyonville is the Charles V. Stanton County Park. One exciting feature here is the children's playground which includes a special helicopter built just for the kids. The park offers some scenic hiking trails.

LONGFIBRE COUNTY PARK

Head south from Canyonville to Azalea and from there it's just five miles east to Cow Creek Road to Longfibre County Park. The hiking here is excellent and it's an ideal place for a picnic near the mountains.

MILO ACADEMY COVERED BRIDGE

This location has sported a covered bridge since 1920. The current bridge was built in 1962 and is Oregon's only steel bridge housed in wood. The 100' long bridge can be reached by taking State 227 out of Canyonville heading east past Day's Creek. It's another seven miles to the bridge which crosses over the South Umpqua River to the Seventh Day Adventist Academy.

CAVE JUNCTION

MIDDLE-EARTH

Middle-Earth is located two miles north of Cave Junction on US 199. The owners of the Middle-Earth gift shop have created a mini-park here inhabited by Hobbits. Visitors are welcome to wander about in this fantasy land. Children really enjoy it and can even venture inside one small house. It's a delightful place to stretch your legs and exercise small children.

OREGON CAVES

At the Oregon Caves you will find many well maintained, marked trails. Some connect with trails in the adjoining Siskiyou National Forest.

No Name Trail is just a little over a mile round trip. It leads past tumbling mountain streams, wildlife, mossy cliffsides, wildflowers and dense forests.

Another short trail is the Cliff Nature Trail. Here, signs identify the plantlife. The Big Tree Trail is 3 miles round trip and offers a longer alternative return route. Walk in the solitude of a virgin conifer forest with mountain views to see the grand old Douglas fir measuring r.early 13' thick and estimated to be between 1200 and 1500 years old.

COTTAGE GROVE

CHAMBERS COVERED BRIDGE

This railroad bridge was built in 1936 to bring logs to the Frank Chambers Mill in Cottage Grove. It crosses the Coast Fork Willamette River. It is the last covered railroad bridge in Oregon and no longer in use. Follow US 99 through Cottage Grove to Main Street. Head west thru town and turn left on South River Road.

COTTAGE GROVE HISTORICAL MUSEUM

This general museum is housed in a former Catholic church built prior to 1897. Here you can see mining equipment, working models of an 1870 stampmill and an 1960 sawmill, photographs, Indian artifacts and items representative of pioneer home life, farm and industry. The building also has some beautiful stained glass windows.

Hours: July & August -- Open Wednesday thru Sunday from 1:00 p.m. to 5:00 p.m. September thru June they are open weekends only from 1:00 p.m. to 5:00 p.m.

Donations welcome.

COTTAGE GROVE LAKE

Cottage Grove Lake is located on the Coast Fork of the Willamette River five miles south of Cottage Grove. The US Army Corp of Engineers maintains four public parks along its shoreline giving visitors easy access to the clear blue water. Piped water, restrooms and picnic facilities are available. This is a popular area for fishing, swimming and water skiing and offers two boat launching ramps.

CURRIN COVERED BRIDGE

The Currin Covered Bridge is east of Cottage Grove four miles on Row River Road/Layng Road. Built in 1925 it is 105' long and spans the Row River.

DORENA LAKE

Dorena Lake is located in partially wooded hill country five miles east of Cottage Grove. Here you will find three public parks, calm water, picnic tables, boat ramps and swimming beaches. To reach it take the Cottage Grove exit off I-5 and turn left on Row River Road. Keeping right at the Y Dorena Lake is five miles from town.

DORENA TREE NURSERY

This US Forest Service Nursery is on Government Road near Dorena Lake. A phone call to 942-5526 will get you a free tour of the facility.

MOSBY CREEK COVERED BRIDGE

Head east from Cottage Grove two miles to Row River Road and make a right turn to Mosby Creek Road. Drive southwest two miles to Layng Road. The bridge sits over Mosby Creek. It was built in 1920 and is 90' long.

ROBERT B. PAMPLIN
FOREST RESEARCH CENTER

Six miles southeast of Cottage Grove is Georgia Pacific's Tree Experiment Station. This working seed orchard offers a tour of the facilities from April thru October, weekdays between 10:00 a.m. and 2:00 p.m.

STAR/DORENA COVERED BRIDGE

From Cottage Grove, head east five miles on Row River Road. Turn on Government Road for seven miles. The 105' long bridge is spanning the Row River near Dorena. It was built in 1949.

STEWART COVERED BRIDGE

Take Row River Road 1 mile east from Cottage Grove to Mosby Creek Road. The bridge is 2½ miles down this road crossing Mosby Creek. Built in 1930, it is 60' long.

CORVALLIS

AVERY PARK

This city park is located on Marys River off Allen Street. Its 75 acres include picnic facilities, rose gardens, rhododendron gardens, jogging trails, bicycle paths, playground equipment and a sports area.

BENTON COUNTY COURTHOUSE

The Benton County Courthouse is the oldest courthouse in Oregon still used for its original purpose. It was built in 1889. Much of the original detail can still be seen. The ceiling is made up of a plaster radius with cornice at all the edges. An ornate wood and plaster medallion is at the center. Much of the original furniture is still in use including the original judge's bench, jury box, spectator benches, library table and coat rack.

BIKEWAYS

The Corvallis area has several interlinking bike paths. Some, like the Riverfront Path, are separated from the roadway while others consist of bicycle lanes traveling along major traffic routes. Benton County offers a detailed map of area routes. The Riverfront Park path extends all the way to Philomath. Along its way it passes through Pioneer Avery, Bruce Starker Art and Sunset Parks.

CENTRAL PARK

This tiny downtown park has a rose garden and is located across from the downtown library.

OREGON STATE
UNIVERSITY

Oregon State University is Oregon's first college. In existence since 1868 the present day campus covers 400 acres in south Corvallis. Here you will find several free exhibits.

There are two art galleries at OSU. One at Fairbanks Hall and another in Memorial Union. They offer changing displays of sculpture, paintings, ceramics, weaving and graphics.

The Horner Museum first opened in 1925. Exhibits include: Oregon natural history, prehistory and history, artifacts from other cultures and pioneer and Victorian exhibits, birds and animals, rocks, minerals and fossils. Located in the basement of Gill Coliseum they are open at 10:00 a.m. Tuesday through Saturday. They close at 5:00 p.m. weekdays and 2:00 p.m. on Saturday. Sundays they are open from 2:00 p.m. to 5:00 p.m.

Other campus displays include a Herbarium, Entomology exhibits and mounted birds. The latter is located on the first floor of Cordley Hall. To see the Herbarium or Entomology exhibits special arrangments must be made. Call 754-0123 for more information.

Another great place to visit is the OSU Cow Barn. Milking time is from 1:30 p.m. to 4:30 p.m. Drop by any day.

TENNIS

Corvallis offers a great many tennis courts. You will find them at Cloverland Park, Lincoln Elementary, Highland View Intermediate, Western View Intermediate, Corvallis High, Crescent Valley High and Oregon State University.

WILLAMETTE PARK

Picnics and hiking are great pastimes in this 161 acre park on the Willamette River. It is located off Goodnight Road in Corvallis.

E. E. WILSON WILDLIFE AREA

This wildlife area encompasses nearly 1600 acres. A brush-grassland habitat, it attracts over 100 different kinds of large and small birds. It is maintained by the Oregon Department of Fish and Wildlife.

HOSKINS

Hoskins is actually a small town. Many of the original houses and the general store still exist. It is located west of Philomath on State 223. This was the location of Fort Tavern. Established in 1856, time has totally obliterated it. In 1976 a group from OSU organized an archeological dig unearthing a vast number of articles. The dig is on private property.

Nearby Kings Valley is also quite old. The church, cemetery and other buildings remain.

PEAVY ARBORETUM

The School of Forestry at Oregon State University maintains an arboretum seven miles north of Corvallis on State 99W.

(South of the City)

WILLIAM L. FINLEY
NATIONAL WILDLIFE REFUGE

The William L. Finley National Wildlife Refuge is ten miles south of Corvallis along State 99W. It was established to protect and manage the wintering Dusky Canada Geese. The refuge includes over 5,000 acres of Oregon oak, maple, ash and fir growing amid open meadows, pastures and cultivated fields. Waterfowl flock to its marshes and creeks. A self-guided tour provides a look at the area.

125

IRISH BEND COVERED BRIDGE

Just past the wildlife refuge, take a left on Irish Bend Road heading toward Monroe. Over Slough Creek is a 60' covered bridge. It was built in 1954.

(West of the City)

BENTON COUNTY HISTORICAL MUSEUM

Located in Philomath, the Benton County Historical Museum is open noon to 5:00 p.m. Tuesday thru Saturday and 1:00 p.m. to 5:00 p.m. on Sunday.

HARRIS COVERED BRIDGE

Built in 1936, the Harris Covered Bridge takes you over the Marys River. Take State 20 to Wren, then head west on County Road 52 to the bridge.

DALLAS

BLACK ROCK HISTORIC DISTRICT

Eleven miles southwest of Dallas off State 223 you can see some historic homes built in the 1850's. You can also see a ledge of black shale for which the town was named.

DALLAS PUMPING STATION COVERED BRIDGE

This private bridge was built in 1915. The 84' span crosses over Rickreal Creek. To find it, take Eklendale Road out of Dallas for about 2½ miles to Robb Mill Road.

DETROIT/IDANHA AREA

The Detroit/Idanha Area offers many recreational parks. Hiking is particularly enjoyable at Humbug and South Shore Parks, with the latter being in the Breitenbush Springs area. The Breitenbush Hot Springs are found in the Cascades, 11 miles northeast of Detroit. From here you can also enter the Mt. Jefferson Wilderness Area.

You will find great places to enjoy the water at Detroit Dam and Reservoir as well as Detroit Lake State Park. The park is one of the largest on the reservoir. In all, 5 public parks dot its 32 mile shoreline.

You can also take a tour of the Marion Forks Salmon Hatchery. Coho and winter steelhead can be seen 11 miles east of Idanha on State 22.

DRAIN

HISTORIC CHURCH

When driving through Drain you might enjoy stopping at the 100+ year old Church of Christ.

PASS CREEK COVERED BRIDGE

This covered bridge spans Pass Creek near its junction with Elk Creek. It was built in 1925 and is 61' long. Travel First Street through Drain to where it sits adjacent to the schoolground.

ROARING CAMP COVERED BRIDGE

Six miles west of Drain, off State 38, is the Roaring Camp Covered Bridge. It is located along a private road and retains an aged look. The bridge was built in 1929. You can see it from State 38 off to the left.

EAGLE POINT

AGATE LAKE

Agate Lake is a county operated recreational area. It is located off the Crater Lake Highway on Antelope Road.

BUTTE CREEK MILL

In 1872 a water-powered grist mill was established on Little Butte Creek. Today it is listed on the National Register of Historic Places. A small park and museum are located at the site. Museum hours are from 9:00 a.m. to 6:00 p.m. Monday thru Saturday.

CASEY STATE PARK

Enjoy a swim at Casey State Park. This Rogue River park has some lovely picnic spots off State 62.

COLE M. RIVERS FISH HATCHERY

This is the largest fish hatchery in Oregon and the fifth largest in the United States. Approximately five million fish are grown here annually. You will find the hatchery off State 62 just the other side of Casey State Park.

TOU VELLE STATE PARK

This lovely park is located along the Rogue River near White City. The park provides boat access, swimming and picnic facilities.

Table Rock is also located near here. This basalt formation is the result of thousands of years of volcanic activity mixed with erosion. This sheer plateau was the setting for an all-out battle between the Rogue Indians and the white militia. Many Indian men and women jumped from the top to avoid capture by the white soldiers.

ESTACADA

AUSTIN HOT SPRINGS

Upriver from Estacada, along the Clackamas River, is an eleven acre park with many natural hot water springs. Picnic tables, fireplaces, restrooms and piped water to the park area make this a fun place to go.

BAKER LOG CABIN

The Baker Log Cabin is at the junction of Hatton and Gronlund Roads in Carver. The cabin was built in 1856 with stone from the quarry in Baker. Be sure to see the authentic Indian millstone out back where flour was once ground from local nuts, bulbs and seeds.

This is also the location of an old German Church. Built in 1895 it was moved to this spot in 1967.

Near here you will also find a waterfall and caves along Rock Creek.

BARTON PARK

Just south of Barton, by the bridge, you can enjoy 100 acres along the Clackamas River. Facilities include: a boat ramp, restrooms, playground equipment, ball field, horseshoe pits and picnic tables. Take Highway 212 towards Estacada, turn right at the fork and follow signs to the park.

BRYN SEION - WELSH CHURCH

In 1884 the Welsh Community here began their efforts to build a church. This little building in Beavercreek is the culmination of those efforts. Services are still held here. Although now said in English, the service still includes two Welsh hymns done in their native tongue.

An annual song festival is held here on the last Sunday in June. Known as the Gymanfa Ganu, it attracts visitors from far and wide to witness something that has become a tradition. It was first started by early settlers. To find the church take Molalla Blvd. out of Oregon City to Beavercreek.

CLACKAMAS RIVER

The Clackamas River is a favorite for area rafters. Fourteen miles can be rafted in about six hours and the highway parallels the river for easy shuttling. Runnable year round, the river is surrounded by an area peppered with hiking trails.

EAGLE CREEK NATIONAL
FISH HATCHERY

The Eagle Creek hatchery is thirteen miles east of Estacada. Take State 211 south four miles to Wildcat Mountain Road and follow the signs. The hatchery is open daily from 7:30 a.m. to 4:15 p.m. If you can time your visit for fall, you can see spawning operations.

EAGLE FERN PARK

Eagle Fern Park is out toward Eagle Creek approximately five miles to the east of State 211/224's junction. As Clackamas County's largest park, it covers 300 acres in one of the largest old growth stands of Western Red Cedar and Douglas Fir. Covered picnic facilities, restrooms, playground and nature trails are all found here.

PHILIP FOSTER HOUSE

On the third Sunday of every month, this historic old residence is open to the public from noon till 5:00 p.m. Located just east of the Eagle Creek Post Office, it was once an important supply stop for pioneer wagons coming over the Barlow Road.

METZLER PARK

Metzler Park is shaded by huge Cedar and Douglas Fir tess. A picturesque foot bridge and enchanting hiking trails entice you to this 180 acres of land on Clear Creek. Approximately 5 miles south of Estacada, the park is west of State 211 off Holman and Springwater Roads. Baseball, volleyball and basketball facilities, horseshoe pits, restrooms, picnic tables and running water are all provided.

PROMONTORY PARK

Take Clackamas River Road east out of Estacada to North Fork Reservoir. At this PGE park you will find picnic tables, fireplaces and running water plus a special Small Fry Lake. Here youngsters under 14 years of age can catch up to 3 fish per day in a stocked 1 acre pond.

RIVER MILL PARK

PGE also operates River Mill Park along the Clackamas River, one mile west of Estacada. A short trail, playground equipment and picnic tables make it an ideal place for families. The two-mile long reservoir behind the dam, Estacada Lake, has a boat launching ramp.

ROCK LAKES BASIN

You'll find high mountain backcountry southeast of Estacada off State 224. To get there you leave the highway at Promontory Park and follow Forest Service Roads S45, S457 and S456. This takes you along the historic Abbott Road route. Although the road is rough in spots, the views are exceptional. This area has several outstanding lakes, hiking trails and scenic vistas. Located in the remote headwaters of the Roaring River, it offers solitude with some spectacular trees and spring flowers. A trail map is available from the Mt. Hood National Forest Service.

ROCKHOUNDING

The river bed above Estacada produces gem quality cinnabar, petrified woods and dark green bloodstones. Although many of the stream beds are on private land, careful inquiry will sometimes get you permission for casual rockhounding.

EUGENE

ART GALLERIES

Eugene has several fine art galleries with names like Soaring Wings, Designworks, Original Graphics, Kairos, Visions & Perceptions, Emerald Empire, Gallery 30 and Opus 5.

Housed in an 1895 Presbyterian church, is the Maude Kerns Art Center open 9:00 a.m. to 5:00 p.m. weekdays and 11:00 a.m. to 5:00 p.m. Saturday and Sunday.

EUGENE PARKS

Amazon Park, at 27th and Hilyard, offers picnic facilities, tennis courts, playground equipment, wading pool and sport areas on 80 acres of land.

At Summit and Skyline Drive you will find the Hendricks Rhododendron & Azalea Garden. The 80+ acres include some spectacular gardens along with all the usual park amenities.

Owens Municipal Rose Garden is small, but offers a lovely rose garden and picnic tables.

Skinner Butte has an observatory at the top along with picnic areas and playgrounds. This is part of Skinner's original Donation Land Claim and contains the ruins of the University observatory. A trail to the top will show you Skinner's cabin site and a replica of the cabin itself.

Sladden Park has tennis courts and a play area.

Spencer Butte is at the southern edge of Eugene and offers a short trail to the summit. Take Willamette Street, two miles south of the city limits to this 305 acre park.

EUGENE SATURDAY MARKET

Every Saturday, rain or shine, from early April through Christmas you can view handmade and homegrown products at Eugene's Saturday market. Located in the parking lot across from the County Courthouse, downtown, it opens at 10:00 a.m. Festivities often include: puppet shows, clowns, jugglers and musicians. This is also a great spot for "people watching".

HISTORIC BUILDINGS

The following listings are historical buildings belonging to private parties. They can be viewed from the outside only, but for those interested in architecture they provide an interesting tour.

Smeede Hotel (1884)
767 Willamette Street

Shelton-McMurphy House (1888)
303 Willamette Street

330 High Street (1860)

260 High Street (1850's)

205 East 3rd Avenue (1890's)

252 Pearl Street (1900's)

246 East 3rd Street (1870's)

170 East 12th Avenue (1855)

129 East 13th Avenue (1867)

1361 Pearl Street (1880's)

1389 Pearl Street (1890's)

1611 Lincoln Street (1869)

2056 Lincoln Street (1890's)

2050 Madison Street (1857)

1006 Taylor Street (1891)

1268 Jackson Street (1870's)

HINMAN VINEYARDS

You can take a tour of the facilities and taste the fine wines made here from April thru September. Open weekends from noon to 5:00 p.m. they are located off Territorial Road on Briggs Hill Road in Eugene.

LANE COUNTY CLERK'S OFFICE

This is the oldest authenticated building in Lane County. It is also one of the oldest public buildings still standing in the state. Built in 1853, it is an example of Greek Revival architecture which was so popular in Oregon at that time. The building rests on the original hand-hewn sills, and the original clapboard siding shows the vertical cut marks of a whip saw. Located at the fairgrounds.

The local Masonic Cemetery was also started about that time with the oldest burial recorded at 1854. Eugene's I.O.O.F. Cemetery was established in 1873.

LANE COUNTY PIONEER MUSEUM

This museum has a fine display of local history which includes a manuscript and photograph collection. They are open Tuesday through Friday from 10:00 a.m. to 4:30 p.m. and on weekends from 1:00 p.m. to 4:30 p.m. Donations welcome.

UNIVERSITY OF OREGON

When the University of Oregon first opened in 1876 it was situated on a barren knoll in a treeless pasture. Donations made since that time have produced a campus sporting over 400 different types of trees and a beautiful setting taking up 250 acres.

A guided campus tour can be taken weekdays at 10:30 a.m. or 2:30 p.m. It starts at the Oregon Hall Information Desk. A self-guided walking tour map is also available.

The campus also houses the University Museum of Art. This is the only state supported art museum in Oregon and holds a significant collection of Northwest art, Oriental art and photography. Hours are from noon to 5:00 p.m. Tuesday thru Sunday from the beginning of fall term through Mid-August. There is sometimes a charge for special exhibits.

The University campus also has a Museum of Natural History. It is open weekdays from 10:00 a.m. to 3:00 p.m. and Saturday from noon to 3:00 p.m.

WILLAMETTE VALLEY FOLK FESTIVAL

This annual event is held late in May and lasts an entire weekend. It all happens on the University of Oregon campus and includes local folk performers, workshops, demonstrations, films and outdoor music performances. A lot of events offered are free.

WEYERHAEUSER TOUR

During the summer you can take a two hour tour of the Weyerhaeuser Springfield mill. It covers the sawmill, paper mill and presto logs. The tour begins at 9:30 a.m. on weekdays. During the balance of the year tours can be arranged for groups by calling 746-2511.

(North of the City)

ERNEST COVERED BRIDGE

Three miles past Marcola, on Marcola Road, turn right onto Pachelke Road to find this 1938 covered bridge located over the Mohawk River.

WENDLING COVERED BRIDGE

From Springfield take 14th Street, which soon becomes Marcola Road, to Marcola. Turn east on Wendling Road. The bridge is situated four miles from here over Mill Creek. Built in 1938, it is 60' long. Nearby you will see the railroad grade remains and deserted camp homes that constitute the site of an early 1900 lumber company mill.

(East of the City)

COYOTE COVERED BRIDGE

Out of Eugene take state 126 east to Crow Road, then turn left. At Territorial Highway, take another left and follow Battle Creek Road to the 60' bridge spanning Coyote Creek. It was built in 1922.

FALL CREEK LAKE

Fall Creek Lake is at the southern end of the Willamette Valley. The shoreline is a blend of forest and grassy meadows. Two parks offer boat ramps, picnic facilities and swimming. Take the Fall Creek Trail for a beautiful four mile hike to view the 286' Salt Creek Falls. This is the second highest waterfall in the state.

LOOKOUT POINT & DEXTER LAKE

These two lakes are found along the middle fork of the Willamette River south of Eugene. At both lakes you will find boat ramps, picnic facilities and swimming areas.

LOWELL COVERED BRIDGE

From Eugene, take State 58 southeast approximately 15 miles to Lowell Road. The 1945 bridge straddles the Middle Fork Willamette River. It is 165' long.

PARVIN COVERED BRIDGE

Southeast of Eugene, at Dexter, follow Lost Creek Road to Parvin Road. The bridge is over Lost Creek. Although traffic now bypasses it, this 1921 bridge was once the scene of much activity.

PENGRA COVERED BRIDGE

From Jasper, head four miles southeast on Pengra Road to Little Fall Creek Road. Turn on Place Road to find the 120' bridge spanning Fall Creek. It was built in 1938.

UNITY COVERED BRIDGE

At the town of Lowell you will find this covered bridge on Unity Place Road over Big Fall Creek. Built in 1936 it is 90' long.

(West of the City)

FERN RIDGE LAKE

Fern Ridge has the most well developed facilities and the warmest water of all Lane County's major reservoirs. More than 9,000 acres of surface offer water skiing enthusiasts a lot of space. The steady winds also please the sailors. A half dozen parks dot the shoreline offering picnic facilities, beach access and boat ramps. One of the finest parks in the Northwest is located at Orchard Point.

To reach the lake head west out of Eugene on State 126 for approximately 12 miles.

FOREST GROVE

HENRY HAGG LAKE & SCOGGINS DAM

The creation of Scoggins Dam along the creek has created a 1,113 acre reservoir. The lake offers four recreational areas along its shores which include boat launching, picnic facilities and running water. A few hiking trails and a winter population of elk and black-tailed deer make it a pleasant year round spot.

PACIFIC UNIVERSITY MUSEUM

Pacific University was originally established in 1848 as a school for orphans. Shortly thereafter it became known as Tualatin Academy and in 1854 it was given it's present title.

138

JANORA BAYOT

Old College Hall has a special place in Oregon history. In fact, it is the oldest building still used for educational purposes west of the Rocky Mountains. The Hall has been preserved almost intact, just as the pioneers built it. The original cupola still identifies the building as it did in 1850.

Inside, the building has seen few changes. You will pass through doorways installed by pioneer carpenters; surrounded by plain plank walls and panes of glass that were brought around Cape Horn on sailing ships.

Upstairs, the Pioneer Room has an exhibit of Indian artifacts as well as numerous possessions belonging to the founders of the school and other Tualatin Valley pioneers. In the Oriental Room you will see pieces representative of many Asian cultures.

The museum is open to the general public Wednesdays from 1:00 p.m. to 4:00 p.m.

GASTON

HISTORIC RESIDENCE

The residence of Mrs. Ray Nixon is the last house on Lee Falls Road and can be seen at no charge by appointment. This private home is filled with antiques and primitive furniture. Nearby is Oregon's largest yew tree. For an appointment call 985-7033.

GLENWOOD

TROLLEY MUSEUM

The Oregon Electric Railway Historical Society operates a small street railway museum complete with running streetcars. There's a charge to ride the trolley, but no charge at all to look or visit the museum.

GLIDE

CAVITT CREEK COVERED BRIDGE

The Cavitt Creek Covered Bridge crosses Little River near its junction with Cavitt Creek. The portals are odd-shaped, to accommodate heavy log truck usage. The bridge has a metal roof and the floor is layered with asphalt. Built in 1943 it is 70' long.

From Glide, take County Road 17A south about a mile. Stay to the left toward Peel. At the intersection of 17 and 82A you will find the bridge.

LITTLE RIVER

When the waters of the Little River collide with those of the North Umpqua River it creates a unique phenomenon. This is one of the few places in the world where two rivers meet head on.

RICHARD G. BAKER MEMORIAL PARK

This park offers some excellent hiking trails along with picnic facilities. It is located seven miles east of Glide on the North Umpqua Highway.

SMITH SPRINGS COUNTY PARK

Ten miles east of Glide, on the North Umpqua Highway, is the Smith Springs County Park. This picturesque picnic site also offers some good hiking trails.

GRANTS PASS

ANNUAL DOLL SHOW

Each year the Rogue Valley Doll Club holds its annual doll show during June. Contact the Grants Pass Chamber of Commerce for the exact date.

BAND CONCERTS

During the months of July and August free band concerts are held in City Park.

CATHEDRAL HILLS PARK

This county operated park offers picnic facilities, restrooms and hiking trails. Less than one mile east of Grants Pass, leave State 99 to turn right on Cloverlawn Drive. After nearly two miles turn left and follow Walker Road to the park.

CHRISTIE HOP YARDS

Visitors are welcome at the Christie Hop Yards on Lower River Road. Here you can follow the fascinating process from the use of the automatic vine stripper and sorters to the drying room and balers. Hop yards have to be seen to be appreciated. The heavily laden vines are at their fullest in late August, topping and sometimes breaking the 12-14' high wire supports.

FISH HATCHERY PARK

This county park offers picnic tables, grills, running water and restrooms. South of Grants Pass leave State 238 to turn right on New Hope Road to Fish Hatchery Road. Follow this past the junction with Wetherbee Road to Fish Hatchery South.

FRY MINT FARMS

The Fry Mint Farms have about 800 acres of colorful emerald green mint. Located on Riverbanks Road, this sea of plants is backed by purple hills and blue waters. Visitors are welcome during harvest time, late August, when the mint is distilled and several hundred barrels of pure mint oil concentrate are prepared for shipment. Children always enjoy the site of the snowy white geese that keep the fields free of weeds and bugs.

JOSEPHINE COUNTY PARKS

The following county operated parks are all located within four miles of Grants Pass.

Chinook Park — picnic tables, grills, water supply, restrooms, boat ramp.

Pierce Riffle Park — picnic tables, grills, water supply, restrooms, hiking trails, boat ramps.

Tom Pearce Park — picnic tables, grills, water supply, restrooms, hiking trails.

Schroeder Park — picnic tables, grills, water supply, restrooms, hiking trails, boat ramp. On the Rogue River.

These parks are all found west of Grants Pass along the Rogue River toward Grave Creek:

Whitehorse Park — picnic tables, water supply, restrooms, hiking trails.

Matson Park — picnic tables, water supply, restrooms. On the Rogue River.

Ferry Park — picnic tables, grills, restrooms, boat ramp to the Rogue River.

Griffin Park — picnic tables, grills, water supply, restrooms, hiking trails and boat ramp to the Rogue River.

Robertson Bridge Access — picnic tables, restrooms, boat ramp. This park offers a scenic view of the Rogue River surrounded by mountains and farmlands.

Indian Mary Park — picnic tables, grills, water supply, restrooms, hiking trails and boat ramp on the Rogue River. This was once the smallest Indian reservation in the United States. A historical marker nearby tells the story. Take the Merlin exit off I-5 to reach this one.

Ennis Riffle Park — picnic tables, restrooms, boat ramp.

Alemeda Park — picnic tables, grills, water supply, restrooms and a boat ramp on the Rogue River.

Grave Creek Access — restrooms, hiking trails. The trailhead at Grave Creek Bridge will lead you along the Rogue River Trail. It's only two miles to Rainie Falls. From there you can continue on or turn back.

LAKE SELMAC

This man-made lake is located in a fairytale wonderland 20 miles south of Grants Pass. The lake is stocked with trout and bass and the park offers picnic facilities, hiking trails, restrooms, swimming and a boat ramp. No speed boats or water skiing allowed. This county park is half mile south of Selma on State 199. Turn left on Upper Deer Creek Road to the park.

MYRTLEWOOD PRODUCTS, INC.

Myrtlewood Products at 6th and D Streets in Grants Pass allows visitors to watch as the craftsmen turn rough, raw myrtlewood into exquisite satin finished gifts. You are welcome to visit Monday through Saturday from 9:00 a.m. to 5:00 p.m.

RIVERSIDE PARK

At Riverside Park you will find the only Oregon lawn bowling green outside of Portland. The park is shaded and has well kept banks and playground. Sports fields and picnic sites are available.

ROGUE RIVER BOATNIK

This Memorial Day Classic includes a parade, queen selection and a 50 mile white water race over a perilous course.

SAVAGE RAPIDS DAM

Six miles south of Grants Pass on State 99 you will find a three mile lake where boating and water skiing can be enjoyed from mid-April to mid-October. Fishing ladders at the dam are great to watch during the late spring and summer as salmon and steelhead make their way upriver.

THE TRAIN GALLERY

The Train Gallery sports one of the largest model railroad layouts and exhibits in the Northwest as well as a fine art gallery. Located at 1951 Redwood Avenue, they are open Tuesday through Friday from noon till 7:00 p.m. and on Saturday from 10:00 a.m. to 5:00 p.m.

HILLSBORO

INDUSTRIAL TOURS

Oak Knoll Winery, Inc.
Located four miles south of Hillsboro along State 219, take Burkhalter Road half mile to winery. Tours are available between 2:00 p.m. and 6:00 p.m., Thursday thru Sunday, or by appointment. Call 648-8198.

Rodgers Organ Company - 648-4181
1300 NE 25th Avenue
The last Thursday of every month the people at Rodgers Organ Company have a tour which allows you to see the manufacturing of one of their fine organs. You will see all

steps involved, from start to finish. They ask that you be over the age of 17 and recommend calling 3-4 days in advance to reserve a spot on the tour.

Trus-Joist Northwest Corp. - 648-6641
550 South Bailey
If you are interested in construction techniques you'll probably find the tour at Trus-Joist interesting. They manufacture roof and floor trusses using both wood and steel. You have to call ahead for an appointment and be prepared to sign a statement that you won't reveal any of their special processes but then you can see everything from the finger joining of the wood to the punch press working the steel and assembly.

WASHINGTON COUNTY MUSEUM

At the Washington County Museum you will find county and regional artifacts, changing displays, photographs and library materials. The museum is located on PCC's Rock Creek Campus, 17677 NW Springville Road. They are open Monday thru Saturday from 9:00 a.m. to 4:30 p.m. The Rock Creek Campus also offers ever changing art displays in the Northwest Room of the library.

INDEPENDENCE/ MONMOUTH

ART GALLERIES

You'll find three free art galleries at Western Oregon State College in Monmouth. At the College Center you can drop by any day - Monday thru Saturday between 8:00 a.m. and 9:00 p.m., Sundays it's noon to 5:00 p.m. Campbell Hall and the second floor Administration Building exhibits are open Monday thru Friday between 8:00 a.m. and 5:00 p.m.

BIKE PATH

There is a 14 mile bike path beginning at Monmouth that takes you all the way to Wallace Marine Park in West Salem.

INDEPENDENCE HERITAGE MUSEUM

This museum covers local history. You will find it at Third and B Streets in the old First Baptist Church building. They are open Wednesday thru Sunday from 1:00 p.m. to 5:00 p.m. Donations are welcome.

MONMOUTH/INDEPENDENCE ARTS FESTIVAL

Every year, in early July, the Monmouth/Independence Community Arts Association holds their annual Arts Festival and Fair. This event offers music, dancing, arts and crafts exhibits and children's activities. Many are free.

A Fourth of July Celebration is sponsored by the Monmouth/Independence Chamber of Commerce. Each year they host a late morning parade as well as fireworks at dusk in Polk Marine Park.

POLK MARINE PARK

Picnicking, boating, softball and swimming are a few things to be enjoyed here at Polk Marine Park.

TENNIS COURTS

Tennis courts are available for public use at Monmouth Elementary, Independence's Henry Hill Elementary plus local high schools and college campuses.

JACKSONVILLE

APPLEGATE PARK

Southwest of Jacksonville, at the town of Applegate, you will find a charming little park with its own swimming hole.

ARMSTRONG HOUSE

This lovely old home is open on Fridays and Saturdays from 1:00 p.m. to 4:00 p.m. at no charge. Built in 1858, it is an excellent example of "salt box" architecture. It is open during the summer only.

BEEKMAN BANK

The Beekman Bank was built in 1863. Over $30 million in gold passed over these counters.

BEEKMAN HOUSE

You can take a guided tour of this 1881 house. It has been fully restored with furnishings throughout the house representing styles from 1881 to 1915. Open daily from 1:00 p.m. to 4:30 p.m. Donations welcome.

GOLD

A marker at Applegate and Oak in Jacksonville shows the original site of the 1851 gold discovery here. The surrounding area was a favorite for gold seekers.

JACKSONVILLE MUSEUM

This building was once the County Court House. Today it serves as a museum. The building itself was built in 1884 but when the county seat was moved in 1927 it became vacant. One outstanding exhibit inside is a collection of Peter Britt Photographs depicting pioneer life. Donations are welcome.

PIONEER DAYS

Every June this town hosts Pioneer Days. A parade, games, entertainment and hand pumper firetruck demonstrations are all features of the event. Contact the Jacksonville Chamber of Commerce for the exact date.

RAILROAD DEPOT

The old railroad depot is now the home of the Jacksonville Chamber of Commerce. Built in 1891, it has been beautifully restored.

TOWN PROPER

This entire town is a National Historic Landmark. Established in 1851, it is steeped in tradition left behind from old gold rush days. Reminders of Jacksonville's colorful past are all around you. Visit the historic old cemetery first put to use in 1859. The Sexton's tool house there was built with a trap door in the floor so bodies could be stored while graves were prepared. The cemetery is also an excellent viewpoint.

Jacksonville offers a chance to view wooden and brick buildings unchanged since the early 1850's when they were built. It has never been a ghost town. After the gold rush, it evolved into a prosperous agricultural center and remains, as always, a living and working reminder of the nineteenth century. Over 70 Victorian homes and buildings dot the surrounding area.

You can take a self-guided tour of the area with the help of a map available at the Jacksonville Museum.

VALLEY VIEW VINEYARD

Just south of Ruch you can take an informal tour of the Valley View Vineyard. They are open daily, from April 15 thru December 31 from 11:00 a.m. to 5:00 p.m. but only on weekends the balance of the year. The hours then are 1:00 p.m. to 5:00 p.m.

JUNCTION CITY

JUNCTION CITY HISTORICAL MUSEUM

The Junction City Historical Museum is only open on the last Sunday of each month. You will find it located in a historical old home on Holly between 6th and 7th Streets.

SCANDINAVIAN FESTIVAL

The second weekend in August, Junction City plays host to a four day event known as the Scandinavian Festival. Each day emphasizes a different Scandinavian group. Swedish, Norwegian, Finnish and Danish are all honored. Free outside stage performances. More information can be obtained by calling 998-3300.

WASHBURNE STATE PARK

Three miles north of Junction City on State 99 is Washburne State Park. It's a good place for a quiet picnic. Another notable picnic spot, Blue Star Pond, can be found five miles south of Junction City on Highway 99.

KERBY

JOSEPHINE COUNTY HISTORICAL MUSEUM

Housed in a picturesque two story 1860's home, the Josephine County Historical Museum reflects life as it was over a hundred years ago. Displays include: historical artifacts, a turn-of-the-century log school house, a blacksmith's shop, and the home's furnishings.

TOWN PROPER

This reconstructed ghost town is complete right down to its wooden sidewalks. According to legend the town got its start when a man packing a pool table by mule from Crescent Ctiy got stuck here when his mule died. This was around 1856.

LEBANON

CENTURY PARK

In Lebanon, at Fifth and Rose Streets, you will find picnic facilities, a ball diamond, lighted tennis and basketball courts and a fenced play area.

FOSTER RESERVOIR DAM & LAKE

Water skiing and rafting are two popular pastimes at Foster Reservoir. Picnic facilities and hiking trails add to your enjoyment.

INDUSTRIAL TOURS

Commodore Corporation — 258-7114
This Lebanon business offers a tour of their mobile home plant. Call ahead to arrange an appointment.

Champion Timberlands Nursery — 451-1460 ext. 291
During the summer you can make an appointment to see stages of growth at this nursery which include seed preparation to year-old seedlings prepared for planting.

Foster Fish Hatchery
No appointment is necessary to visit the fish hatchery. They are open from 8:00 a.m. till 5:00 p.m. To find them just take State 20 half mile from Foster.

Happy Valley Tree Farm — 258-6643
This family owned tree farm offers tours by appointment only. They are real friendly and enjoy showing you everything from seedlings to mature trees.

Lebanon Community Hospital — 258-2147
The Lebanon Community Hospital offers informational tours by appointment only.

Lebanon Fire Hall — **451-1471**
Tours are available here most any time but you must call ahead for an appointment. The firemen here go all out for the children with a tour of the station, engine room and barracks.

Roaring River Fish Hatchery
Located east of Crabtree the Roaring River Fish Hatchery is open to the public from 8:00 a.m. to 5:00 p.m.

LARWOOD PARK & COVERED BRIDGE

Three miles north of Lacomb, on Fish Hatchery Drive, you can swim, fish and picnic in the shadow of Larwood Covered Bridge. The bridge was built in 1939 and is 105' long.

McDOWELL CREEK PARK

McDowell Creek Park is twelve miles southeast of Lebanon on McDowell Creek Drive. Here, in this natural setting, you can enjoy a lovely waterfall, hiking trails and picnic facilities.

ROARING RIVER PARK

East of Crabtree, on Fish Hatchery Road, you will find a delightful little park complete with picnic facilities, nature trails and swimming.

SODAVILLE

This historic little village was an early day mineral spring spa in the 1890's. Here you can visit tiny Sodaville Park, one of Oregon's oldest, established in 1871.

STRAWBERRY FESTIVAL

This annual event got its beginnings in 1909. It is held around the last weekend in May and features the "world's largest strawberry shortcake". Arts, crafts, music and exhibits are just a few of the varied enticements offered during the festival.

WATERLOO PARK

Three miles southeast of Lebanon, on the South Santiam River, you can visit Waterloo Park. It offers a large picnic area, swimming, hiking, nature trails, boat ramp and a children's playground.

LYONS

HANNAH COVERED BRIDGE

This 105' long bridge spans Thomas Creek 8 miles east of Lyons along State 226. Built in 1936, it has partially exposed trusses. This is a feature unique to the Linn County Covered Bridges.

JOHN NEAL MEMORIAL PARK

This small park is exceptional! The most delightful aspect is the beaver colony that resides in the natural area which allows for observation. Picnic facilities, playground equipment, hiking trails and restrooms are available.

McMINNVILLE

AMITY VINEYARDS

South of McMinnville, on State 99, is Amity Vineyards. Visitors are welcome here from June 1 thru September 30 on weekends, and holidays between noon and 5:00 p.m.

DAYTON BLOCKHOUSE

East of McMinnville, in Dayton, at the city park you will find a military blockhouse. Originally built in 1856 at the Grand Ronde Agency by Willamette Valley Settlers, it was known as Fort Yamhill. In 1911, the fort was dismantled and rebuilt here at Dayton.

GLACIAL ERRATICS

A marker, seven miles west of McMinnville along State 18, points out a fine grained rock which was rafted by iceberg from a spot far up the Columbia River, at the close of the ice age. Erratics are so called because they

were brought naturally from their original resting place and are totally unrelated to any local rocks. This is one of the largest of many found in the Willamette Valley.

LINFIELD COLLEGE

This Baptist college was incorporated in 1858 and renamed Linfield College in 1922. Pioneer Hall was built in 1882.

Stop in at the observatory, the oldest in the northwest and see an 1890's telescope. Visitors are welcome Monday thru Thursday from 9:00 a.m. to 10:00 p.m., Friday from 9:00 a.m. to 5:00 p.m. and Saturday from 1:00 p.m. to 5:00 p.m.

The Renshaw Art Gallery displays contemporary art. They are also open Monday thru Thursday from 9:00 a.m. to 10:00 p.m., Fridays from 9:00 a.m. to 5:00 p.m. and Saturday from 1:00 p.m. to 5:00 p.m.

McMINNVILLE AIRPORT

McMinnville Airport offers tables for picnickers, plus a second-floor observation deck looking out over the runway. A city park is found at the west end of the airport offering nature trails, picnic tables, and restrooms.

YAMHILL COUNTY HISTORICAL
MUSEUM

Northeast of McMinnville, in Lafayette, you can visit the Yamhill County Historical Museum. Here the historical

society maintains the old Poling Memorial Church built in 1893, as well as a Farm Tool Museum. Exhibits relate to historical events of the area. Their summer hours are Wednesday thru Sunday from 1:00 p.m. to 5:00 p.m. During the balance of the year they are open weekends only from 1:00 p.m. to 4:30 p.m. Donations are welcome.

MEDFORD

ANNUAL BUG-IN

Every August, Medford is host to an all Volkswagen car show sponsored by the Southern Oregon VW Club and Central Import Parts. This happening is open free to the public. Contact either of the above, or the Medford Chamber of Commerce, for details.

ANTELOPE CREEK COVERED BRIDGE

Take State 62 north out of Medford to it's junction with State 140, then head east about five miles to Antelope Road. The bridge is one mile from here over Antelope Creek. It is 58' long and was built in 1922.

CRATER ROCK MUSEUM

At Central Point, just northwest of Medford, you can view gold nuggets, Indian artifacts, fossils and geological exhibits. They are open Monday thru Saturday 9:00 a.m. to 5:00 p.m. and Sundays from 1:00 p.m. to 5:00 p.m. Donations are welcome.

INDUSTRIAL TOURS

Just west of I-5, at the Barnett Road exit, are two companies that welcome visitors. Both offer guided tours of their facilities weekdays from October 15 thru December 15 from 8:30 a.m. to 10:30 a.m. and 1:00 p.m. to 3:30 p.m.

Harry & David's is the world's leading shipper of food and fruit gifts.

Jackson & Perkins' are the world's largest rose growers. Visit their 33,000 square foot Test and Display Garden. It features award winning roses, daffodils, tulips, iris, lillies, gladiolus, dahlias, dianthus, daylillies and more. Each spring, Jackson & Perkins ship over 6,000,000 rose bushes out of their Medford plant. Most are grown in the San Joaquin Valley.

LOST CREEK COVERED BRIDGE

Take State 140 north of Medford to the Lake Creek exit. From here you will follow S. Fork Little Butte Road to Lost Creek Road. The Lost Creek bridge is a half mile south. Built in 1919, the 39' bridge is the shortest covered bridge still standing in Jackson County.

LOST CREEK DAM

The upper waters of the Rogue River offer spectacular views and some excellent fishing. At Lost Creek Dam you will find a lovely lake, park and fish hatchery. Enjoy a picnic at McGregor Park beside the rushing river, tour the hatchery or just relax and enjoy the water. All three are located north of Medford along State 62.

McKEE COVERED BRIDGE

Leave Medford on State 238. At Ruch, turn south on Applegate Road. You will find this 122' covered bridge on the Applegate River about 8 miles down the road. Built in 1917, it provides a lovely swimming hole and picnic area.

McKEE JAMBOREE

McKee is the host for a jamboree held each year in September. It features contests galore! Be on hand to watch as participants compete in horseshoe pitching, cribbage, cow patty throwing, watermelon eating, bubble gum blowing and more.

MEDFORD CITY PARKS

Bear Creek is probably the most popular of all of Medford's city parks. Picnic facilities, restrooms, tennis courts, bike trail access, fitness trail, nature study area and lots and lots of room to play all are offered. The Bear Creek Bike & Nature Trail is three miles long and offers a brochure keyed to numbered signs pointing out plants, viewpoints and small animal trails. The fitness trail covers one mile.

Tennis courts are also found at Holmes, Howard, Jackson and Union Parks as well as Medford Senior High. Nature study areas are offered at both Holmes and Wilson Parks. Jefferson Park also offers a fitness trail.

MEDFORD CORPORATION

Just north of Medford on State 99 is the Medford Corporation. Tours are available at this lumber plant year round. Visit the facilities weekdays between 7:00 a.m. and 10:30 a.m. and between noon and 3:00 p.m. Tour passes and self guided brochures are available at the office.

PEAR BLOSSOM FESTIVAL

Each year, Medford plays host to the beautiful Pear Blossom Festival. Happening in April, events include a grand parade complete with floats, equestrian units and marching bands, street fair, 20 kilometer run, bicycle races and displays throughout the city.

ROCKHOUNDS

The area around Medford is rich in moss and dendritic agate, jaspers, and milky chalcedony. The Medford Chamber of Commerce has a listing of good hunting locations.

ROGUE VALLEY ART ASSOCIATION

This art gallery is located at 40 South Bartlett. Summer hours are Monday thru Saturday 9:00 a.m. to 4:00 p.m. During the balance of the year, they are open from 10:00 a.m. to 5:00 p.m.

MILL CITY

FISHERMEN'S BEND PARK

This scenic river area offers picnic tables at one of the area's favorite fishing spots.

MAPLES WAYSIDE

At Maples Wayside you can enjoy some scenic hiking, or just relax and watch as fishermen practice their craft.

MINTO PARK

Minto Park offers a beautiful view. Fishing and hiking are two favorite activities here.

NIAGARA PARK

Niagara Park is a historic site. The Niagara Dam was built here in 1898-9, by Italian stonemasons, for the O'Neil Brothers wheat and straw paper mill. You can walk to the bottom and look back at the dam's remains. Besides an interesting nature trail the park also offers picnic facilities.

PACK SADDLE PARK

Another scenic area park is Pack Saddle. Fishing, picnics and relaxation may all be enjoyed here.

160

MILWAUKIE

HAGER POND

At 2746 SE Washington, just off 99E, you can visit Hager Pond located behind a stately old home. This fresh water pond and stream contain a picturesque water wheel, ducks and animals. Visitors are welcome anytime during the summer and weekend afternoons the balance of the year.

HISTORIC TREE

Behind the City Hall you will find an ornamental peach tree tree. This was the first in the northwest and was sent from China in 1869.

MILWAUKIE CITY LIBRARY DUCK POND

Directly behind the Milwaukie City Library, you will find a shady pond filled with resident ducks. Be sure to bring some bread for a chance to watch these friendly beggars feed.

MILWAUKIE HISTORICAL MUSEUM

Located in an 1865 farm house at 3737 SE Adams, the Milwaukie Historical Museum includes an 1872 horse-drawn street car, among its displays. Open weekends only, 11:00 a.m. to 3:00 p.m.

MOORE'S FLOUR MILL

At Moore's Flour Mill you can watch as they grind flour. Displays explain the process. The first mill uses a stone made from quartz, mined in Paris, France. The stone measures 48" in diameter. It is made up from 22 separate pieces and was brought around Cape Horn in 1872. It was originally used in Dufur, Oregon. They are open weekdays and Saturday from 9:00 a.m. till 5:30 p.m.

RISLEY PARK

At Risley Park, just west of River Road on Risley Street, you will find a small area offering picnic tables, a tennis court, soccer and baseball fields.

RIVERSIDE PARK

Riverside Park is located on the north side of the Clackamas River, one mile upstream from Gladstone. Facilities include a boat launching ramp, ball diamond, soccer field, picnic tables and restrooms.

MT. HOOD NATIONAL FOREST

The Mt. Hood National Forest covers a vast area. Multnomah Falls cascades near its northwest corner. The east boundary is just outside Hood River. To the south it ends around the Clackamas/Marion County line from near Burnt Mountain at the western corner, to the Olallie Lake area at the east end.

A map of the area can be viewed at any of the Mt. Hood forest offices located in Gresham, Dufur, Maupin, Estacada, Troutdale, Mt. Hood or Zig Zag. These offices also offer information sheets on the more popular hiking trails in the area.

BAGBY HOT SPRINGS

To find Bagby Hot Springs, take the Timothy Lake turnoff from US 26. At Timothy Lake, continue to State 224. Head due south, 4 miles to the junction of the Collowash River with the Clackamas. From here you can follow the signs. It's 3½ miles up to the Collowash on Forest Service Road S63, then a right onto S70 for another 5½ miles. Park at the Nohorn Campground and walk to the hot springs. It is about a half hour hike but well worth the effort!

BARLOW TOLL ROAD

In 1845, Samuel K. Barlow began this wagon route which crossed the south shoulder of Mt. Hood. It was opened in 1846 with the gate located at Wamic. You can still find traces of the road.

At Laurel Hill just west of the summit, you can see scars on tree trunks where wagons were roped down slopes, at several places. This is just west of Government Camp.

Tollgate, southeast of Rhododendron, is where the pioneers paid their fee for the use of Barlow's road. This amounted to $5 per wagon. A replica of the original tollgate marks the spot just east of Tollgate Campground.

BULL OF THE WOODS

This 10,200 acre area is located in the remote headwaters of the Clackamas River. Spectacular mountain scenery and numerous high lakes abound in the isolated, roadless setting. In the early 1900's an influx of mining activity began here which left old mine shafts, tunnels and rusting equipment throughout the area. Any Mt. Hood National Forest Service office can provide you with a map showing trails, lakes, streams, mines and mountain peaks.

CROSS COUNTRY SKI TRAILS

Another brochure, available at local forest service offices will provide you with in depth information on the area's cross country ski trails. It lists 16 separate routes and includes a map as well as hiking tips. These trails range from 1-10 miles in length.

ELIOT GLACIER

At the end of Forest Service Road S12 you will find a trail leading to Eliot Glacier. It is located on the north slope of Mt. Hood.

HIKING TRAILS

You can also contact the Mt. Hood National Forest offices for information on trails through that area. The Columbia River Gorge alone, has over 150 miles of trails, unveiling unsurpassable views and hidden waterfalls. The district office in Troutdale can provide maps showing easy hikes like Latourell Falls, the Multnomah-Wahkeena Loop and Elowah Falls Trails. If you're more experienced ask about the Ruckel Creek trails or Nick Eaton Ridge. If you really like to make work out of hiking, try Gorton Creek or Mt. Defiance.

This national forest is divided into 7 districts, and each has its own listing of trails. Offices are located as follows:

Barlow District at Dufur; Bear Springs District at Maupin; Clackamas District at Estacada; Columbia Gorge District at Troutdale; Estacada District at Estacada; Hood River District at Mt. Hood-Parkdale; and Zig Zag District at Zig Zag.

Each area has its own fascinating scenery. Mountain glaciers, waterfalls, hidden lakes and panoramic views will delight nature lovers all along the way.

HORSETAIL FALLS

Horsetail Falls is 33 miles east of Portland in the Columbia Gorge. Continue past Multnomah Falls nearly 3 miles along State 30 to where the falls are located. One look will tell you why it was so named.

LOST CREEK NATURE TRAIL

Special mention should be made for this paved path through the forest. It provides handicapped access for a journey along the creek to a beaver dam. It's northeast of Zig Zag.

MT. HOOD

Mt. Hood was known to the Northwest Indians as Wy'east; a mountain god who spouted fire and hurled boulders to the sky. It stands 11,235' above sea level and sports twelve glaciers and five ridges. Men and women have been meeting the challenge of the climb since the mid 1880's. The mountain is the most frequently climbed glaciated peak in North America.

There are four routes taken up the mountain. Each takes ten to fourteen hours and are only for the very experienced.

Be sure to visit Timberline Lodge on the south side of the mountain. This monument of massive stonework and carved wood was built during President Franklin D. Roosevelt's WPA project. Roosevelt himself dedicated the building in 1937.

MT. HOOD LOOP

For a scenic tour of the Mt. Hood area, pick up the Columbia Gorge Scenic Route east of Troutdale. This will take you past the 1917 Crown Point Vista House. From here, you can view the Columbia River 725' below with a panoramic look at the gorge to the east and west. Driving further, you will pass Latourell Falls, Bridal Veil Falls, Wahkeena Falls, Multnomah Falls, and Oneonta Gorge before picking up I-84 to Hood River.

Head south at Hood River on State 35. Panorama Point is a good stop as well as the road off to the west for Cooper

Spur and Cloud Cap Inn. Pick up US 26 westbound for a drive past Barlow Pass, Government Camp, Tollgate, Zig Zag and Sandy as it leads back to Portland.

A brochure detailing this drive is available at the National Forest Service office.

MT. HOOD WILDERNESS AREA

The first land set aside here was known as the Mt. Hood Primitive Area. This was in 1931. Today, that land has grown to over 47,000 acres. Zig Zag and Parkdale offices of the National Forest Service can give you information on visiting this area, help you with maps, and issue a wilderness permit for hiking the land.

MULTNOMAH FALLS

Multnomah Falls is the second highest waterfall in the United States. Located 31 miles east of Portland along I-84, it can be seen from the freeway. Pull off and take a short walk to the lower falls. It's just a bit further to the next viewpoint, and the more industrious can hike all the way to the top. A visitor's information center is also located here.

ONEONTA GORGE

Take State 30 from Multnomah Falls, a quarter mile to view Oneonta Gorge. This picturesque site was caused by an ancient earthquake. Follow the creek back to enjoy a lovely secluded waterfall.

WHITE RIVER GAME MANAGEMENT AREA

Black tailed deer, elk and wild turkey are provided with range here along the east boundary of the Mt. Hood National Forest. The area covers over 440 square miles, managed by the Oregon State Game Commission. Information on access to this area can be obtained through their Portland office.

MT. JEFFERSON WILDERNESS AREA

The Mt. Jefferson Wilderness Area, is part of a volcanic plateau containing several large, steep sided, extinct volcanoes. The largest include Mt. Jefferson and Three Fingered Jack.

This 100,208 acre area has more than 160 miles of hiking trails including a 36 mile stretch of the Pacific Crest National Scenic Trail. The Deschutes, Mt. Hood and Willamette National Forests meet together here to form the wilderness area. Forest offices for any of these can give you information and show you maps of the area.

MT. WASHINGTON WILDERNESS AREA

Land from the Willamette and Deschutes National Forests are included in this wilderness area. It contains 46,655 acres providing a rugged retreat for hikers and mountain climbers. The desolate country is dominated by Mt. Washington's sharp rise above the lava strewn plains.

The only entry to this area is by foot or horseback. It offers solitude and primitive recreation upon a land once crossed only by Indian trails along McKenzie Pass.

Offices for both the Deschutes and Willamette National Forest will be able to give you detailed information on hiking into the area.

MYRTLE CREEK

NEAL LANE COVERED BRIDGE

Take Main Street in Myrtle Creek to County Road 46. Neal Lane Covered Bridge is at the intersection of County Roads 46 and 124. It spans Myrtle Creek, is 42' in length, and was built in 1929.

OAKLAND

OAKLAND MUSEUM

At the Oakland Museum you will see historical exhibits which include photographs, tools, household items, clothing and furniture. They are open afternoons except for Mondays and holidays.

While in Oakland, be sure to check out the rest of the town. Built in the 1890's it is listed in the National Register of Historic Places.

O'BRIEN

WIMER & McGRAW WAGON ROADS

The Wimer and McGraw wagon roads ran to Crescent City. A road, now known as the Lone Mountain Road, follows the original trail used from 1853 until the 1920's to bring supplies from California to Southern Oregon. You will find this road just off US 199 at O'Brien.

OREGON CITY

BARCLAY HOUSE

This was once the home of Dr. Forbes Barclay and now serves as the Oregon City Chamber of Commerce Visitors Center. The house was built in 1850. The public is welcome daily from 10:00 a.m. to 4:30 p.m. The Barclay House is located at 719 Center Street.

FEYRER MEMORIAL PARK

Two miles east of Molalla, just outside of Oregon City, take Robbins Road off State 211 to this county operated park. Here you will find twelve acres on the Molalla River complete with picnic facilities, playground, horseshoe pits, ball field, running water and restrooms. This park has many beautiful coniferous and deciduous trees, native to Western Oregon.

HISTORIC HOMES

Oregon City was founded in 1829 and incorporated in 1844. In fact, it has the distinction of being the first incorporated city west of the Rocky Mountains. At that time Portland had only one house, Seattle was but an Indian village and San Francisico still a Spanish fortress.

Oregon City holds the title for many notable "west of the Rocky Mountains" firsts. These include - first government, first newspaper, first public school, first library, first Protestant church, first mint, first water-powered industry, first Catholic Archdiocese, first Masonic lodge and first court of record - to name but a few.

It's a lovely place for a historic driving tour. You can simply explore on your own or, for a minimal charge, purchase a mapped out driving tour brochure from the Oregon City Chamber of Commerce. A few notable area homes include 224 (1869) and 713 (1846) Center Street; 308 (1881), 415 (1874) and 902 (1893) Jefferson Street; 316 (1867), 402 (1862), 416 (1867) and 604 (1866) McLoughlin Blvd.; 215 (1858) Jerome Street; 215 (1859) Miller Street; 502 (1867) 4th Avenue; and 536 (1858) and 567 (1898) Holmes Lane.

MUNICIPAL ELEVATOR

There are less than a half dozen municipal elevators in the entire world. Oregon City built their first in 1913 to connect downtown Oregon City with upper residential levels. It was run by water pressure. The current elevator was built in 1954 and travels upward 90' where it commands a sweeping view of Willamette Falls, the 100-year old locks (which are still in use), Main Street and a panorama which includes Mt. St. Helens on a clear day. There is no charge to ride the elevator. It operates Monday thru Saturday from 6:30 a.m. till midnight and on Sundays from 6:30 a.m. to 8:30 p.m.

NEW ERA

Eight miles south of Oregon City off State 99E, you can visit New Era. This historic district contains several old buildings and a grist mill.

PACIFIC NORTHWEST LIVE STEAM
RAILROAD

In Molalla, 13 miles out of Oregon City, you can take a ride on an 1/8 scale gondola car pulled by a real steam engine. The train operates on Sunday between noon and dusk, from May through October. Other exhibits include a miniature sternwheeler. To reach this tiny railroad simply take East Main Street, in Molalla, and follow the signs from there.

JANORA BAYOT

WAGON WHEEL PARK

Located in Mulino, south of Oregon City, you can find Wagon Wheel Park. Here you can visit an old schoolhouse, church, and flour mill.

PEDEE

RITNER CREEK COVERED BRIDGE

Built in 1927, this covered bridge was moved in 1976 when the State Highway Division deemed it too narrow and dangerous for highway traffic. It now sits 60' downstream from State 223 south of Pedee. Its 75' spans Ritner Creek. Polk County operates a lovely picnic park here.

PORTLAND

(AND NEARBY VICINITIES)

ALPENROSE DAIRY

During the summer Alpenrose Dairy offers a special place for all of us. They sponsor lots of nice annual events which include kite flying and frog jumping contests, quarter midget car racing, an Easter egg hunt and Family Day in May. On Family Day they have many special exhibits and pony rides for the children.

Their Velodrome offers amateur bicycle racing most weekends, all summer long. The 42° banks on this track make it one of the steepest in the United States. It is used for local, state, regional and national competitions.

AMERICAN RHODODENDRON SOCIETY GARDEN

You can see over 2500 rhododendrons and azaleas here in this five acre woodland setting on Crystal Springs Island. Located in southeast Portland's Eastmoreland Park, it's free every day but Mother's Day weekend. Open from 8:00 a.m. to 4:30 p.m. from April thru September, the best viewing is in April and May when everything is in its peak blooming period. The lake here is home to many ducks, so be sure to bring along some bread or kernels of corn and watch their antics as they scramble for the food.

ARCHERY RANGES

You will find public archery ranges at Washington and Delta East Parks but you'll have to bring your own targets and equipment.

ARCHITECTURAL PRESERVATION GALLERY

At the Architectural Preservation Gallery you will see rotating exhibits on Portland's architectural history. Located at 26 NW 2nd Avenue, on the second floor, they are open Tuesday thru Friday from 10:00 a.m. to 3:00 p.m. and on weekends from noon to 4:00 p.m.

ART GALLERIES

The City of Roses is chock full of art galleries. The phone book has seven columns under that listing. Here you will find paintings, sculpture, drawings, ceramics, photography, woodwork, jewelry, weaving, batiks and pottery. It would take days to see it all. Most feature Northwest artists. Many change exhibits monthly.

Portland State University, Portland Community College, Reed College, Oregon School of Arts & Crafts, Portland

Center for the Visual Arts and the University of Portland all offer art showings. Downtown office buildings have also put their artwork out where the public can see it. Paintings line their walls and sculptured works and fountains enhance their entrances and courtyards.

ARTQUAKE

Each September, Portland plays host to this fantastic cultural happening. Artists, craftsmen, performing artists, musicians and restaurants put out their best and people flock to take part in the events. It gets bigger and better every year. Downtown streets are blocked off and the crowds roam about freely, taking it all in.

AUDUBON SOCIETY

Every Sunday, the Audubon Society puts on a free nature program at 2:00 p.m. Concerned with preserving habitats for wildlife and providing environmental awareness programs they manage the Audubon Bird Sanctuary here complete with pond, nature center and short trails. They are located at 5151 NW Cornell Road and are open daily.

BENJAMIN FRANKLIN MUSEUM

Located in the Benjamin Franklin Plaza, at SW First and Jefferson, this little museum houses Ben Franklin artifacts. The principal exhibit is a porcelain sculpture entitled "Declaration of Independence" Original signatures and authentic reproductions of several of his inventions are other highlights.

BIRD WATCHING

Besides the already mentioned Audubon Society sanctuary, there are many other great places for bird watching in the Portland area. Sauvie Island offers views of wintering waterfowl, sandhill cranes and great blue herons. Oaks Bottom, in southeast Portland, is currently being developed as a wetland bird sanctuary and the Pittock Wildlife Sanctuary is a good place to see the pileated woodpecker. The area's many lakes and parks offer refuge to many winged creatures.

BLM RECREATIONAL SITES

The Bureau of Land Management offers more than 70 recreational areas throughout the state. At their headquarters at 729 NE Oregon Street you can obtain information and maps on using this land. Over 15 million acres are managed by Oregon's BLM people. They offer visitors opportunities for outdoor recreation from the sea to the eastern desert; from the Columbia River to the California border.

CAMASSIA NATURAL AREA

Located in West Linn just east of the high school, this spot is of great interest to geologists and naturalists. The 22½ acre area is an excellent record of the Missoula flood which took place at the end of the Ice Age. It was so vast, it extended all the way from Montana to Oregon. The area is preserved by the Nature Conservancy and contains more than 300 species of plants, several erratics, ponds and small animal life. It is open to visitors at any time.

CAMELLIA SHOW

For over 40 years the Oregon Camellia Society has been opening up their annual camellia show to the public. Held in April, it gives flower lovers the opportunity to see and smell the lovely blooms. Contact the Portland Chamber of Commerce for exact date.

CEDAR CROSSING COVERED BRIDGE

This bridge was built in 1982 to span Johnson Creek. It is 65' in length and can be found by following Foster Road to 136th to Deardorff.

CHILDREN'S ART MUSEUM

In Portland, children are special people too; and at the Children's Art Museum it's obvious. Located at 3037 SW 2nd, they are open Monday thru Thursday from 10:00 a.m. to 6:00 p.m., Fridays from 9:00 a.m. to 5:00 p.m. and Saturday from 10:00 a.m. to 4:00 p.m. Miniatures, dolls, natural history exhibits and a live zoo are all there for children to discover on their own. Closed during September.

CITY HALL

The city hall building was completed in 1894. Located at 1220 SW 5th, tours are available to those who make arrangements in advance. Wednesday or Thursday are the best days to come, when you can combine the tour with a visit to the city council meeting. Call 248-4210 for reservations.

COUNCIL CREST PARK

Council Crest is the city's highest viewpoint with nearly 38 acres of hilltop, 1,073' above Portland Heights. To get there, take Southwest Broadway to Broadway Drive. Turn left on Greenway and follow the signs to the top. Mt. St. Helens, Mt. Rainier, Mt. Adams, Mt. Hood and Mt. Jefferson can all be seen if the weather is right.

When visiting the park, be sure to stop for a look at a relic of Portland's old transportation system. This trolley car was once an important part of many Portlander's lives.

The park also sports a combination drinking fountain, sculptured statue. The woman and child gracefully enhance the park's atmosphere as she dances barefoot across the grass lifting her child up to the joys of nature.

176

FARELESS SQUARE

You can contact Tri-Met offices to get a map of downtown areas serviced free by bus. The area stretches from the Willamette River to the Stadium Freeway and from Market Street to the other side of old town. Maps are posted downtown or available free from Tri-Met. Call 233-3511.

FIRE BOATS

Weekday afternoons anyone over the age of twelve can take a half hour tour of one of Portland's fire boats. This is not a ride but offers a unique opportunity for adults and older children to inspect an operating fire boat. Call 227-6175 for more information and location.

FIRST NATIONAL CENTER

Portland's tallest building offers a collection of over 400 paintings, sculptures and prints on view throughout the 40 story building. Inside the 4th Avenue entrance you can visit a small money museum maintained by the Oregon Historical Society. The building is at 1300 SW 5th Avenue.

FLAG DAY PARADE

Each year, Gresham hosts this annual parade which includes marching units, bands, equestrian groups and floats. If you enjoy celebrating this American holiday, then Gresham is the place to be.

FOREST PARK

At over 5,000 acres, this is the largest park in the Portland metropolitan area. Forest Park adjoins Macleay Park, making it the biggest wilderness preserve within city limits in the entire United States. Many trails traverse the area with the longest being Wildwood. This 14½ mile hiking trail stretches across the west hills, taking you north through the Hoyt Arboretum and Pittock Acres, before plunging deep into a Macleay Park creek canyon. With the Audubon Bird Sanctuary also close at hand, many side trips can be taken. There are 25 miles of trails in all.

Park headquarters are located at 2960 Upshur, where a self guided tour brochure can be obtained.

FOUNTAINS

Portland is full of fountains. I guess a city with this much rain has to have some place to display it all! The Elk Fountain, across the street from the Multnomah County Courthouse, was presented to the city in 1900 as a watering place for horses. Since the land here was once a feeding ground for elk, it's a very fitting piece.

Skidmore Fountain was dedicated in 1888. The bronze maidens of the fountain sit surrounded by grass which is surrounded by sycamores, old fashioned carriage lamps and rhododendrons. It is located at SW First and Ankeny.

Downtown Portland streets offer drinking fountains, with a touch of class. Simon Benson, an early Portland lumber baron, donated the first of these during prohibition. Additional fountains were added at a later date. These are spread throughout downtown.

Ira's Fountain, SW 3rd and Clay Street, was designed by landscape architect Lawrence Halprin. It is located directly across from the Civic Auditorium in a block-square park. It sports an 18′ high waterfall, is 80′ wide, and is flooded with water at a rate of 13,000 gallons per minute.

Other special fountains include the Shemanski Fountain in the South Park Blocks and Lovejoy Fountain at Portland Center. Many downtown office buildings sport their own artistic fountains. The Georgia-Pacific Building, O'Bryant Square and The Bank of California are a few.

THE GROTTO

At the Sanctuary of our Sorrowful Mother, on Sandy Boulevard just east of 82nd Avenue, you will find one of Portland's most attractive landmarks. It is filled with sunken gardens overshadowed by a towering cliff. The lower area is free, and includes a Catholic altar set into a large cavelike opening hewn from volcanic rock. Outdoor masses are offered here Sundays at noon from May through September. This is an international shrine dedicated to all mothers.

HARBOR BUS TOUR

On Tuesdays and Wednesday afternoons, mid-June thru August, you can enjoy a two hour bus ride around the waterfront. This is a chance to see and hear the sights and sounds of Portland's waterfront at work. This tour is sponsored by the Port of Portland. You'll need to call 3-4 weeks in advance for this popular tour - 231-5000, ext. 208.

HIDDEN VALLEY BULB RANCH

Late in August, the Hidden Valley Bulb Ranch allows visitors to cut the blooms from their crop of bulbs. Over 1½ million flowers cover the fields, showing off over 150 different varieties of Dahlias. They are located 2.2 miles off I-5, west of the Woodburn exit. Watch local papers for a date and time. Any time in August is a great time to view these fields in full bloom but be sure to wait for the invitation before cutting your own.

HISTORIC DISTRICTS

For those interested in historical buildings there are several areas around the city. You might start downtown in the Skidmore Fountain/Old Town areas. This pioneer business section has many Victorian commercial structures built before the turn of the century.

The Yamhill/South River Front area runs from Stark to Yamhill from the river to SW 3rd. Many early Portland business establishments were built here prior to 1900. Notable buildings include the Pioneer Post Office, Calvary Presbyterian Church, Multnomah County Central Library, Union Station, and the Spaghetti Factory. Some are outside the basic district.

Further into northwest Portland, you will find older Vistorian homes and churches. King's and Lair Hills are two areas to the southwest with Ladd's Addition and Laurelhurst being southeast.

HOYT ARBORETUM

More than 500 varieties of trees and native shrubs grow at the Hoyt Arboretum. Covering 216 acres, this woodland preserve contains one of the country's best collections of needle bearing and deciduous trees.

The arboretum is above Washington Park on Fairview Boulevard, situated at the location of the former county poor farm. It includes 7 miles of trails for which a self-guided tour map is available. Picnic facilities are also available.

INDUSTRIAL TOURS

Many Portland businesses offer tours; however most require advance notice. A variety of industries are covered.

Blitz-Weinhard Company
1133 West Burnside
At this old Portland business you can view the complete brewing process. The one hour tour takes you from raw hops to the bottled product and includes a hospitality room. Tours operate weekdays at 1:00, 2:30 and 4:00 p.m.

Kandel Knitting Mills
4834 North Interstate (288-6975)
Call ahead to arrange a tour of Kandel Knitting Mills. Available weekdays to groups whose members are age ten and over.

KATU
2153 NE Sandy Boulevard (231-4610)
Weekday mornings you can be part of KATU's "A.M. Northwest" audience. Anyone over six can attend, but generally you need to call ahead at least two weeks before to make reservations. This is a popular Portland show hosted by local celebrities Jim Bosley and Margie Boule.

National Biscuit Company
100 NE Columbia Blvd. (285-2571)
Anyone in the 6th grade or above can tour the National Bisquit Company. The 1½ hour tour is given from October 1st thru May 31st afternoons (1:15 p.m.). Please call ahead for reservations.

Pendleton Woolen Mills
Milwaukie Garment Factory
801 River Road
During a tour here you can watch the complete manufacturing of a shirt, from the cutting of the fabric to the boxing of the finished product. Tours last 45 minutes and are given weekdays to small groups over the age of 12. Reservations are required - 226-4801.

Portland Fire Bureau
55 SW Ash (232-8135)
The firemen here are happy to see children visit their fire station. Fire trucks and emergency equipment are always of interest to youngsters.

Portland International Airport (231-5000 ext. 422)
A walking tour is given by the Port of Portland that includes a slide presentation and tour of the terminal. Tours are given daily but you'll have to call at least two weeks in advance for a spot on one of their tours.

Post Office
715 NW Hoyt (221-2363)
The main post office, downtown, will give tours to anyone age 10 and over. This one hour tour takes you through workrooms where mail is sorted and sent on its way. Call ahead for reservations. It's easiest to get in well after the end of the month in the afternoon. Some branch offices offer tours for younger children. Call your local post office to inquire about these.

Oregon Health & Science University
3181 SW Sam Jackson Road (225-8231 - Tour Coordinator)
You have a choice of four different tours at OHSU. Although most tours are intended for small groups they are happy to schedule individuals into planned tours.

First, there's the General Tour. This is designed to give visitors a basic look at OHSU's facilities and functions. The Educational Tour is for those interested in career oriented information. It includes a look at classrooms and laboratories as well as basic information. A Clinical Care Tour takes you through Dornbecker Hospital, the Crippled Children's facilities, Dental School and various clinics. A Research Tour covers basic information as well as a look at ongoing research activities.

These tours are not for young children. They ask that all participants be in junior high or above. The tours are available throughout the academic year.

INTERNATIONAL ROSE TEST GARDEN

These famous rose gardens overlook the city from the beautiful western hills of Washington Park. From here you can take in a magnificent view of the city while enjoying the heady fragrance of roses. More than 400 varieties grow here with over 8,000 roses filling the scene. This is one of only 24 official test gardens in the country. Each year approximately 40 new numbered introductions are planted here. During their two year testing period they are judged for color, size, disease resistance and other attributes that go in the make up of an outstanding rose.

Visit the Gold Medal Awards Garden, Shakespeare Garden, Queens Walk and the Royal Rosarian Garden. Each offers its own unique attractions.

JOGGING TRAIL

The Park Bureau maintains a two mile exercise and jogging trail that starts on Terwilliger Boulevard, about a quarter mile north of the 5700 block. The track takes you toward downtown with twenty exercise "stops" along the way. The trail is well marked.

KELLY POINT STATE PARK

On the east side of the Willamette River, where it joins the Columbia, you will find Kelly Point Park. From here you can watch passing ocean-going ships while enjoying the city maintained beaches, meadows, wooded areas and fields. Picnic tables and grills, along with paved bicycle paths make it a great place to bring the family.

KITE FLYING

There are two places in Portland where kite flyers join together to practice their craft. Delta Park in north Portland, just off the I-5 freeway near Jantzen Beach and

Waterfront Park. Waterfront Park plays host to the annual kite flying festival held each March as well as regular Sunday kite flying sessions. Some of the creations aloft here are both unusual and amazing.

LAKE OSWEGO

Lake Oswego is located southwest of Portland and deserves special mention. Here you can visit Bishops Close, a thirteen acre garden open daily from dawn to dusk.

At George Rogers Park you can look over the remains of an old pig iron smelter stack. You will also enjoy the trails, playground equipment, ball field, picnic facilities, tennis courts and gardens. On the opposite end of the lake you can picnic at Waluga Park.

Each year the community holds a parade to celebrate Armed Forces Day. This happens in May and marks the opening of the Arts & Flowers Festival which is a display for all phases of the arts.

LAURELHURST PARK

This is a great in-town park! Its 33 acres include a lake that is home to hundreds of ducks, tennis courts, lots of grass and trees, and a large children's playground. It's just north of Stark Street at 39th Avenue.

MOCKS CREST

Mocks Crest offers an excellent view of Portland's busy harbor. The Willamette River, Port of Portland dry docks, and the industrial area of Swan Island can all be seen. To get there take Portland Boulevard to North Willamette. Turn right to the viewpoint located just east of the University of Portland campus.

MT. HOOD COMMUNITY COLLEGE

MHCC has a lot to offer. Call 667-7317 for a customized tour of the campus. You can also have free use of the gym, handball and racquetball courts and weight room. For information on these call 667-7350. The college also has two art galleries. They are open during the academic year. The Art Mall Gallery can be enjoyed Monday thru Thursday between 8:00 a.m. and 7:30 p.m., Fridays they close at 5:00 p.m. The College Center exhibit is accessible Monday thru Thursday from 8:00 a.m. to 9:00 p.m., Friday and Saturday they close at 5:00 p.m.

MT. TABOR PARK

Mt. Tabor Park provides 200 acres of trees, grass and water within the city limits. Rolling grassy hills surround three reservoirs located at the site of a long extinct volcano. A small amphitheater has been built at the north end in the charred, eroded cone.

The park, which is 643' high has some excellent viewpoints. At the top you will find a statue of Harvey W. Scott, the Oregonian's pioneer editor. Picnic tables, walking trails and a children's playground are also there. During the summer months the Portland Bureau of Parks sponsors musical events here.

The park is located just east of 60th Avenue between Yamhill and Division Streets.

MULTNOMAH COUNTY CENTRAL LIBRARY

The Multnomah County Library building is listed in the National Register of Historic Places. Designed by Albert Doyle in 1912, the building pays homage to philosophers, poets, artists, and all those who help to put a book together. Many names are etched into the outside of the building.

185

Inside, besides all the usual library items, you will find art, special reference collections including Oregon and Northwest material as well as many historical books, manuscripts and maps. Check their schedule for story times and special offerings.

MULTNOMAH COUNTY COURTHOUSE

The courthouse is open Monday thru Friday from 9:00 a.m. to 5:00 p.m. Visitors are welcome to sit in on most trials and hearings. Wander around the fifth floor and visit trials in rooms 512, 526, 544. On Tuesday and Thursday mornings at 9:30 a.m. you can sit in on the Board of County Commissioners meeting in room 680. This is a first rate chance to see how a county operates.

OAKS PARK

There is no admission charge at Oaks Park. Located near the foot of the Sellwood Bridge you will find picnic tables, restrooms and an old locomotive. The Oaks Pioneer Museum is near here as well as St. John's Episcopal Church which was built in 1857.

THE OLD CHURCH

The Old Church at 1422 SW 11th is an example of "carpenter gothic". Built in 1882 it was a place of worship until the 1960's. It is now a historic landmark.

Drop in any Wednesday at noon for the "sack lunch recital". You will be treated to music played on an organ brought around Cape Horn from Boston in 1883. This is the oldest standing church structure on its original site, in Portland.

OREGON HISTORICAL SOCIETY

The Oregon Historical Society offers an everchanging display of Pacific Northwest history. Besides the

ELEPHANT EARS

JANDRA BAHOT

changing exhibits on the first floor there are permanent displays on the second floor and some things to see in the basement. The top floor houses a non-circulating library. Maps, manuscripts, photographs, rare books and genealogical reference sources are held here. Visitors are welcome.

OREGON/WASHINGTON BICYCLE PATH

A $1 million bike lane on the I-205 bridge provides cyclists with a safe route over the Columbia River. On a clear day the view includes glimpses of Mount St. Helens and a spectacular angle on Mt. Hood.

The bridge is uphill all the way from Oregon to Washington. Allow at least 40 minutes for the crossing. The downhill return trip can be done in half the time.

OVERLOOK HOUSE RAVEN MUSEUM

At 3839 North Melrose you can visit a hands on natural history museum daily between 4:00 p.m. and 6:00 p.m.

PENINSULA PARK

Peninsula Park is one of North Portland's oldest showplaces. Wide stone steps lead down to the beautiful Sunken Garden with its ornate music pavillion and six acres of formal rose gardens. The park is located at 6400 North Albina.

PIONEER COURTHOUSE & POST OFFICE

Built between 1869 and 1873 this was the first federal office building in the Pacific Northwest. When first built, the building was thought by many to be too far from the business district; today it is Portland's central landmark. The building was extensively remodeled in the 1970's to provide an elegant Victorian Courtroom on the second floor for the 9th Circuit U.S. Court of Appeals. The building is located at 555 SW Yamhill and open to the public during the regular business hours.

PITTOCK WILDLIFE SANCTUARY
& AUDUBON HOUSE

This 25 acre wilderness tract offers 5 miles of trails which interconnect with others in the surrounding parks. A trail map and bird list is available, showing over 100 species spotted in the area. Many small animals are also sighted here. The Audubon House is closed Wednesdays and Saturdays but open from 9:00 a.m. to 5:00 p.m. the balance of the week. The sanctuary is at Cornell Road and 53rd Drive.

PORTLAND ART MUSEUM

The Portland Art Museum, at 1219 SW Park Avenue, has free admission on Tuesday nights between 4:00 p.m. and 7:00 p.m. The balance of the week there is a small charge. This is one of the finest art museums in the nation and includes collections of Renaissance Art, Classical Antiquities, Northwest Indian Art, Japanese Prints, English Silver, Chinese Paintings and a pre-Columbian exhibit of stone sculptures. Pacific Northwest artists are also well represented here.

PORTLAND MALL WALK

Tri-Met publishes a map for a Portland Mall Walk. It starts at the Pioneer Courthouse and takes you past sculptured artworks, modern office buildings, historical sites, fountains and public buildings. It can be obtained through Tri-Met or the Portland Chamber of Commerce.

PORTLAND PARKS

Portland Parks and Recreation offer 7500 acres of public parks in 160 locations throughout the city. They have everything from the smallest park in the world to the largest urban wilderness within an American city. They publish a map and listing which is available through their offices, or those of the Portland Chamber of Commerce.

Totally, these parks provide more than fifty miles of hiking trails. They offer jogging trails, an exercise course, archery ranges and casting pool. Thirteen locations have fountains; everything from a downtown waterfall to memorial fountains.

Seven parks have gardens, at some you can feed the ducks, others offer fantastic mountain views and yet others just offer a place to sit and rest, or enjoy a picnic lunch.

PORTLAND POLICE MUSEUM

Early police uniforms, badges, photos and other police memorabilia are featured. Museum hours are Wednesday thru Friday 10:00 a.m. to 3:00 p.m., weekends noon to 4:00 p.m. The address is 80 NW 2nd Avenue, second floor.

PORTLAND STATE UNIVERSITY

Portland State University (PSU) has three free art galleries. They offer changing art exhibits throughout the academic year. Gallery 299 is located on the second floor of Newberger Hall. They are open weekdays from 9:00 a.m. to 5:00 p.m.

In the Smith Center, second floor, you will find two more galleries. The Littman Gallery is open noon to 5:00 p.m. weekdays. White Gallery, which is a photographic display, can be viewed weekdays between 8:00 a.m. and 9:00 p.m.

If you'd like a tour of the campus, it's just a phone call away. One of the PSU counselors will schedule you for a personal tour when you call 229-3511. These tours are only available during the academic year.

ROCKY BUTTE

Rocky Butte offers a stone viewing platform from which to view the Portland airport. It's a great place to watch the Vancouver fireworks on the Fourth of July, too. Head east off 82nd Avenue on Fremont to the park. It was named for the quarry on the east slope.

ROSE FESTIVAL

Portland is indeed the "City of Roses" and when June rolls around, the entire city celebrates with the annual Portland Rose Festival. The festival had its beginning just after the turn of the century and gets more festive every year.

The coronation of the queen and her court kicks off a ten day string of events that include three parades; the Starlight Parade, Junior Parade and Grand Floral Parade. Other no charge events include Lawn Bowling and Milk Carton Boat Races at Westmoreland Park, tours of American and Canadian Navy ships at the seawall, exhibits throughout the city and a downtown Fun Center.

The newspaper prints a schedule of events listing numerous musical groups, televised coronation of the queen, a starlight fun run, art exhibits, junior tennis tournaments, model boat races, wheelchair and river parades, bicycle races, a boomerang tournament, float display and more. All for free.

It happens each June and runs for ten days.

SATURDAY MARKET

Portland has its own open-air market. Here you can see thousands of quality handcrafted items. Wood, stoneware, leather, glass, silver, embroidery, copper, silken fabrics, natural fibers, feathers, brass and driftwood are some of the items used in their creation. Strolling entertainers give it a festive atmosphere with musicians, jugglers, acrobats, pantomime artists and clowns dropping by from time to time.

It all happens every Saturday and Sunday from the first weekend in April through the last weekend before Christmas. Located under the west end of the Burnside Bridge, in the heart of Old Town, the hours are 10:00 a.m. to 5:00 p.m. on Saturday and 11:00 a.m. to 5:00 p.m. on Sunday.

What a colorful way to meet people!

SCULPTURE & STATUES

Portland is full of sculptured art work. You will see a myriad of styles ranging from equestrian statues of Joan of Arc and Theodore Roosevelt to modern works done all in metal. Downtown streets hold many, with more on display in city parks. You will find work done before the turn of the century, and pieces done only yesterday. North of Jefferson, downtown, between SW 10th and Park you will even find a sculpture mall.

STEAM ENGINE

In front of the Western Forestry Center you can see a Shay locomotive that was brought around Cape Horn to be used for logging operations. No longer in use, it sits here complete with a flatcar loaded with specimens of Northwest timber, to provide children and adults with the opportunity to get close to a piece of yesterday. You are welcome to climb aboard, at you own risk, for a real feel of how it must have been.

TRYON CREEK STATE PARK

Between Lewis and Clark College and Lake Oswego sits Tryon Creek Park. This 600 acres of wilderness offers peace and quiet to the city's nature lovers.

The park's nature center is open Wednesday thru Sunday and conducts tours at 1:00 p.m. and 3:00 p.m. on weekends. The center also features park history and natural phenomenon within the park. You will find eight miles of hiking trails, three miles of horse trails and a one mile bicycle path here.

WASHINGTON PARK

This is one of Portland's oldest parks. It contains 145 acres just up the hill from downtown, and offers city dwellers a place to unwind. Mountain views, shaded walkways, statues, tennis courts, playground equipment, picnic tables and groves of tall Douglas firs provide an inviting scene.

This is also the setting for the International Rose Test Garden. During the summer, the Washington Park Amphitheater and surrounding area offer live musical theater, opera, big bands and symphony in the open air most evenings and some afternoons.

WASHINGTON PARK ZOO

Three miles from downtown Portland, just off Highway 26, is the Washington Park Zoo. Tuesdays, after 3:00 p.m., they offer free admission. This doesn't give you much time during the winter but allows almost four hours to explore in the summer since the zoo closes one hour before dusk.

The Washington Park Zoo boasts the largest breeding herd of Asian elephants in all the zoo world plus one of the world's largest captive colonies of chimpanzees and another of Humboldt's penguins. The newest exhibit here features plant and animal life of the Cascade Mountains.

WESTMORELAND PARK

Westmoreland Park also deserves special mention. People congregate here for model plane flying, model boat racing, fly casting, bowling on the green, bocci ball, softball and baseball. It's a pleasant place to spread out a picnic while enjoying these activities. You will find the park at SE 22nd and Bybee.

WILDWOOD TRAIL

This 14½ mile trail begins at the Western Forestry Center and winds its way through the Hoyt Arboretum and Pittock Acres to end deep in Forest Park on Saltzman Road. It has been designated a scenic trail by the National Trail Act and joins other area trails for a variety of hikes.

WILLAMETTE RIVER

Two parks sit on the west bank of the Willamette River, Willamette Park and Powers Marine Park. At either one you can stroll beneath a variety of trees -- Western red cedar, Pacific madrone and poplar. Picnic tables are available.

One other Willamette River park is Waterfront Park which runs between Front and the river on the eastern edge of downtown.

WILLAMETTE STONE

The Willamette Stone is the surveyor's monument marking the intersection of the Willamette Base Line and the Willamette Meridian. All lands in Oregon were sectionized from these guidelines. The stake was put in the ground in 1851 and the stone marker laid in 1885.

PROSPECT

JOSEPH P. STEWART STATE PARK

The Joseph P. Stewart State Park sits at the meadow's edge of Lost Creek Lake. Here you will find over eight miles of hiking and biking trails, including one which connects with the famed Pacific Crest National Scenic Trail.

Playground equipment, picnic facilities, swimming beaches, restrooms, horseshoe pits, tennis courts, softball field and a boat ramp are also located here.

The park is six miles southwest of Prospect via State 62.

MILL CREEK FALLS SCENIC AREA

In Prospect, take Mill Creek Drive to this scenic area. A walk down the steep path will lead to some pretty impressive giant boulders that have been worn smooth by the rushing water.

PROSPECT WAYSIDE

Just off State 62, this state owned land has picnic tables and hiking trails.

RAINIER

TROJAN NUCLEAR PLANT

If you're interested in how a nuclear plant works you can visit the Trojan Visitors Information Center. This is the only nuclear generating plant in Oregon. They offer educational displays on energy. A combination of films, slide shows and static graphics are all put to use. The center is open Monday thru Saturday from 9:30 a.m. to 5:00 p.m. and Sundays from noon to 6:00 p.m.

Visitors can also get a drive through tour of the plant area around the cooling tower, a walking tour inside the turbine-generator building and a view of the control room. The facility also offers a wildlife viewing shelter and picnic area.

Trojan is located southeast of Rainier along US 30 on the Columbia River.

RICKREALL

BASKETT SLOUGH NATIONAL
WILDLIFE REFUGE

From Rickreall, take State 22 approximately two miles to the Baskett Slough refuge. Here you can enjoy wildlife observation and study, as well as photography while the natural inhabitants roam over its 2500 acres. Located in the lush Willamette Valley the area is full of green hillsides, oak covered knolls and grassy fields. Morgan Lake and Baskett Slough are also enticing attractions for migrant waterfowl.

ROGUE RIVER

ANNUAL ROOSTER CROWING CONTEST

This event is great fun! Each year, on the third Saturday in June, Rogue River holds this eye opening contest. Prizes go to the owner of the rooster crowing the most times in a thirty minute period. Check with the local Chamber of Commerce for details.

WIMER COVERED BRIDGE

From Rogue River, follow Madrone to East Evans Valley Road. Take this north for eight miles to the town of Wimer. The bridge is here over Evans Creek. Wimer was settled prior to 1887. This 1927 bridge was rebuilt in 1962 and is 85' long.

ROGUE RIVER NATIONAL FOREST

The Rogue River National Forest offers some very isolated public lands. A good portion of the land has been left unaltered by man where visitors will find only an occasional camp site, trail sign or fellow traveler along the trails. They also offer some very highly developed areas as well, and everything in between.

This National Forest runs from just west of Grants Pass to Crater Lake and from the California border to north of Union Creek. The main office, for maps and information on trails throughout the area, is located in Medford. District offices are in Butte Falls, Prospect, Jacksonville and Ashland.

ROSEBURG

AMACHER PARK

Take the Winchester exit off I-5 and continue across the old bridge to Amacher Park. Here you will find one of the few Myrtlewood groves located in Douglas County. Picnic on the North Umpqua River below Winchester Dam. Playground equipment and a boat ramp are available.

While you're there, take a trip down to the Winchester Dam. Underwater viewing windows allow you to observe migrating fish. The fish ladder is also easy to view.

DAVE BUSENBARK COUNTY PARK

The cool semi-wilderness of old-growth trees, wildflowers and a spring make this Douglas County park an ideal picnic spot. You will find it ten miles west of Lookingglass on Coos Bay Wagon Road.

DOUGLAS COUNTY MUSEUM

You'll find this museum near Umpqua Park in Roseburg, take the fairgrounds exit off I-5. The museum features exhibits of pioneer logging equipment, agricultural tools, Indian artifacts, early Oregon fur industry tools and natural history displays. They are closed most holidays. Open daily from 8:30 a.m. to 5:00 p.m.

HILLCREST VINEYARD

Ten miles west of Roseburg, off Garden Valley Road, you will find Hillcrest Vineyard. Stay left, as Garden Valley becomes Melrose Road to turn left on Cleveland Hill Road. A left on Orchard Lane and right again on Elgarose Road will get you there with ease. They offer tours of the facility, and samples when you visit their tasting room. Visitors are welcome daily from 10:00 a.m. to 5:00 p.m.

LANE HOUSE

This was the home of General Joseph Lane. In 1848 he became the first territorial Governor of Oregon. They are open weekends from 1:00 p.m. to 5:00 p.m. and at other times by appointment. Call 673-7082. Located at 544 SE Douglas Street. Donations are welcome.

O. C. BROWN COUNTY PARK

Five miles east of Roseburg, on North Deer Creek Road, is the O. C. Brown County Park. This is a great picnic spot for families with its well-developed children's playground.

SINGLETON COUNTY PARK

Another well-developed park is the Singleton County Park northwest of Roseburg. Take Garden Valley Road to Curry. The park is situated at the forks of the Umpqua River and is a popular picnic site on warm summer days.

RIVER FORKS PARK

Also located at the Umpqua forks you will find River Forks Park. Picnic facilities, boat ramp and an imaginative old west playground for the children complete with a cannon, teepees, covered wagon and log fort make it a great place to spend the day.

RIVERSIDE PARK

The Lotus Knight Memorial Gardens are located at Riverside Park in downtown Roseburg. Located between the Oak and Washington Street bridges, on the South Umpqua River, the gardens feature azaleas, rhododendrons and a fountain.

ROSEBURG ART GALLERY

You can visit the Roseburg Art Gallery from 11:00 a.m. to 4:00 p.m. Monday thru Saturday. Located at 1624 West Harvard they display work done by local artists.

WHISTLER'S BEND COUNTY PARK

You'll find excellent hiking trails at Whistler's Bend County Park. With 3 miles of river frontage, this 175 acre county park offers the outdoors person plenty to do. You'll find it 15 miles east of Roseburg off North Umpqua Highway.

SALEM

ANKENY NATIONAL WILDLIFE REFUGE

The Ankeny National Wildlife Refuge is located ten miles south of Salem between the Willamette River and the I-5 freeway. Drive out some early morning to catch a look at a great blue heron or white egret. Many other birds can also be seen here.

ARCHAEOLOGY MUSEUM

You'll find the Archaeology Museum at the Robert S. Allen Western Baptist College. Some of the artifacts displayed here are up to 4000 years old. They are open to the public during normal business hours. You will find the college at 500 Deer Park Drive SE.

ART

The city of Salem has a public art collection valued at over $200,000. You will find it on display in the Salem Public Library, City Hall and the outside plaza area of the Civic Center complex. Anyone can view this collection during normal business hours.

There are also several local art galleries. The best known is the Bush Barn Gallery located at 600 Mission Street SE. They are open weekends from 1:00 p.m. to 5:00 p.m. and Tuesday thru Friday from 9:30 a.m. to 5:00 p.m. This lovely old converted barn displays Northwest artists. Other local galleries include High Street, Keller and Window Gallery.

BOISE CASCADE CORPORATION

At Salem's Boise Cascade you can take a 45 minute tour of the facilities. It all starts at the guard's office, on the corner of Front and Trade Streets. Weekdays at 2:00 p.m. No children under twelve are permitted. Call 362-2421 for more information.

DEEPWOOD GREENHOUSE
EXPLORATORIUM & NATURE TRAIL

Behind the Deepwood House is a ¼ mile loop trail for public enjoyment of this natural setting.

If you're there Tuesday through Friday between 9:00 a.m. and 4:00 p.m., or Sunday between 1:30 p.m. and 4:30 p.m., stop in at the greenhouse exploratorium. It is also free to the public. Here you can view a collection of exotic plants.

FIRST UNITED METHODIST CHURCH

This is the oldest Methodist Church west of the Rockies. It was organized in 1841. The present church was built in 1879. Call 364-6709 for information on touring the building.

HONEYWOOD WINERIES

This is Oregon's largest commercial winery. Both fruit and berry wines are produced here. Visitors can call ahead to arrange for a tour weekdays between 9:00 a.m. and 4:00 p.m. The number is 362-4111 and they are located at 501 14th Street SE.

LINCOLN HISTORIC DISTRICT

Off State 221 north of West Salem you will find what remains of an old riverboat landing.

NOTABLE TREE

In Willamette Mission State Park, about nine miles north of Salem, you can view the largest cottonwood tree in the continental United States. The tree is 26' 3" in circumference.

OREGON STATE ARCHIVES

This is the location of federal, state and local governmental records pertaining to Oregon. These records date from 1836 to the present. They are open to the public during normal business hours. The archives are located at 1005 Broadway NE.

SALEM PARKS

The city of Salem operates 40 parks offering everything from tennis courts, jogging paths, hiking trails, bicycle paths, horseshoe courts and playground equipment to picnic tables. You can call 588-6261 for information and location.

7-UP/RC BOTTLING COMPANY

You can take a tour of this soft drink bottling company located on Southeast Pringle. It includes a short slide program and a trip through the plant. Tours are by appointment only. Call 585-2822.

STATE CAPITOL

A tour of the state capitol includes the marble and bronze rotunda, governor's office, senate, and house of representatives. The legislature is in session from the

second Monday in January until the end of May during odd numbered years. All committee meetings are open to the public, so check with the information desk to see what's happening.

Take a walk to the top of the tower where a 24' gold leafed statue entitled "The Pioneer" looks out over the capitol city. You may also tour the park-like grounds.

Visitors are welcome at the capitol from 8:00 a.m. to 5:00 p.m. weekdays and from 9:00 a.m. to 5:00 p.m. on weekends. Guided tours run the middle of June thru Labor Day. The balance of the year they are self-guided.

VALENTINE PARTY

Each year the Friends of Deepwood hold their annual Valentine party on the second Sunday of February at the Deepwood Mansion. It runs from 1:00 p.m. to 5:00 p.m. and includes displays of both antique and newly created valentines. Donations welcome.

WALLACE MARINE PARK

Located on the Willamette, at the end of Musgrave Lane, is Wallace Marine Park. You will find a boat ramp, horseshoe pits and picnic facilities here.

ZENA HISTORIC DISTRICT

Five miles northwest of Salem off State 221 is the Zena historic district with its pioneer church and cemetery. It was named for Arvazena Cooper, a pioneer woman who lived here in 1863.

SANDY

MARMOT HISTORIC DISTRICT

Leaving Sandy on US 26 east, turn left onto Ten Eyck Road. Proceed two miles and turn right on Marmot Road. From here it's a short distance to an old log cabin and the remains of the saw mill. This area was settled in 1883.

ROSLYN LAKE PARK

This is a great spot for family picnics. Roslyn is a shallow lake suitable for small children, inflatable rafts and inner-tubes. The 140 acre lake is part of the Bull Run project operated by PGE. Picnic tables, fireplaces, electric stoves, toilets, a playfield and horseshoe courts are available for public use. There is a minimal charge on weekends and holidays. The park is located 3½ miles north of Sandy on Ten Eyck Road.

SAUVIE ISLAND

BYBEE HOWELL HOUSE

This 1856 Antebellum house was built for one of the original Donation Land Claim holders. It has been restored and furnished as a pioneer homestead. The house is open for tours from May thru October, daily from 10:00 a.m. to 5:00 p.m. You can also tour the grounds and visit the pioneer orchard. Donations are welcome.

SAUVIE ISLAND WILDLIFE AREA

Nearly 12,000 acres of public land can be found in the Sauvie Island Wildlife Area. The wetlands here attract thousands of migrating waterfowl. The area has shallow lakes, marsh, grassland, oak-ash woodlands and cultivated fields which entice the wintering birds.

You can obtain a wildlife checklist from the Oregon Department of Fish & Wildlife office located on the island. They will also advise you as to the usage of the land.

SCAPPOOSE

CITY HALL

The Scappoose City Hall is located in one of the area's historic old homes. You will find a small museum in the lower part of the house.

SCAPPOOSE POW WOW

Held each year in mid-June, this four day event features a children's parade, exhibits and lots of celebration. Contact the Scappoose Chamber of Commerce for the exact dates and information on free events.

SCIO

BOHEMIAN HALL COVERED BRIDGE

This is one of three Oregon covered bridges housed entirely in sheet metal. Built in 1947, it is 120' long. Local residents refer to the bridge as "Richardson Gap Bridge". From Scio take State 226 east to Richardson Gap Road. The bridge is to the south, 3½ miles.

GILKEY COVERED BRIDGE

Until 1960 there were two covered bridges at this location. The other, a railroad bridge, is now gone. This bridge was built in 1939 and is 120' long. From Scio, take State 226 south a half mile to County Road 628. At the intersection of County Road 629, turn right and travel a half mile to the bridge.

HOFFMAN COVERED BRIDGE

From Scio, take State 226 south three miles to County Road 647. The Hoffman Covered Bridge is two miles to the west. It measures 90' and was built in 1936 to cross Crabtree Creek. The design includes gothic-style windows. The entry portals have been enlarged to allow passage of large loads.

MT. JEFFERSON WOOLENS

This woolen mill is located west of Scio at Jefferson. Here you can tour a facility that uses the shearings from approximately 1200 sheep each week. See the carding, spinning, dyeing and weaving of the wool into bolts of designer fabrics. Open weekdays from 9:00 a.m. to 4:00 p.m.; take the Talbot Road exit off I-5 to 1827 Talbot Road SE. Call ahead for an appointment, 327-2203.

MT. PLEASANT CHURCH

The Mt. Pleasant Church was organized in 1854. This structure was built of lumber logged in the area, hauled by wagon to Oregon City for sawing and hauled back to the building site. The church is a historical landmark, yet still holds services. To reach the church simply take the Stayton-Scio Road north out of Scio and turn right on Ridge Drive.

ROARING RIVER FISH HATCHERY

Southeast of Scio, near Larwood Covered Bridge, the Roaring River Fish Hatchery has been in operation since 1924. Visiting hours are from 10:00 a.m. to dark. This is a good opportunity to learn a little about fish and how the Oregon State Game Commission works to manage them. Picnic facilities including tables and outdoor fireplaces are available as well.

SHELBURN HISTORIC DISTRICT

Two miles northwest of Scio you will find a few abandoned houses, a school and a church in what was once a thriving logging town.

SHIMANEK COVERED BRIDGE

The first bridge at this location was built in 1861 and came complete with a two-hole toilet built into the foundation. This 130' descendant across Thomas Creek was constructed in 1966. It is the fifth bridge at this location and is currently the only red covered bridge in Oregon. To find it take State 226 east out of Scio to Richardson Gap Road. Turn left. The bridge is nearby.

WEDDLE COVERED BRIDGE

The Weddle Covered Bridge is also known as the Devaney Covered Bridge. Built in 1937, it is 120' in length and spans Thomas Creek. From Scio, take Market Road 4 west to County Road 622. The bridge is to the left.

SILVERTON

ANNUAL EVENTS

Three terrific annual events are held in Silverton. First, every June the Silverton Hills Community Club holds their Strawberry Festival. This event features loads of exciting activities. In August it's the Silverton Art Association's annual Homer Davenport Days. Named for a local man, the world's highest paid newspaper cartoonist around the turn of the century, it offers local artists and craftspeople a chance to display and demonstrate their talents.

The last, and perhaps best known, occurs during the third week in September. The Mt. Angel Octoberfest serves as an excellent introduction to the Swiss-Bavarian culture. This event includes Bavarian dancing, singing, music concerts, glass blowing and art exhibits.

GALLON HOUSE COVERED BRIDGE

This 1916 bridge crosses the Abiqua Creek north of Silverton. It is Marion County's last remaining covered bridge. To find this 84', shingle roofed bridge, take State 214 north to Hobart Road. Turn left to Gallon House Road. The bridge is half mile to the right.

SCOTTS MILLS MUSEUM

In Scotts Mills, 7 miles northeast of Silverton, the local historical society has converted an old church into a museum. It illustrates the early Quaker settlement of the area and includes local artifacts, photographs and geneological information. They are open only the second Sunday of each month from 1:00 p.m. to 5:00 p.m. and by appointment. (873-5949)

SILVER FALLS STATE PARK

Silver Falls State Park is the largest state park in Oregon. Located 15 miles east of Silverton, it covers over 8300 acres and displays fourteen spectacular waterfalls. There is a minimal charge on weekends and holidays, April thru October.

The park contains an extensive trail system winding its way through Douglas fir and hemlock interspersed with lush meadows full of wildflowers and giant ferns.

The "Trail of Ten Falls" follows the north and south forks of Silver Creek and offers an incredible display of cascading waterfalls along Silver Creek Canyon. The park also offers fourteen miles of horse trails and a four mile bicycle path.

If you are alert you can see a variety of wildlife here. Deer, beaver, rabbits, birds, squirrels and chipmunks are often sighted.

Each May, the park sponsors an annual Mother's Day Wildflower Show.

SILVERTON COUNTRY MUSEUM

At 428 South Water Street, in Silverton, you can visit the Silverton Country Museum. The buildings, which include one of the area's older homes and a former railroad depot, house a collection spanning time from the days of Oregon's early pioneers to the present. Hours are Thursday and Sunday only 1:00 p.m. to 4:00 p.m. During the winter they are open every Thursday but only the first Sunday of each month.

ST. LOUIS HISTORIC DISTRICT

Three miles north of Gervais, in the Silverton area, you will find what remains of this pioneer settlement. Catholic records show a Jesuit missionary visiting the settlement in 1844. In 1845 he built a log church here. A parish home, cemetery and a few scattered houses mark the site. The remains of Madame Marie Dorion, famed pioneer woman, are interred at the St. Louis Church cemetery.

SISKIYOU NATIONAL FOREST

The Siskiyou National Forest has been called a botanists' paradise. With over 1400 varieties of plants, trees and shrubs which include many rarely found elsewhere in a wild state; it's easy to see why.

This public land also allows access to the Rogue River, one of eight waterways in the United States officially designated under the National Wild and Scenic Rivers System. The river winds its way through some impressive rock gorges.

Forest Service offices are located in Brookings, Grants Pass, Gold Beach, Cave Junction and Powers, Oregon. Information on hiking trails, river access and maps can be found at any location.

ST. HELENS

COLUMBIA COUNTY HISTORICAL MUSEUM

At the Columbia County Historical Museum you will see pioneer artifacts which include a complete kitchen, bedroom and living room, books, records and photographs. The museum is open Wednesday thru Friday from 1:00 p.m. to 5:00 p.m. You will find it at the courthouse, overlooking the Columbia River.

While there, be sure to stop in at the old courtroom down the hall. It remains much the same as it did when first used.

ST. PAUL

ST. PAUL CATHOLIC CHURCH
& CEMETERY

During the late 1820's this land was settled by some retired Hudson's Bay Company trappers and their families. They farmed the land. In 1839 the St. Paul Catholic Mission was established here. In 1846 they built the first brick church west of the Rocky Mountains. Many noted early French-Canadian settlers as well as local Indians are buried in the church cemetery. You can see a replica of the 1836 log church which once stood here.

STAYTON

FINE ARTS FESTIVAL

Each February the North Santiam Fine Arts League sponsors the Santiam Fine Arts Festival. This two-day festival includes exhibits and demonstrations. Musical performances are also featured. Contact the league for more information.

PARIS WOOLEN MILLS

The Paris Woolen Mills have been in Stayton since 1880. They produce quality woolen products. Tours of the mill's operations are given Monday thru Friday between 7:00 a.m. and 3:00 p.m.

SUTHERLIN

COOPER CREEK COUNTY PARK

This county operated park is located east of Sutherlin at Cooper Creek. It offers picnic facilities, two boat ramps and some good hiking trails.

ROCHESTER COVERED BRIDGE

Three miles northwest of Sutherlin, the Rochester Covered Bridge spans the Calapooya River. Take State 138 west two miles, turn right on County Road 10-A. The 80' bridge is one mile down this road. The original construction took place in 1933 with extensive remodeling done in 1969.

SWEET HOME

CLEAR LAKE

Clear Lake was formed 33,000 years ago when the Belknap Crater Lava Flow dammed the area. The water here is so clear you can see the bottom. The water temperature is a constant 41°. Clear Lake is also the headwaters of the McKenzie River.

From Sweet Home take State 20 east. The lake is located south of its junction with State 126, 35 miles east of Sweet Home.

CRAWFORDSVILLE COVERED BRIDGE

The Crawfordsville Covered Bridge crosses the Calapooya River at Crawfordsville, southwest of Sweet Home. Built in 1932, it is 105' in length. It was bypassed by State 228 in 1963. A county park there commemorates its historical significance. McKercher Park offers picnic facilities and swimming. Crawfordsville was established in 1870.

EAST LINN MUSEUM

This lovely pioneer museum is located in a former Sweet Home church. It is open from mid-June till mid-September, Tuesday thru Sunday from noon to 5:00 p.m. The balance of the year, it is open Thursday thru Sunday from 1:00 p.m. to 5:00 p.m. The address is 746 Long Street.

LINN COUNTY HISTORICAL MUSEUM

These early store buildings have been turned into a museum with the re-creation of pioneer rooms and shops. Winter hours are 1:00 p.m. to 5:00 p.m. weekends only. From June 1 thru the end of September they are open every day but Monday from 2:00 p.m. to 5:00 p.m.

Located west of Sweet Home, at 106 Spaulding Avenue, in Brownsville. Exhibits include over 3,000 pioneer life artifacts. Period rooms are furnished with authentic pieces. One room has been devoted exclusively to mining equipment and a rock collection. A saddlery, blacksmith shop and logging tools are also important parts of this display.

LINN COUNTY PARKS

Linn County has several fine parks. In the Green Peter/Foster Lakes area you will find five parks offering picnic facilities, boat ramps and lake access. While there, you can contact the Corps of Engineers for a tour of the dam facilities — 367-5124.

Other area parks include McDowell Creek, northeast of Sweet Home, where you can view two scenic waterfalls and Waterloo to the north.

MOYER HOUSE

In Brownsville you can visit an 1881 Italian villa style residence at 213 North Main Street. They are open Tuesday thru Sunday, May thru September, from 2:00 p.m. to 5:00 p.m. The balance of the year they are open weekends only.

PIONEER PARK

Pioneer Park is located in Brownsville along the Calapooya River. This was once the south end of the local ferry. It was over this trail that supplies were carried to town. The ten acre park has sandy shores, a nice grove of shade trees and picnic facilities.

Every June, the park plays host to the annual Linn County Pioneer Picnic. This is the oldest community celebration in the state.

NORTHSIDE CITY PARK

You will find tennis, handball and basketball courts at the Northside City Park in Sweet Home. Facilities also include ball field, picnic facilities and a swimming area.

QUARTZVILLE

Quartzville was a big gold mining area in the 1860's. The townsite was platted in 1864. A stamp mill was erected the same year. Although there are no buildings at this site it could prove an enticing spot for gold panning or off the road exploration. The Santiam mines were located near here. The Quartzville site was 25 miles north of Sweet Home.

SHORT COVERED BRIDGE

This is the last of the covered bridges to span the South Fork of the Santiam River and one of only a few remaining bridges to have a wood shingle roof. Built in 1945 it is 105' in length. From Sweet Home, take US 20 east toward Cascadia. Turn on High Deck Road to the bridge.

SOUTH SANTIAM FISH HATCHERY

Visitors are welcome to tour the facilities at the South Santiam Fish Hatchery. They are open Monday thru Saturday from 8:00 a.m. to 4:30 p.m. The hatchery is located 1 mile east of Sweet Home, on the north side of Foster Lake, at the foot of the dam.

SOUTH SANTIAM TREE FARM

You can give yourself a self-guided tour of this tree farm located 7 miles east of Sweet Home on Highway 20. You'll need to stop at the Sweet Home Ranger Station first for details. Call 367-5168 for more information.

WHITE'S ELECTRONIC MUSEUM

At White's Electronic Museum you can take a historical look at metal detectors, plus old coins, rocks, gold nuggets and various other items unearthed by them. The museum can be found at 1011 Pleasant Valley Road. Hours are from 8:00 a.m. to 5:00 p.m. weekdays and 9:00 a.m. to 4:00 p.m. Saturday.

TANGENT

PREHISTORIC BURIAL MOUNDS

Along the Calapooya River, between Tangent and Shedd, are the burial grounds of the "Mound Builders". The Mound Builders is a race of people who once dwelled here. They are thought to have originally come from Siberia which is the only other place in the world where burial mounds like these have been found.

TUALATIN

TUALATIN VINEYARDS

At Tualatin Vineyards you can take a tour and enjoy a trip to the tasting room every weekend between 1:00 p.m. and 5:00 p.m. To reach the vineyards take State 8 out of Forest Grove. Turn right on Kansas City-Thacher Road, left on Clapshaw Hill Road and right on Seavy Road.

UMPQUA

JAMES WOOD COUNTY PARK

The James Wood County Park is six miles downstream from Umpqua. Picnicking and hiking are very popular here along the Umpqua River.

UMPQUA
NATIONAL FOREST

This national forest was named for the Indians who once fished its rivers and roamed its hills. Over 988,000 acres ranging from timbered mountain slopes to lowland farms make up this southwestern Oregon forest.

You can travel miles of forest roads leading to secluded waterfalls and quiet retreats. Hiking trails thread their way through the trees offering peace and solitude. Information and maps can be seen at Forest Service offices in Roseburg, Cottage Grove, Idleyld Park, Glide or Tiller. People there will tell you how to find waterfalls like Steamboat, Fall Creek, Grotto, Toketee, Watson, Lemolo, Clearwater, Shadow and Cow Creek. The Umpqua National Forest offers many scenic wonders.

VERNONIA

FOSSIL BEDS

Northeast of Vernonia you will find some interesting fossil beds.

COLUMBIA COUNTY HISTORICAL
MUSEUM

At 511 East Bridge Street you can see pioneer and Indian relics, mineral specimens and a grand old Shay Engine. The historical society also operates a library here. Summer hours are Tuesday thru Sunday from 1:00 p.m. to 5:00 p.m. but they are closed the fourth Wednesday of each month. From November 1 thru May 31 they are open Friday thru Sunday only, from 10:00 a.m. to 5:00 p.m.

SCAPONIA PARK

Located between Scappoose and Vernonia it's easy to see how this BLM park got its name. A wooden footbridge leads to this shady spot along Scappoose Creek. Picnic tables, restroom facilities and water make it a pleasant stop. Trails provide some excellent bird watching. The park is located off State 47 northeast of Vernonia.

VIDA

BELKNAP COVERED BRIDGE

From Vida, head east on State 126. Turn south at the town of MacKenzie Bridge along McKenzie River Drive. It is one mile to the Belknap Covered Bridge over the McKenzie River. Built in 1966, the bridge is 120' long.

BLUE RIVER LAKE

Blue River Lake is a small but beautiful lake nestled among steep mountain slopes. Take State 126 east from Vida past Blue River. Here you will find a boat ramp and swimming area.

COUGAR LAKE

Cougar Lake is located in the mountainous Willamette National Forest where wooded slopes plunge to the edge of this man-made lake. Five public sites along its shores offer picnic facilities, boat launching and swimming. You will find Cougar Lake south of State 126 just past Blue River.

GOODPASTURE COVERED BRIDGE

Goodpasture Covered Bridge spans the McKenzie River at Vida. Built in 1938, it is 165' long. This is probably the most photographed covered bridge in Oregon. The town of Vida was established before the turn of the century.

HORSE CREEK COVERED BRIDGE

East of Vida, at the town of McKenzie Bridge, head southeast on Horse Creek Road to this quaint covered bridge. Built in 1930, the 105' span was bypassed in 1968 when a concrete bridge was added to better carry the traffic.

LEABURG FISH HATCHERY

Cutthroat trout, rainbow trout and summer steelhead are raised here at Leaburg. The facility was built in 1953 to compensate for the loss of natural fish production caused by construction of the upper Willamette River dams. Each year 725,000 rainbow trout, 200,000 cutthroat and over 120,000 summer steelhead pass through here. The large fish you see are resident brood fish.

The hatchery is just west of Vida along State 126. There is a park nearby.

WILD ROGUE WILDERNESS

The Wild Rogue Wilderness covers 36,000 acres within the Siskiyou National Forest. The Rogue River flows through the heart of this wilderness.

Two main trails are found here; Panther Ridge Trail and the Rogue River Trail. The latter parallels the river and allows the backpacker to share the territory and campsites with those who are floating their way down this wild and scenic river. Horses are not allowed on this trail due to is narrowness and steep canyon walls.

Two maps entitled "Wild Rogue Wilderness" and "The Wild and Scenic Rogue River" are available at National Forest offices in Grants Pass, Brookings, Gold Beach, Cave Junction and Powers. The rangers will help you with trail selection and brief you on the area.

WILLAMETTE NATIONAL FOREST

This 1,600,000 acre national forest covers 110 miles along the western slope of the Cascade Mountain Range. It is home to countless deer, elk, bear, rabbits, chipmunks, squirrels, gophers, porcupines, wolverines, fox, coyote, cougar, raccoon and skunk as well as numberless species of birds.

Ranger stations in Eugene, Blue River, McKenzie Bridge, Detroit, Sweet Home, Lowell, Westfir and Oakridge can provide information on area usage.

For family recreation ask about Waldo Lake. Oregon's second largest natural lake; it covers 6,700 acres. Or check into one of over 90 hiking trails. Most were laid out years ago and will reveal wild rhododendron, fern and bear grass, western hemlock, western white pine, Pacific yew, grand fir, sugar pine, white fir, vine maple, lodgepole pine, madrone, ponderosa pine, western red-cedar, incense cedar, noble fir, alder and bigleaf maple.

WOLF CREEK

GOLDEN

In 1892 over 150 people lived here along Coyote Creek. A church, carriage house and general store were soon built and in 1896 a post office opened under the name of Golden. Today that church, carriage house, store and several other small buildings are still standing. It is indeed a picturesque site.

This historic area is located four miles east of Wolf Creek on Coyote Creek Road.

GRAVE CREEK COVERED BRIDGE

Also known as the Sunny Valley Covered Bridge, this span was built in 1921 to cross Grave Creek. Take the Sunny Valley exit off I-5 and head under the freeway to view the 105' bridge.

If you turn right on Placer Road, just beyond the bridge, you can drive to the town of Placer. The area is currently occupied but you will see a half-dozen old structures including a school house which once held 24 students. This was once a large community that included three stores. At that time over twenty stills were said to be producing whiskey along the creek. Many of the old buildings have burned down over the years.

WHISKEY CREEK CABIN

The Whiskey Creek Cabin is on the National Register of Historic Places. It is the oldest known standing miners cabin in the remote lower Rogue River Canyon. Visitors can look through the windows and wander around. The "cabin" consists of a main house, pantry, blacksmith shop, generator shed, solar shower, toolshed and outhouse. Water runs by gravity through a pipeline to an outside tap. The solar heated shower, fir floor and sawdust insulated pantry were not part of the original construction.

The flume ditch near the cabin was dug around 1890. It begins a half mile up Whiskey Creek and ends at the gully just behind the toolshed.

The cabin is along the Rogue River three miles downstream from Grave Creek, just off the Rogue River Trail. By car take the Mt. Reuben-Whiskey Creek Access Road. You will have to hike the last ¾ mile down to the cabin along a steep dirt road.

WOLF CREEK TAVERN

Wolf Creek Tavern is representative of the stagecoach inns that once peppered the early roads and trails of Oregon. It was situated on the Portland-to-Sacramento line and built between 1868 and 1873.

It is now owned by the Oregon State Parks and Recreation Department who lease it to be operated as a restaurant, hotel and banquet facility. It is not a museum.

The south wing was added in 1927 to make room for additional sleeping rooms. Two earlier inns were once operated at Wolf Creek. Known as Six Bit House, the first was built in 1853 east of town. It stood within the Southern Pacific Railroad's hairpin curve. The second Six Bit House was also close to the railroad at the north end of town.

SECTION III
ALL ALONG US 97

All Along US 97 covers the very heart of Oregon, the center of the state. Bend, Crater Lake, Hood River, Klamath Falls, Madras, Prineville, Redmond and The Dalles can all be found here. This is where you will meet some of the friendliest people, see a variety of geological wonders and have the opportunity to visit places where those who traveled the Oregon Trail left their mark.

The terrain ranges from high mountain forests to wide expanses of desert offering a variety of temperatures. The mountains hold back the clouds making Central Oregon a haven for sun seekers.

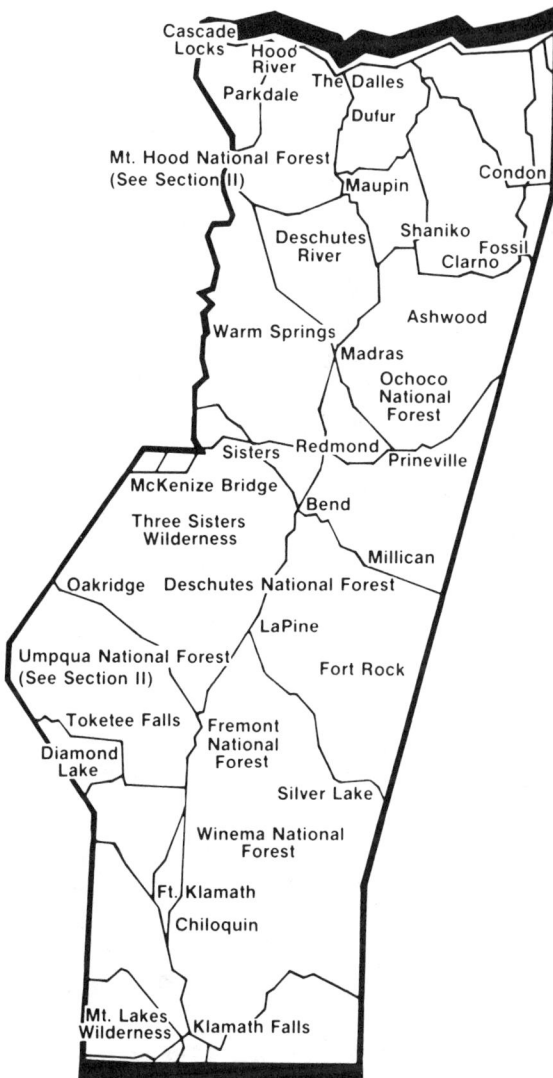

Cascade
Locks
Hood
River
Parkdale
The Dalles
Dufur
Mt. Hood National Forest
(See Section II)
Maupin
Condon
Deschutes
River
Shaniko
Fossil
Clarno
Ashwood
Warm Springs
Madras
Ochoco
National
Forest
Sisters
Redmond
Prineville
McKenize Bridge
Bend
Three Sisters
Wilderness
Millican
Oakridge
Deschutes National Forest
LaPine
Umpqua National Forest
(See Section II)
Fort Rock
Toketee Falls
Fremont
National
Forest
Diamond
Lake
Silver Lake
Winema National
Forest
Ft. Klamath
Chiloquin
Mt. Lakes
Wilderness
Klamath Falls

ASHWOOD

This historic old town can be reached by leaving US 197 two miles south of Willowdale. Signs point the way as you pass fifteen miles of beautiful countryside along back roads. When you enter the valley of Trout Creek the road suddenly makes a left turn and there you are.

The church building directly in front of you, as you make that turn, was built in 1897. At that time it was known as McCallum's Saloon. Thirty years later it was converted by the Baptists into a church. Looking through the windows you feel like you've slipped into the past.

This area was first settled in the 1870's. Other buildings include a hotel/saloon which later became the country store/gas station. An old restaurant amidst the trees, the Ash Butte Grange Hall and bygone residences can also be seen. The town once had a population of 300; today only a handful of people inhabit the area.

If you continue along this road, past the end of town, after fifteen miles you will find yourself in Horse Heaven. This was once a large mercury mining operation where 200 million pounds of cinnabar ore was pulled from the hillsides. The loading tipple that was used to crush and roast the ore to produce the liquid mercury still stands. Other interesting remains dot the surrounding area.

BEND

AREA HIKING TRAILS

The Bend area is loaded with nature walks and hiking trails. Some, such as the Lava Lands Visitor Center Trail, Lava Cast Forest Nature Trail, Newberry Crater Obsidian Trail and Smith Rock State Park Trail, are revealed under other area listings.

The Mt. Bachelor Trail leads from Sunrise Lodge, 2½ miles, to the 9050' summit of Mt. Bachelor. The 2 mile Black Butte Trail is located the other side of Sisters out Forest Service Road (FSR) 1139. At the trail's end you will find a lookout station and an outrageous view.

The Dee Wright Memorial Trail is 15 miles west of Sisters on Highway 242. This paved, ½ mile trail provides views of the Cascade mountains and information on this recent lava flow. To reach the Head of Jack Creek Nature Trail take Highway 20 15 miles west of Sisters, FSR 1138 to FSR 1211 to FSR 1210 to the trailhead.

You can get more information on these and other trails, like those found at the head of the Metolius River, from the Sisters Ranger District (549-2111).

ART GALLERIES

You'll find quite a few small art galleries in and around Bend. For a current listing and addresses check the Bend yellow pages.

ANNUAL SUMMER
FESTIVAL OF THE ARTS

Each July, Bend plays host to the annual Summer Festival of the Arts. Held at Drake Park, events include puppetry, music, arts and crafts, demonstrations, and entertainment. It is hosted by the Central Oregon Arts Society and the Bend Metro Park and Recreation District.

BROKEN TOP LOOKOUT

From Broken Top Lookout you have a clear view into the crater. A trip there in July or August will reward you with a brightly colored display of wildflowers. Snow generally makes this lookout inaccessible until early July.

CASCADE LAKES DRIVE

Take Cascade Lakes Drive off US 97 near Bend for a scenic tour that takes you past forests, mountains and lakes. The route traverses through stands of ponderosa and lodgepole pine.

CITY PARKS

Drake Park has eleven acres of lawn and trees bordering the Deschutes River in Bend. Abundant waterfowl and picnic facilities make it a lovely family park.

Another Deschutes River park is Pioneer Park. A children's fishing area surrounded by lawn, trees and flower gardens plus picnic tables make it very appealing.

Juniper Park has twenty-three acres of spacious lawns and recreational facilities which include a fine children's playground, horseshoe pits and tennis courts.

At Shevlin Park, five miles out of Bend, along Tumalo Creek, you can wander through 388 acres of natural forest. The park includes Shevlin Park Hatchery Pond.

DESCHUTES HISTORICAL CENTER

The Deschutes Historical Center is located in Reid School. The building itself was completed in 1914 out of native stone quarried west of the Deschutes River. On display, you will find relics of the county's colorful past.

They are open Thursday thru Saturday from 1:00 p.m. to 4:00 p.m.

FOREST SERVICE NURSERY

At the Forest Service Nursery you will find seventy acres used for starting ponderosa and lodgepole pines. These trees are then used in national forests throughout eastern Oregon and Washington. To find the nursery, take Butler Market Road out of Bend to Deschutes Road.

JOGGING TRAILS

At Central Oregon Community College you will find two and three mile jogging trails complete with exercise stations. The Ponderosa Park Par Course at Northeast 15th Street is a one and a half mile course with exercise stations. At Hillside Park, northwest Trenton and 12th Street, you will find a half mile par course with exercise stations. For more information contact the Parks and Recreation people at 389-PARK.

LAVA LANDS

Lava Lands is a 4400 square mile scenic wonderland of sculptured peaks, waterfalls and crystal clear lakes. This is probably the best variety of outstanding volcanic formations anywhere on the continent.

Start your visit at the Lava Lands Visitor Center. Here you will find automated displays and slide shows giving the history and geology of the area. You are invited to take a self-guided tour on the Trail of the Molten Land, Trail of the Whispering Pines, Crater Rim Trail, Trail of Glass, Lava Cast Forest Trail, Lava River Trail or Jack Creek Trail. Brochures are available at the visitors center.

Lava Butte is 11 miles south of Bend. Rising 500' above the forest covered land, the center provides a view into the 150' deep crater. To the west and north is an awesome lava field spreading over 6,117 acres. The center is open from May 15 to September 15.

Nearby you can visit Lava River Caves State Park. Bring a lantern and tour the one mile long lava tube. This cave runs under the highway, averages 35' in height and is 40° year round. Lanterns can be rented at the park.

The turnoff for the Lava Cast Forest is one mile further on US 97. Take Forest Road 1942 east to an area where the flow of lava engulfed a forest. Trees and logs burned out as the lava cooled and hardened. Casts were left in solid rocks, you can see imprints of tree bark and limbs.

232

This area also offers Arnold Ice Cave, Wind Cave and Skelton Cave for the adventurous. They are not that difficult to find and offer a less trampled chance to explore. These are not maintained so be sure to bring good walking shoes and dependable lanterns. To find them take Forest Road 1821 to 1854 for Skelton Cave or 1821 to 1924 for Arnold and Wind Caves.

Newberry Crater shelters two lakes, waterfalls, some huge obsidian flows and Paulina Peak. You will find it near LaPine.

PILOT BUTTE VIEWPOINT

Just east of the city limits, visit the Pilot Butte Viewpoint. Here you will be rewarded with a view of nine snow covered peaks. Mt. Hood, Mt. Jefferson, Three-Fingered Jack, Mt. Washington, North Sister, Middle Sister, South Sister, Broken Top and Bachelor Butte can all be seen.

To reach the viewpoint simply follow Greenwood Avenue east to the base of the butte.

ROCK-O-THE-RANGE COVERED BRIDGE

This is the only Oregon covered bridge located east of the Cascade Range. It was built in 1953 by a private party and spans an irrigation canal. The design was picked from a picture found on a calendar. It is 42' long. Take US 97 north of Bend two miles and turn left onto Bowery Lane to reach the bridge.

SAWYER STATE PARK

Sawyer State Park is off O. B. Riley Road one mile northwest of the city. Picnic sites and hiking trails make this an excellent place to stop along the Deschutes River.

SILVICULTURE LABORATORY

This U.S. Forest Service Silviculture Laboratory is located at Trenton and West 12th Street in Bend. It is open to the public from 7:30 a.m. to 4:00 p.m. Monday thru Friday.

TENNIS

You will find tennis courts at the Bend High School and Juniper Park.

TUMALO FALLS

Deep in a pine forest, you can view the gorgeous 97' Tumalo Falls. From Drake Park, head west on Galveston Avenue. After 11 miles the road turns into a rough forest service road. Another 3½ miles will take you to the falls.

CASCADE LOCKS

BONNEVILLE DAM

This major hydro-electric project is located 23 miles west of Hood River. It stretches 1450' across the Columbia and contains a major fish hatchery, visitors center and fish ladders. You can take a one hour tour any day from June 1 thru September 1. Between April and September is a good time to view the fish ladder.

CASCADE LOCKS HISTORICAL
MUSEUM

At Cascade Locks you can view the original 1896 navigation locks located beside the old canal. Nearby is the old portage road. There is now a city maintained museum in what was once the lock tender's residence. This community was started prior to the 1880's.

At the museum you can see the story of the mighty sternwheeler. Other items of interest include the first steam locomotive on the Pacific Coast, an 1872 wagon road and many pioneer artifacts. This area is a National Historic Site.

FORT RAINS BLOCKHOUSE

East of Bonneville you will find a replica of the 1853 Fort Rains Blockhouse.

CHILOQUIN

COLLIER STATE PARK
& LOGGING MUSEUM

Collier State Park is 33 miles north of Klamath Falls on US 97. The park is located at the junction of the Williamson River and Spring Creek. This beautiful setting offers picnic facilities, restrooms, a children's playground, hiking trails and a museum.

The Collier Logging Museum is open year round displaying log houses, old logging equipment, steam locomotives, horse drawn logging sleighs, steam tractors, a steam donkey engine and more. It contains over 500 exhibits and is the largest museum of logging equipment in the entire United States. The park covers 350 acres.

KLAMATH FOREST NATIONAL WILDLIFE
REFUGE

The Klamath Forest National Wildlife Refuge is 25 miles north of Chiloquin, off US 97. This is a very important nesting area for the Sandhill Crane consisting of 15,427 acres of natural marsh.

KLAMATH INDIAN MEMORIAL MUSEUM

The Klamath Indian Memorial Museum is located at the Chiloquin City Hall. It is open Tuesdays and Thursdays only, during the winter, from 1:30 p.m. to 5:00 p.m. From June 1 thru September 15 they are open daily between 1:00 p.m. and 5:00 p.m.

CLARNO

JOHN DAY FOSSIL BEDS
NATIONAL MONUMENT

A visit to the John Day Fossil Beds will reveal a variety of rock and hill formations opening up panoramic views of a brightly colored landscape. This national monument stretches from John Day, along the John Day River, northwest to Clarno.

Just beyond Dayville is Sheep Rock. Here you will find flat topped hills with names like Rattlesnake Formation. Remains of a single-toed horse, the last known rhinos in North America and bear-like dogs as well as prehistoric bears, cats, rabbits and squirrels have been found here.

Along State 19 you travel through Picture Gorge toward Thomas Condon Viewpoint. The viewpoint was named for an 1860's minister who brought this geological paradise to the public's attention. The view across the river, toward Sheep Rock, is of 18 million year old lava formations. At one time the surrounding area's high cliffs and canyon walls revealed Indian pictographs. Few remain.

At the Cant Ranch, you will find a three-story square ranch house which the National Park Service operates as a museum. They also maintain exhibits along the highway. At Turtle Cove the colors are astounding. You'll see 40 million year old formations containing teeth and bones from saber-tooth cats, three-toed horses, the huge pig-like entelodont and giant land tortoises remaining from a time when this was a hot, moist, tropical jungle. This area also contains a 70 million year old rock wall known as Goose Rock; made up of many round rocks deposited here when a shallow sea covered the area.

Turtle Cove offers trails and picnic facilities. This is the only trail open to the public because of the fragile nature of the fossil beds. Those with aspirations of finding their own fossil will have to look outside the park's boundaries.

Near Clarno are more interesting rock structures along with the Oregon Museum of Science and Industry's Camp Hancock.

One other area within the John Day Fossil Beds which is worth a stop, is the Painted Hills. Northwest of Mitchell, they are almost indescribable. At the road's end you will find colors, textures and delicacy only nature and time can sculpt from the earth.

CONDON

CITY PARK

At the Condon city park you can enjoy a rousing game of tennis, let the children run or just settle down to a quiet picnic. Condon was established as a trading center in 1883.

CONDON MUSEUM

On Main, between Gilliam and Summit Streets, you will find Pete the Barber's Museum. It contains memorabilia of a bygone day and is open free to the public.

DEVIL'S BACKBONE

Along State 19, near milepost 44, you can find traces of the old stage coach road that once ran from Condon to Fossil. It's easy to spot along Thirtymile Creek.

LONEROCK

Lonerock, Oregon is 22 miles southeast of Condon. It was named for one huge rock that dominates an otherwise flat valley. Not only the town, but the stream and valley were all named for this 100' high landmark. The area was populated before the 1880's.

A tiny Baptist church built here before the turn of the century, and the Methodist church from 1898, are both still standing. Silent play equipment sits in front of the large school building. A deserted main street, jail and area homes stand in various stages of decay. The town is partially inhabited.

MOUNTAIN IDENTIFIER

At milepost 24, along State 206, you can stop at the mountain identifier for a view of Mt. Hood, Adams, Jefferson, Rainier, St. Helens and the Three Sisters.

OLEX

Olex is another one of Oregon's historic towns. Established in 1874, it contains the oldest, and only country school still in operation in Gilliam County as well as a few old buildings, cemetery and Jeremiah Crum's Mill. You will find this town north of Condon.

PETERSON'S MUSEUM

Another Condon museum is Peterson's. This little place is packed full of Indian artifacts and antiques.

RICHMOND

Richmond is 19 miles northeast of Mitchell just off State 207. The town was begun in 1890. Still standing are a house with a corner porch, and the still handsome Methodist church. The long building once housed a post office, boarding house and general store with a covered porch running the front length. Oregon's first shopping mall?

On the hillside, northwest of town, stand several large homes. Most are vacant except for the small critters that can be heard scurrying about.

DESCHUTES NATIONAL FOREST

Offices for the Deschutes National Forest are located in Bend, Crescent and Sisters, Oregon. Here you will find maps and information on hiking trails. Ice caves, a lava cast forest, volcanic peaks and craters, scenic rivers, streams and springs can all be visited. Ask about Lavacicle Cave with its stalagtites and stalagmites or Osprey Point with its abundant waterfowl. During the winter, cross-country skiers will enjoy the Swampy Lakes Shelter, Tumalo Lake Road or Tumalo Falls Tours.

With more than 200 lakes and reservoirs, this national forest is popular with fishermen and water enthusiasts. Canoeing, sailing, floating streams, swimming, diving and water skiing can all be enjoyed. Suttle, Cultus and Crescent Lakes along with Wickiup Reservoir are most popular with water skiers while Elk Lake entices more sailors. Many well-developed and un-developed recreational sites abound in this national forest.

DESCHUTES RIVER

Information on floating the Deschutes River can be obtained from the Deschutes National Forest offices, the Bureau of Land Management or the Oregon State Parks & Recreation office. The BLM has an office in Portland and the State Parks Division can be reached at 1-800-452-7813. It is not wise to raft the river without knowledge of the area as the water is very cold and a few stretches are quite dangerous and must be portaged.

There are many places where you can put ashore to relax along this scenic waterway. Maps from the above listed offices will point out the hazards and locations of campgrounds and land boundaries.

DIAMOND LAKE AREA

With Mt. Bailey and Mt. Thielsen towering over this 3000 acre natural lake, the view is exhilerating. Diamond, and the nearby Lemolo Lake, offer city dwellers a civilized brush with nature. The broad valley was created more than a million years ago when lava dammed the area. Many thousands of years later, melting snow and glaciers filled the pockets with water. The area is operated by the Umpqua National Forest. Trails range from a half mile walk to the Diamond Vista Viewpoint to longer hikes along Howlock Mtn., Mt. Bailey, Rodley Butte and Mt. Thielsen. They vary in difficulty. Information can be obtained at the district ranger's office in Idleyld Park.

DUFUR

BOYD

Just one mile northeast of Dufur, on Fifteen Mile Creek, is Boyd. It was so named for T. P. Boyd who, with his sons, operated a flour mill here in 1883. The creek once supplied enough water to power the now idle grist mill. A three-story millowner's residence overlooks the mill and granary. You will also find a small cluster of elegant nineteenth century homes along this road.

DUFUR

Dufur's first townsite, 1852, was actually 4 miles from the town's current location. David Imbler built a farmhouse at this site in 1863. Andrew J. and E. Burnham Dufur laid out their farm in 1872. When a post office was established in 1878, the Dufur name was selected for the town. A few historic buildings still stand.

FORT KLAMATH

FORT KLAMATH MUSEUM

South of Fort Klamath on State 62, you will find a reconstructed 1863 guardhouse along with photo displays and memorabilia. This frontier post was maintained to protect southern emigrant trains from Indian attack. It was an important position during the Modoc Indian War of 1872-3. The museum is open from June through September, daily, from 9:00 a.m. to 6:00 p.m. Nearby Kimball State Park provides a delightful place for a picnic at the head of the Wood River.

FORT ROCK

FORT ROCK STATE MONUMENT

Fort Rock State Monument is the site of a fractured volcanic crater that resembles an ancient fort. More than 10,000 years ago the area was inhabited by Indians. Picnic facilities are available.

HOLE IN THE GROUND

Hole-in-the-Ground is a geologic rarity for which there are two possible explanations. Volcanic explosion or meteorite collision. The hole is 500' deep. Located northwest of town.

LAVA TUBES

At South Ice Cave you will find ice year round. Other area caves include the Lavacicle and Fort Rock Caves. At the latter 75 sagebrush sandles said to be over 9-13,000 years old were found. This cave faced a great lake that spread all the way to Picture Rock in ancient times.

FOSSIL

ASHER'S OLD CAR MUSEUM

This privately operated display is located in the town's old blacksmith shop. Cars range from an early Model T to a 1940 Packard. Ask here for direction to find "The Goose", an odd looking rail bus that once carried passengers between the towns of Willamina and Grande Ronde. Hours are not regular here but summer weekends seem to be the best opportunity for a guided tour.

FOSSIL HISTORICAL MUSEUM

This city museum offers items of both local and regional interest. It contains material illustrating a time when Fossil was part of an important sheep ranching region. Museum hours are 10:00 a.m. to 5:00 p.m. daily.

Ask them about a local display of old barber equipment. They can also tell you about the Wheeler County Courthouse, one of the oldest and most colorful county buildings in the state. If it's time for lunch you may enjoy a brief stop at the city park. It offers picnic tables and restroom facilities.

WILLIAMS ROCK DISPLAY

The Williams Rock Display is a privately owned exhibit which welcomes the public.

FREMONT NATIONAL FOREST

The Fremont National Forest covers nearly two million acres of land once occupied by Paiute, Modoc, Klamath and Achumaur Indians. Camping, hunting, fishing, hiking, skiing, snowmobiling and rock collecting are now popular activities here. At Forest Service offices in Bly, Lakeview, Paisley or Silver Lake you can go over maps with the staff for up-to-date information on local trails.

Visit Winter Ridge Viewpoint with its view of Summer Lake and numerous fault cliffs, or the Slide Mountain Geologic Area where you will have an opportunity to observe volcanic geology. Once a large dome-shaped volcano, Slide Mountains was scarred by a giant prehistoric slide. This can be viewed from State 31, north of Paisley. Spectacular views can also be enjoyed at

Albert Rim Viewpoint, North Warner Viewpoint, Drake Peak Lookout, Crane Mountain Viewpoint and Mount Vida Vista Point.

HOOD RIVER

ANNUAL EVENTS

Hood River plays host to several annual events. In April, when the orchards reach their full bloom, you can enjoy the Hood River Blossom Festival. Head south to Mt. Hood Meadows in May for the Spring Carnival which features an obstacle course ski race among its attractions. At Port Marina Park, in Hood River, you can enjoy an old fashioned Fourth of July celebration. You can witness a cross channel swim, sailing regatta, 10,000 meter Road Run, annual Fly-In and other activities during the Labor Day weekend. Check with the Hood River Chamber of Commerce for details.

AREA PARKS

In 1855 Nathaniel Coe planted the first fruit trees here which led to Hood River becoming a major agricultural area. Commercial orchards have been in existence since 1876. Fruit trees make this an area of extreme beauty from spring thru fall. Many nearby picnic parks will help you enjoy this beauty at your leisure.

In the city, you can stop at Waucoma, Jackson or Gibson Parks. To the west, along I-84, visit Ruthton, Wyeth, Viento or Starvation Parks. Along State 35 parks include Panorama Point, Toll Bridge, Tucker Bridge, Sherwood, Polallie and Robin Hood. Each has its own special attraction.

ART GALLERIES

Two notable art galleries in Hood River are Columbia Art Gallery and the Fruit Tree Art Gallery. Several other studios are open for viewing as well. Check the local phone book for addresses.

HOOD RIVER COUNTY HISTORICAL
MUSEUM

The Hood River County Historical Museum is located at the Port Marina Park. To reach it simply take exit 64 off I-84. At the museum you can view agricultural antiques

representative of both the fruit and lumber industries, photographic displays and an outstanding Indian and Japanese artifacts collection. They are open May thru October, Wednesday thru Sunday from 10:00 a.m. to 4:00 p.m.

Another attraction here is the Hood River Visitors Center. A large relief map of the gorge, local art, and historical and industrial displays will further your knowledge of the area.

INDUSTRIAL TOURS

Diamond Fruit Growers, Inc.
11 Third Street (386-3111)
Wednesday, Thursday and Friday, September thru December, Diamond allows visitors to watch as pears are processed. Tours are available by reservation only.

Hood River Wastewater Treatment Plant
818 Riverside Drive (386-2432)
Tours of this secondary treatment plant are given week-days with prior reservation.

Krieg Millwork, Inc.
755 Frankton Road (386-2929)

Krieg manufactures molding and kiln dry lumber for cabinet making. Between customers, 8:00 a.m. to 4:00 p.m., they will show you through their facilities.

Luhr Jensen & Sons, Inc.
400 Portway (386-3811)
For a look at how fishing lures and equipment are made visit Luhr Jensen's between 11:00 a.m. and 1:30 p.m. some Tuesday, Wednesday or Thursday.

Lava Nursery
5301 Culbertson Road, Parkdale (352-7303)
Planting and harvesting of forest trees can be watched weekdays, 9:00 a.m. to 3:00 p.m., during late February and March. Call ahead to be sure work is in progress.

Heritage Boat Works
1331 Country Club Road (386-1526)
Call ahead for a chance to see the operations of this custom boat builder. They are open 8:00 a.m. to 5:00 p.m. weekdays.

KOBERG BEACH

One mile east of Hood River you will find the sandy beach known as Koberg. The only entrance off I-84 is from the westbound direction. Here you can enjoy swimming, fishing, sun tanning or just picnic beside the Columbia River.

PANORAMA POINT

For a great view of Mt. Hood and the Hood River Valley, stop at Panorama Point, three miles south of the city along State 35.

PORT MARINA PARK

This seems to be the focal point for summer activity. Hood River is sometimes called the wind surfing capital of the northwest. Water skiing, fishing, swimming and boating also entice a great many people. Picnic facilities and a fully equipped playground are available.

KLAMATH FALLS

ANNUAL EVENTS

From January thru October, Klamath Falls and the surrounding area play host to over two dozen annual events. Many have parades and other free activities for the general public. Dog sled races, snowmobile races, art shows, and festivals are included. The biggest of all is the State of Jefferson Days in early August. Contact the Klamath Falls Chamber of Commerce for dates and a listing of events.

ART GALLERIES

In Klamath Falls you can visit the Klamath Art Gallery or Ruse Art Gallery. Klamath is on the corner of Main and Riverside and open Tuesday thru Sunday from 1:00 p.m. to 4:00 p.m. with changing exhibits. Ruse is at 803 Main Street and features monthly shows Monday thru Saturday from 10:00 a.m. to 5:00 p.m.

Check the yellow pages of the Klamath Falls phone book for other small galleries.

KENO PARK

West of Klamath Falls on State 66 Pacific Power & Light Company has developed a delightful little park along the Klamath River. Here, swimming and picnicking are two great pastimes.

KLAMATH COUNTY MUSEUM

At 1451 Main Street, you will find the Klamath County Museum. Displays here tell the story of the Klamath Country with exhibits covering geology, biology, anthropology and history. Special sections include wildlife, the logging industry, early Indian and Pioneer cultures and the Modoc Indian War. They are open Tuesday thru Saturday from 9:00 a.m. to 5:00 p.m.

LAKE OF THE WOODS

Lake of the Woods is west of Klamath Falls near Mt. McLoughlin. During the summer water sports are the attraction, but winter brings cross country skiers and snowmobilers to haunt the area. Maps are available through the U.S. Forest Service for winter use.

LAVA BEDS NATIONAL MONUMENT

These lava beds are actually over the California border but you're so close it's worth mentioning. Hikers and spelunkers alike enjoy this spot. A comparatively recent lava flow here left miniature volcanoes, tunnels, natural bridges and caves filled with ice. A natural fortress used during the Modoc War in 1872-3 is also found here. It's all located 40 miles south of Klamath Falls.

LOWER KLAMATH NATIONAL
WILDLIFE REFUGE

The Lower Klamath National Wildlife Refuge is a major stopover for migrating waterfowl along the Pacific Flyway. Millions of ducks and geese pass through the area annually. Drive south on US 97 to State Line Road then head east where you may view a wide variety of birds.

MOORE PARK

On the shore of Upper Klamath Lake you will find a 435 acre park. Playgrounds, tennis courts, archery range, picnic tables, nature trail, bird sanctuary, boat ramp and splendid viewpoints can all be enjoyed here. Special sledding and snowmobile areas are set aside during winter. Consistent winds entice many sail boats to the lake and several regattas are held here each year.

OREGON STATE FISH HATCHERY

Take State 62 north of Klamath Falls. A few miles south of Ft. Klamath you will find the hatchery. Visitors are welcome year round.

OUXKANEE LOOKOUT

Ouxkanee Lookout offers a panoramic view of Spring Creek Valley, a picnic area and historical displays. To reach it take US 97 north of Klamath Falls 27 miles.

UPPER KLAMATH NATIONAL
WILDLIFE REFUGE

The Upper Klamath National Wildlife Refuge is located 35 miles northwest of Klamath Falls. This marshy area of 12,457 acres provides an excellent habitat for white pelicans, herons, egrets and other colonial nesting birds as well as several species of ducks.

WIARD PARK

Wiard Park offers tennis courts and a children's wading pool. Drive south on State 140 and turn right on Wiard Street in Klamath Falls for a cooling stop.

LaPINE

ART GALLERY

While in LaPine visit Gordon Gallery on Foss Road. It is open weekdays from 10:00 a.m. to 6:00 p.m.

CRANE PRAIRIE OSPREY
MANAGEMENT AREA

Crane Prairie Reservoir is located near LaPine and is one of the few remaining Osprey nesting areas in the United States. June and July are the best times to view the nests and witness the feeding of the young. Bald eagles, blue herons, deer and other animals also inhabit the area. An observation point has been set up between Quinn River and Rock Creek Campground. Hiking trails abound.

This management area is a cooperative venture by the U.S. Forest Service and the Oregon State Game Commission. Its purpose is to provide the Osprey, a potentially endangered species, with a safe place to live and rear their young.

NEWBERRY CRATER

Newberry Crater is the caldera of an ancient, massive volcano that collapsed upon itself. It is the largest of all the Ice Age volcanoes in Oregon east of the Cascades. Two lakes, East and Paulina, are located within this crater. An overall view is available from Paulina Peak which reaches nearly 8000' above sea level offering views of the entire Cascade Mountain Range and portions of four states.

The outer slopes hold some of the Pacific Northwest's most spectacular lava flows which includes one that engulfed forests of pine trees forming strange tree molds known as "lava cast forests". Volcanic cinder cones, spatter cones, fissures and caves can also be found here. You can see an obsidian flow which spilled to the basin floor from a high vent leaving behind frozen cataracts of black, volcanic glass. Newberry is considered to be a dormant volcano, not extinct. Future volcanic activity is possible but many events would give ample warning of its coming.

When visiting the peak you may wish to take a side trip to the spectacular Paulina Falls. This hiking trail and the one leading around the lake shore allow you some close up looks at the land.

PRINGLE FALLS EXPERIMENTAL FOREST

This Pacific Northwest experimental forest and range experiment station is found seven miles west of US 97 near LaPine. They practice selective cutting, thinning and planting with ponderosa and lodgepole pine.

MADRAS

COURTHOUSE MUSEUM

This 1917 courthouse holds a small museum open Thursday thru Saturday from 1:00 p.m. to 4:00 p.m. Outside, to the rear, you will find the 1918 county jail. Though it is now used only for storage, you can still feel what if must have been like to be shut away here in this small box with its barred windows and metal shutters.

COVE PALISADES STATE PARK

The Cove Palisades State Park is located ten miles out of Madras in a land of gently rolling plains dotted with low hills and flat-topped buttes. At the conjunction of three rivers -- the Deschutes, Crooked and Metolius great gashes have been cut into the plain, laying open some spectacular views of a remarkable geological area. The 7,000 acre park shows off 10 million years of geologic history.

In 1960, the Round Butte Dam was constructed on the Deschutes River just below the mouth of the Metolius. This rock-fill dam raised the water level nearly 400' above the bottom of the canyon and created a body of water known as Lake Billy Chinook. Roads lead you through the canyon and over the Crooked River arm of Lake Billy Chinook alongside towering cliffs. You can see a large petroglyph here that was saved from below before the area was flooded. Found near the former rapids of the Crooked River, its age and meaning are unknown but the designs etched into this massive rock are similar in design to many found along the Columbia River. A geologic tour brochure is available through the State of Oregon's Department of Geology.

MAUPIN

SHERAR'S BRIDGE

Out of Maupin take the Sherar's Bridge junction off US 197. It is seven miles to this historic site. Halfway to the bridge you will find a small state park located down a tree lined road. At its end you can view a delightful waterfall. A spillway on the side with pipes that once directed the water and the remains of an old dam make it an interesting stop. Restrooms, running water, picnic tables and a backdrop of plateaus and tableland covered with green sage make it a worthwhile stop.

At the current Sherar's Bridge you will find a marker giving the history of this spot. It was once the site of an ancient Indian trail. Early explorers mentioned an Indian bridge at this point in 1826. In 1860 John Todd built a toll bridge here at the gateway to central Oregon. Sherar bought it in 1871. Fishing platforms along the Deschutes worked by Native Americans add atmosphere to the scene.

McKENZIE BRIDGE

Near the town of McKenzie Bridge, along State 126, you will find two very beautiful waterfalls; Koosah and Sahalie. Further north you will encounter Clear Lake at the headwaters of the McKenzie River. Near the junction with US 20 you can view lava beds.

MILLICAN

PINE MOUNTAIN OBSERVATORY

The Pine Mountain observatory is operated by the University of Oregon. It is open to visitors Thursday thru Sunday from 2:00 p.m. to 5:00 p.m. year round and during the summer from 7:00 p.m. till one hour after dusk. The road is sometimes closed during the winter. Take US 20 east out of Bend and turn south just beyond Millican.

PREHISTORIC RIVER

Four miles west of Millican a marker denotes the area where a prehistoric river once flowed across the high desert country of this rocky canyon. It drained the large ice age lake which cut this rocky gorge and has long been the site of Indian encampments.

MOUNTAIN LAKES WILDERNESS

The Mountain Lakes Wilderness landscape was created several million years ago by a series of volcanic eruptions. Volcanic forces, glacial periods, wind and running water have left only remnants of the rim and portions of the base of a mountain which once towered 12,000' and covered 85 square miles. Over 23,000 acres are included in this wilderness area, offering solitude and peace for those who truly desire to get away from it all. Maintained trails give access to broad valleys, lake basins and steep, rugged remnants of the old volcano. Located within the Winema National Forest, the office in Klamath Falls can provide hiking information and a look at the wilderness map.

OAKRIDGE

HILLS CREEK LAKE

Hills Creek Lake is set in rugged mountain timber country just southeast of Oakridge, off State 58. The U.S. Forest Service operates four parks here along both sides of the lake. Boat ramps, swimming and picnic facilities make it enticing to those interested in water sports.

OAKRIDGE FISH HATCHERY

Just one mile east of Oakridge, off State 58, you can view a fish hatchery where spring chinook salmon are raised.

OFFICE COVERED BRIDGE

At Westfir, just northwest of Oakridge, the Office Covered Bridge was built in 1944. It is 180' long.

SALT CREEK FALLS

At Salt Creek Falls the water makes a sheer drop of 286'. It's located 19 miles east of Oakridge. Look for the observation point just past the rock tunnel on the Willamette Highway.

OCHOCO NATIONAL FOREST

Offices for this national forest can be found in Prineville, Paulina and Hines. The rangers will be happy to show you maps of the area and direct you to hiking trails and recreational sites. The forest covers 845,855 acres and is managed along with the Crooked River National Grassland's 106,000 acres. Roads and trails lead you through forest and meadowlands carpeted with colorful wildflowers, streams and trees. The forest is the center of one of the best known rockhound areas in the nation. Winter finds it a haven for cross-country skiing and sledding.

Indians have long known the area but records show the first visit made by white men was in 1824 with the coming of Peter Skene Ogden and his party of Hudson's Bay Company trappers. American exploration began in 1834 with Nathaniel Wyeth's expedition.

PARKDALE

HUTSON'S ROCK MUSEUM

At the Hutson's Rock Museum, outside of Parkdale, you can view two dozen cases displaying rocks. They are open daily and located at the corner of Condor and Cooper Spur Roads.

LAVA BEDS

Two miles southwest of Parkdale you can see many interesting rock formations in an area simply known as the lava beds. They cover quite an extensive area and are readily accessible.

PRINEVILLE

A. R. BOWMAN MEMORIAL MUSEUM

Located at 3rd and Elm, this old stone building was once a bank. The original counter and teller's windows still remain along with historical exhibits of both local and regional interest. Outside are old wagons and an early day log cabin. The museum is open from May 31st thru Labor Day, Wednesday thru Sunday from noon to 5:00 p.m. The balance of the year they are open Wednesday thru Saturday.

CENTRAL OREGON TIMBER CARNIVAL

This annual festival features a beard contest, parade, logging equipment shows and a variety of competitions involving logging equipment. There is no admission charge for any of the events. The carnival takes place in May. Contact the Prineville Chamber of Commerce for details.

HOWARD

This historical early Oregon town is about 28 miles northeast of Prineville via US 26. The post office was closed in 1909. Town remains include log and frame buildings as well as the old gold mine. The original 1870's townsite is near the mouth of Scissor's Creek. It was named for the man who found gold there in 1872.

OCHOCO LAKE STATE PARK

This state park is located 8 miles east of Prineville off the Ochoco Highway. It offers 9 miles of shoreline, 900 acres of water, pine trees, sagebrush, picnic facilities and a wonderful place to enjoy water sports.

PIONEER PARK

This tiny city park is the location for the Pioneer Historical Museum. Here you will find an 1880 log cabin furnished with artifacts from original Crook County pioneers. The museum is open weekdays from 8:00 a.m. to 4:00 p.m. They are also open Saturdays from June thru September.

PRINEVILLE RESERVOIR STATE PARK

Prineville Reservoir is 16 miles southeast of the city. This 3,000 acre lake offers swimming and boat ramps for those interested in water sports. Over 40 miles of shoreline offer Russian olive and locust trees adding shade to the natural sagebrush vegetation.

ROCKHOUNDING

Central Oregon is a rockhound's paradise. Thunder eggs, plume, carnelian and moss agates, petrified wood and a jasper-like material called Morrisonite are all to be found in nearby areas. The land surrounding the

Prineville Reservoir an Ochoco Lake State Park are some of the most productive sites in the state, although no digging is allowed within state park boundaries. The Prineville Chamber of Commerce operates over 1,000 acres where amateur enthusiasts can dig for thunder-eggs, green jasper, agates, dendrites, petrified wood and obsidian. Contact them for more information.

STEIN'S PILLAR

Northeast of Prineville, in Mill Creek Valley, is a 350' high rock with a 120' diameter. It stands there all alone. To reach it take Forest Service Road 1334 to the trail leading to the foot of Stein's Pillar.

REDMOND

OPERATION SANTA CLAUS

Two miles west of Redmond, on State 126, you can visit a real live reindeer ranch. Open daily from dawn to dusk, visitors are welcome to drive in and look around. The reindeer get their new antlers around August and are most rambunctious in September and October. There are about forty reindeer in the herd. All are native Oregonians although the original stock came from Lapland via Alaska. This is the world's largest commercial reindeer ranch. The animals make guest appearances throughout Oregon during the Christmas season.

PETERSEN ROCK GARDENS

Rasmus Petersen began this creation of his in 1935. Since then it has become a collection of rock bridges, towers, terraces, buildings and ponds. The grounds have been made more beautiful with the addition of flowers, trees and lagoons and at night it is lighted.

Located five miles south of Redmond visitors are welcome from 7:00 a.m. to 9:00 p.m. April thru October. Winter hours are 8:00 a.m. to 5:00 p.m. daily.

RAY JOHNSON PARK

This 40 acre park offers picnic facilities and a children's fishing pond. You will find it south of Redmond.

REDMOND AIR CENTER

You can take a tour of the Redmond Air Center. This is the Northwestern Fire Equipment Center for smoke-jumpers, helitack crews and fire retardant planes. Its warehouse holds enough fire equipment for 4,000 firefighters. They also have a specially equipped shop for the maintenance and repair of fire pumps. The Air Center is located two miles east of Redmond on US 26.

SMITH ROCK STATE PARK

Smith Rock State Park is found between Madras and Redmond. This is a spectacular area where canyon walls are colored by sedimentary rock formations. The Crooked River winds its way between breathtaking formations layered in orange, burnt red, green and purple.

Hiking trails wind throughout the park, along the cliff's rim and on both sides of the river. Practicing mountaineers frequent this mini-mountain range where the technical rock climbing is considered among the best in Oregon. Monkey Face's 400' vertical wall is a favorite for both climbers and viewers. Three miles farther north is the Crooked River Gorge which is 403' deep. It provides another unequalled view.

SHANIKO

TOWN PROPER

Shaniko is probably Oregon's grandest ghost town. The area was populated prior to the 1880's. Still standing is the Shaniko Hotel, the 1902 schoolhouse and a good portion of the town proper. This was once a prosperous center where shopkeepers supplied the area sheepherders and railroad men with a variety of wares. The two-store firehouse, an old livery barn, the marshall's office where iron doors still mark the cells and a large wagon yard all prove it was once a busy communty.

SILVER LAKE

PICTURE ROCK PASS

At the summit between Summer and Silver Lakes are some Indian petroglyphs for which the area was named. Arrowheads, fossils and agates are all found around here. A hot mineral spring is located near the southeast tip of Summer Lake.

THE DALLES

ANNUAL EVENTS

The Dalles plays host to many annual events. Most have numerous free activities and parades. Some notable happenings include the Northwest Cherry Festival in April, Fort Dalles Days and the Fort Dalles Rodeo in July.

ART GALLERIES

The Dalles Art Center is housed in the beautifully restored Carnegie Library at 220 East 4th. Outside, the aged bricks are covered with old growth ivy while inside the wood beams gleem and the warmth of the building is greatly enhanced by the work of Oregon artists. A careful look along the floor reveals where bookshelves once lined the walls in this historic landmark. They are open Tuesday thru Saturday from 10:00 a.m. to 4:00 p.m.

At the Wasco County Library, on Court Street, just to the right of the entrance you can view the work of local artists. This small gallery is open from 10:00 a.m. to 7:30 p.m. weekdays and 10:00 a.m. to 6:00 p.m. Saturdays. Outside in the courtyard is a delightful wood bear sculpture.

A look at the local telephone directory will also reveal a few private galleries.

CELILO CONVERTER STATION

The Celilo Converter Station sits on a bluff overlooking the Columbia River and the city of The Dalles. It serves as the northern terminus for the world's longest direct current transmission line. This line stretches 846 miles to southern California.

The Bonneville Power Administration offers a self-guided tour showing prepared exhibits and displays. It also includes a second floor viewing gallery.

CITY NATORIUM

The Natorium has a large children's play center with lots of play equipment where children can burn off energy. Tennis courts with a background of old homes provide entertainment for adults. The Natorium is located next door to the Old Wasco County Courthouse.

Additional tennis courts can be found at the high school at 10th and Union and Howe Park on East 13th.

CITY PARK

At 6th and Union you will find the official end of the Oregon Trail. This is the trail which served to bring early pioneers west and The Dalles has erected a log archway to commemorate its end. The park offers picnic tables and children's play equipment in a shaded setting.

FORT DALLES MUSEUM

The Fort Dalles Museum at 15th and Garrison is housed in the original surgeon's quarters of historic Fort Dalles. Built in 1856, it sits on its original site. The surrounding historical buildings have all been moved to this location to provide the city with one large historical exhibit.

Fort Dalles was one of the most active army posts in the West during the Indian Wars of the 1850's. Inside this one-and-a-half-story house you can see some of the original construction of the building from viewing windows built into the walls. The kitchen has been restored to nearly original with its wood range and hand pump. A fine collection and displays are also housed here. Yellowed photographs and clippings add to its authenticity.

Outside, on the northwest corner of the property, you will find a long open shed which shelters a collection of horse drawn vehicles ranging from farm wagons to Conestogas. The setting is a grassy acre amid chestnut, mulberry and ponderosa pine trees.

The museum is open every day but Monday, May thru September from 10:30 a.m. to 5:00 p.m. The balance of the year it's noon to 4:00 p.m. Tuesday thru Friday and 10:00 a.m. to 4:00 p.m. on weekends.

OLD ST. PETER'S LANDMARK

St. Peter's Catholic Mission was built in 1897. Construction is of red brick and pure Gothic in style with stone steps. The steeple towers 176' above the ground and is topped by a 6' weathervane rooster. The inside is a monument of marble and stained glass. The church has been deconsecrated and can be toured weekdays 11:00 a.m. to 3:00 p.m. Weekends 1:00 p.m. to 3:00 p.m. It is located at 3rd and Lincoln.

A drive around town will reveal many other historic homes and buildings. Most are Victorian and Italinate in style. A few date from the 1860's. The clock tower on 3rd belongs to a former county courthouse. Built in 1883 it now houses the Masonic Lodge.

ORIGINAL WASCO COUNTY COURTHOUSE

The original Wasco County Courthouse, 406 West Second, was built in 1859. This was once the seat of government for the largest county ever formed in the United States.

Inside you will find displays on local history, slide shows and restored jail cells complete with thick wooden doors. Ask about the slideshows featuring local events and the oral history cassettes.

PULPIT ROCK

You will find Pulpit Rock behind the local high school. This natural rock pulpit was used by early pioneer missionaries. Many a legendary preacher stood here to deliver his sermon. It is now used only for Easter Sunrise Services.

ROSCO LOOKOUT

If you don't mind driving a little out of your way, you will be rewarded with a spectacular view of the valley. Take the Chenowith Area exit off I-84 and turn right on Chenowith Road. Turn right again on 10th and follow the signs to Rosco Lookout. All along the way you will be treated to views of surrounding forests and valleys. There's not much traffic up here and it's a great place for some hill top solitude.

ROWENA VIEWPOINT

At exit 69, off I-84, you can take a nine mile loop that winds between Mosier and Rowena. It's an excellent excursion that will take you from cherry orchards outside of Mosier to the rocky cliffs and Rowena Viewpoint. Here you will be treated to a spectacular view. Cliffs tower above and the Columbia River Gorge spreads out below. Near Rowena you can stop at Mayer Park. A rustic wooden bridge leads you over the train tracks into a lovely area with plenty of picnic tables amidst the trees. You'll even find a nice swimming beach here.

SOROSIS PARK

This 15 acre park overlooking the city has lots of room and offers another great viewpoint. Take Scenic Drive to its highest point where you will find picnic tables, cooking facilities, a shelter house and playground equipment with plenty of room for frisbie and running around. Tennis courts are also located here.

This park sits on the bottom of ancient Lake Condon which existed several million years ago. The sediment found here has been reported to be as deep as 1400'. The bones of three types of camels, the ancient horse and mastodons were found near here.

THE DALLES DAM

At The Dalles Dam you can enjoy a free train ride. It operates from May thru September, every half hour from 10:00 a.m. to 5:00 p.m. At the far end you can watch the fish being counted and see them making their way up the fish ladders. A guide will lead you inside the powerhouse where you can see the generators and some self explanatory displays. The grounds also offer picnic tables, a duck pond and fountains.

Before the construction of The Dalles Dam the rock cliffs of this and surrounding areas were filled with Petroglyphs and Pictographs. These rock carvings and paintings were said to number over 400. Their age and purpose remains a mystery.

A few of these ancient canvases were removed before the rising waters claimed the land. A small collection is displayed along the wall at the dam. One has been mounted and displayed, upside down, as a historical marker.

THREE SISTERS WILDERNESS

There are approximately 240 miles of trail within the Three Sisters Wilderness area. These lead to mountain climbing takeoff spots, alpine meadows and over 300 lakes in the nearly 200,000 acres. Flower-filled meadows, snowfields, 14 glaciers including Oregon's largest, spectacular viewpoints and waterfalls will delight the hiker. Not all are long hikes, either. Upper and Lower Proxy Falls are just a short walk from State 242.

The wilderness is part of both the Deschutes and Willamette National Forests. Information and maps can be obtained at offices in Bend, Sisters, Eugene and McKenzie Bridge. The staff there can direct you to recreation sites and hiking trails suited to your experience and desires.

TOKETEE FALLS

Toketee Falls is a beautifully graceful waterfall along State 138. A half mile trail leads to the viewing platform. Four miles west of the waterfalls look for some unusual columnar basalt rock formations as you travel toward Toketee Lake. At the lake you will find more trails leading from the campground.

If you take the road around the lake one mile past the far end and turn right on Forest Service Road 2646 for three miles you can visit Umpqua Warm Springs. An old Indian springs; the surroundings are very pristine.

WARM SPRINGS

WARM SPRINGS NATIONAL
FISH HATCHERY

Fourteen miles north of Warm Springs is the turnoff for the Warm Springs National Fish Hatchery. Here they raise 400,000 spring chinook and 140,000 steelhead yearly along with 75,000 rainbow trout. All are released in reservation waters. The facilities are open daily from 8:00 a.m. to 4:30 p.m. and offer an interpretive display as well as fish viewing.

WINEMA
NATIONAL FOREST

Winema was a great Indian heroine of the Modoc War of 1872. She was credited with saving many lives. The Winema National Forest offers land for public use which is relatively unchanged since her day. The Sky Lakes area is a 20,000 acre high-mountain plateau of gentle land, full of lakes and ponds. It is reached by trail only. Spring Creek, Miller Lake, Mountain Lakes Wilderness, Fourmile Lake, Lake of the Woods and Yamsay Mountain are other outstanding features of this area. Information and maps are available at the National Forest office in Klamath Falls.

SECTION IV
US 395; BORDER TO BORDER

Two outstanding wildlife areas are located in the southern portion of Section IV. The Hart Mountain National Antelope Refuge and Malheur National Wildlife Refuge both offer an opportunity to view native animals in their natural surroundings.

Desert lakes, abrupt mountains, fossil beds, hot springs and geysers, lava faults, the Alvord Desert and towns left behind by early settlers and gold seekers are all highly visible here.

Much of this section is public land managed through Forest Service, Bureau of Land Management and other federal and state operated agencies. By following the simple guidelines set forth by them, you can freely enjoy the sights and sounds found here.

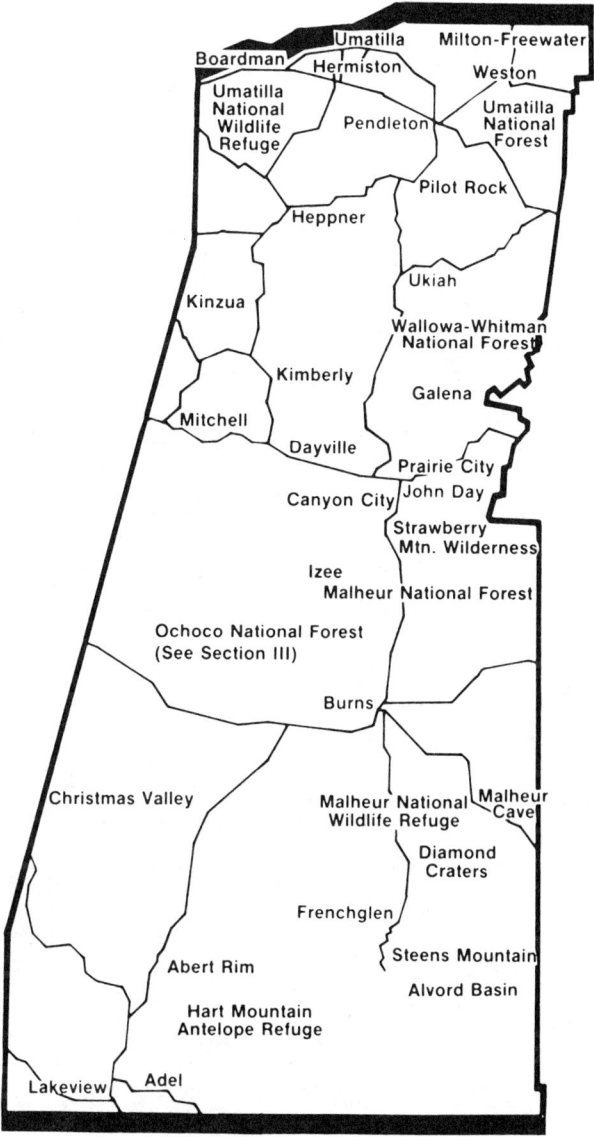

Umatilla
Milton-Freewater
Boardman
Hermiston
Weston
Umatilla
National
Wildlife
Refuge
Pendleton
Umatilla
National
Forest
Pilot Rock
Heppner
Ukiah
Kinzua
Wallowa-Whitman
National Forest
Kimberly
Galena
Mitchell
Dayville
Prairie City
John Day
Canyon City
Strawberry
Mtn. Wilderness
Izee
Malheur National Forest
Ochoco National Forest
(See Section III)
Burns
Christmas Valley
Malheur National
Wildlife Refuge
Malheur
Cave
Diamond
Craters
Frenchglen
Steens Mountain
Abert Rim
Alvord Basin
Hart Mountain
Antelope Refuge
Lakeview
Adel

ABERT RIM

Abert Rim is a 30 mile long exposed fault. It rises 2000' to tower above Lake Abert and Crooked Creek Valley. The top 600' is practically straight up and down. This is the largest exposed fault in North America and second largest in the entire world. This is actually a fracture in the earth's crust accompanied by displacement of one side of the fracture with respect to the other side.

The surrounding area is a rockhound's paradise. Arrowheads, thunder eggs, Hart Mountain nodules, fire opals, sunstones, petrified wood, uranium, cinnabar, agate and jasper have all been found.

ADEL

GEYSER

At the Crump Ranch in Adel, you will find a man-made geyser. It was created in 1956 when a well was being drilled in the hot springs area. It sprouts at approximately two hour intervals.

PLUSH

This town has some buildings from the early 1900's. It is located north of Adel which was established in the 1890's.

ROCKHOUNDING

Sunstones, fire opals, quality agate nodules, various crystals and jasp-agates can all be found in the Hart Mountain area.

STONE BRIDGE

In 1867 General George Crook, then only a lieutenant-colonel, ordered a bridge to be built out of chunks of lava at the Hart Lake Narrows north of Adel. It was built so he could move his men from their camp atop Hart Mountain to a site on Honey Creek, west of Warner Valley.

Warner Valley is 12 miles wide by 42 miles in length. It contains a string of lakes and swamps and is peppered with cattle ranches.

ALVORD BASIN

The Alvord Basin offers a unique out-of-doors experience. It is walled on all sides by mountain ranges. The Steens tower more than a mile above with ragged abrupt cliffs and rims, and massive pinnacles. Other ranges include the Pueblos, Trout Creeks and Pine Mountain.

The Alvord Desert is a vast expanse of white. It is one of the largest and most perfect playas in the world. A playa is a flat-floored bottom of an undrained desert basin. The brightness at this one is startling. You will find sand dunes, desert pavement, purple hills, marshes, hay meadows, snow-melt streams lined with trees and a land that has yielded gold, silver, mercury and borax. The new wealth lies in the area's geothermal resources.

The nearby Alvord Ranch is the second largest in Oregon. This 100+ year old ranch is notable for the numerous stone barns, cabins and walls. Two of the original buildings are still standing. Others were built in the 1940's. The old town of Andrews is another nearby historical site.

BOARDMAN

BOARDMAN CITY PARK

You can picnic at Boardman City Park and they furnish the barbecue pit. Playground equipment and a ball field make it a nice family stop.

BOARDMAN COUNTY PARK

Just off I-84 you will find this wide open county park complete with wood stoves, drinking water, boat ramp and dock, protected swim area and restrooms. Water sports are popular since the protected lake offers miles of surface just off the Columbia River.

Near the swimming area you will find four petroglyphs which were moved to this location so that more people might enjoy them.

HARVEST FESTIVAL

This three day event is held each year in early September. Festivities include a talent show and parade, boat races, a watermelon seed spitting contest and other fascinating events. It all happens at the Marine Park. For further information contact the Chamber of Commerce.

PORTLAND GENERAL ELECTRIC
COMPANY

Call 481-9351 to make an appointment to tour PGE's coal-fired generator plant here at Boardman. The one hour tour is offered Tuesday thru Saturday at 10:00 a.m., 1:00 p.m. and 3:00 p.m.

U & I

At U & I you can tour a food processing plant where frozen french fries are the end product. Call ahead for an appointment — 481-2011.

BURNS

HARNEY COUNTY MUSEUM

The Harney County Historical Museum is at 18 West "D" Street. There you can see exhibits which include an old printing press, early hospital operating table, pioneer kitchen utensils, heirloom quilts and an arrowhead collection. They are open from June through October. Hours are 9:00 a.m. to noon on Saturdays and 9:00 a.m. to 5:00 p.m. Tuesday thru Friday.

HISTORICAL WALKING TOUR

At the Burns Chamber of Commerce you can obtain a map to take you on a walking tour of the town's historical buildings. Three of these homes are "triplets". All were built around 1898. The map also gives the location of the 1899 Voegtly Building which was built of local bricks; and the 1896 Brown Building made from cut stone. The tour covers a one mile route.

PON'S PONDEROSA RANCH

If you want a glimpse of a remnant of the Old West, take a drive out US 395 north of Burns 25 miles. At Pon's Ponderosa Ranch a herd of over 2500 American Bison grazes. They can be easily seen from the road. The ranch is well known for its experimental cross breeding.

ROCKHOUNDING

There's a quarry south of Burns, near the Narrows, on the road to Malheur Wildlife Refuge. Agates by the ton can be found here.

CANYON CITY

HISTORICAL BUILDINGS

Canyon City was once home to nearly 10,000 people. Some of the original buildings are still standing. One church building dates back to 1877.

ROCKHOUNDING

Gold was discovered here in 1862 and can still be found by panning near Canyon Creek. You can see the huge trench at Humbolt Diggins made by placer nozzles and tunnels built by Chinese coolies. These also provided safety for the villagers when Indian bands came rampaging through their town.

"Canyon Jade" is in abundance in the nearby mountains.

CHRISTMAS VALLEY

Christmas Valley is rich in geological wonders. The Fossil Lake area, on the western edge of the sand dunes, has yielded bones of ancient birds, fish, three-toed horses, camels and other life from ancient times. Arrowheads are also found in this area. The sand dunes are referred to as Oregon's Sahara. The location has been used by movie companies. In fact, a well was once drilled here to create a movie oasis.

277

The Lost Forest covers seven square miles and has been described as a relic of an ancient forest which once covered a much greater area. It is isolated by over 35 miles from other ponderosa forests. Legend says a lone cowboy once left a rock at the local assay office, never to return, which was rich in gold and said to have been found within the Lost Forest.

Crack-in-the-Ground is another unique attraction. It is a deep fissure in a lava field about 8 miles north of Christmas Valley. It gives you an awesome view into the earth, as far down as 70'. It measures up to 15' wide. Near here you will see four lava cones which remain from early volcanic blow-outs.

DAYVILLE

ANTONE

Antone is a genuine ghost town. Out of Dayville, take US 26 east toward Mitchell. Turn left onto a gravel road leading past Pine Hollow and Rock Creek. The buildings at this 1860's settlement straddle the creek. The little building between the two frame houses was a post office from 1894 to 1948. The town was named for Antone Francisco, a Portuguese pioneer settler.

If you continue along the back roads toward Dayville you will also find the Spanish Gulch Cemetery; a square fort-like structure down a steep canyon. The square house was once a home and the canyon the center of local gold mining mania. All that remains today are weathered granite and wood tombstones. Many abandoned homesteads, including "Murderer's Cabin" dot the gorges of upper Rock Creek.

Dayville itself was established in 1868. The original Dayville post office was located three miles west of the current townsite.

DIAMOND CRATERS

Diamond Craters is said to have the best and most diverse basaltic volcanic features in the entire United States. All are within a relatively small and accessible area. An auto tour guide is available through the Bureau of Land Management or the Burns Chamber of Commerce.

The drive starts off at the town of Diamond and leads you past domes and craters. One, Graben Dome, wears a crown of juniper trees; others are of red cinder. In all, you will make twelve stops along the forty mile route. This is an isolated place with no water so be prepared. You will also find an interesting array of plants and animals. Watch for the western fence lizard with its unusual black coloring brought on by a life on the black lava of Diamond Craters. The most recent flow here occurred less than 1000 years ago. Desert Trail is open to hikers.

FRENCHGLEN

BLITZEN

Blitzen is just one abandoned town among many in the high desert country. It is a reminder of the many homesteaders who were unsuccessful in the dry Catlow Valley. You will find its remains southeast of Frenchglen.

Take Blitzen Road 12½ miles past Frenchglen. Turn right and keep to the left for approximately 8.3 miles. A sagebrush trail leads into Blitzen which was deserted around 1917.

FRENCHGLEN HOTEL

Frenchglen is made up of aging houses, the most prominant being the historic Frenchglen Hotel. You can't miss its picket fence and screened-in porch. First opened in the early 1900's it is now operated as a wayside by the State Parks Department.

KRUMBO RESERVOIR

Krumbo Reservoir is located northeast of Frenchglen off State 205. Approximately three miles before the turnoff, near the junction of Central Patrol Road, you can see many rimrocks and caves. The caves were once used by local Indians as shelter. One has been partially excavated by archeologists and has a smoke blackened ceiling, grinding mortars and obsidian flakes.

Near the reservoir is a man-made brood pond where waterfowl can rest and feed. Along the road you will also find a large boulder etched with petroglyphic drawings. Then at last you will arrive at the 200 acre lake where you will find cormorants, eared grebes and eagles.

NARROWS

This was once a lively town, started in 1892 by C. A. Haines. A few turn of the century buildings still remain.

One mile past the Narrows Bridge, turn left on Double O Road. After five miles, turn right into the parking area near the base of the cliffs for a look at some Indian pictographs. The drawings are done with a red pigment and include a six-legged lizard.

PETER FRENCH RANCH

In 1872 Peter French came to eastern Oregon to buy land for his soon to be partner H. J. Glenn. A small ranch using a "P" branding iron became his headquarters. Much of it still stands today. The most well known feature of the

Peter French Ranch is the round barn. It was built sometime before 1884 and includes 250 tons of lava stones hauled from the Diamond Craters area. It is 100' in diameter and requires nearly 50,000 shingles to cover the roof. It is located northeast of the "P" Ranch headquarters.

The headquarters of the cattle baron's empire now serves as a substation for the Malheur Wildlife Refuge. A few historical remains can be seen, including the original chimney of the French house, beef wheel, restored willow corrals, the long barn and a fire tower where vultures come to roost at sunset.

To reach the ranch, take State 205 .3 miles past its junction with Krumbo Road and turn right onto Central Patrol Road. After approximately 11.5 miles you will come to the ranch.

SUNSET CEMETERY

Take Double O Road off State 205 for 6.2 miles to the Sunset Cemetery. This pioneer cemetery holds the grave of a child who died while travelling with Meek's "Lost Wagon Train" sometime in 1845.

WRIGHT'S POINT

Just over ten miles down Double O Road's junction with State 205, you can see an example of inverted topography. More than 2.4 million years ago two separate lava flows created this awesome site when they made their way through a stream bearing valley. The surrounding land mass has eroded away leaving the former valley floor, with its protective cap of lava, as the top of Wright's Point. The flat-topped ridge is 6 miles long, 250' high and from 600-1800' wide. Cuts made during the construction of the highway revealed fossilized plant remains, fish bones, a pelecypod and a camel tooth as well as exposing its makeup.

The point was named for Camp Wright established here in 1865. It was located close to the east end of Silvies River. It was only fortified for a very short time.

GALENA

The first group of miners settled here in 1862 when gold was found along the Middle Fork of Day River and up Elk Creek. Nuggets weighing up to five pounds were picked up in the area. Since most miners preferred to sleep on their claims the town proper never grew very large. The town was once active enough though, to see 5000 people come in to vote on the selection of a county seat. Several old residences and a couple of stores still stand on the south side of the road.

Up the narrow Elk Canyon are more sparse remains. An old stamp mill along with other asundry buildings spread out over nearly a mile. This was once considered the upper camp with the post office being down below. Around the turn of the century, when the lower camp was known as Susanville, the upper camp residents removed the entire post office to their camp. With it went the name and the lower camp was renamed Galena.

HART MOUNTAIN
NATIONAL ANTELOPE REFUGE

The Hart Mountain National Antelope Refuge was established in 1936 to save the last of the pronghorn antelope grazing here. Today this 270,000 acre wildlife preserve is the home of one of the largest herds of pronghorns on the North American continent. Although this animal was once almost extinct it can be seen almost any time of the day at the refuge. California bighorn sheep, mule deer and sage grouse also inhabit the area.

Indian petroglyphs, hot mineral springs and General

Crook's stone bridge are also in this area. Arrowheads have been found quite frequently as well as opals and jasper agate.

HEPPNER

ANSON WRIGHT COUNTY PARK

This county operated park is 27 miles south of Heppner along State 207. Picnic facilities, wood stoves and a large fireplace barbecue make it a great place for group picnics. Pond and stream fishing, swimming, rockhounding and a nice children's play area help to make it fun.

CITY PARKS

Both the Heppner City Park and the Courthouse Park are enjoyable stops. The first, offers playground equipment while the latter has picnic tables, barbecue areas and plenty of shade.

CUTSFORTH COUNTY PARK

Hikers will love exploring Hell's Half Acre and Old Baldy Mountain. Fishermen will enjoy lake and stream fishing. Everyone will enjoy swimming and looking for prize rocks. Picnic facilities, drinking water, wood stoves and restrooms are all available. You will find the park off State 74, 17 miles southeast of Heppner on Willow Creek Road.

HARDMAN

Twenty miles south of Heppner is the ghost town of Hardman. This was once a regular stage stop. The community opened its post office in 1881 naming it for a pioneer ranching family.

HARRY DUVALL MUSEUM

Here you can view Indian artifacts, antique furniture, household items and farm tools. They are located in the Public Library Building on North Main Street. Hours are from noon to 4:00 p.m. Monday thru Wednesday, 10:00 a.m. to 5:00 p.m. Saturday and 1:00 p.m. to 5:00 p.m. Sunday.

HERMISTON

COLD SPRINGS NATIONAL
WILDLIFE REFUGE

About 7 miles east of Hermiston are over 3,000 acres of open water, marsh, sagebrush, grass lands and trees where wintering Canadian Geese and ducks can find food. Pheasants, quail and mule deer also make their home here. A paved ramp lets fishermen in to catch sturgeon, salmon, crappies and bass. You will also find plenty of wild asparagus. For more information contact the refuge headquarters in Umatilla.

HERMISTON CITY PARK

If you're looking for a place to picnic while in the city try the Hermiston City Park on West Orchard Road. Picnic facilities include a barbecue; and the children could be entertained by the large, well equipped playground.

INLAND EMPIRE BANK MUSEUM

Indian artifacts from Columbia River and Alaskan tribes can be seen on the lower floor of the Inland Empire Bank building. A totem pole, wall hangings, photographs and other art items are on display here at 101 East Main Street. If you call ahead they will be happy to give you a tour — 566-2291.

J. R. SIMPLOT COMPANY

This Hermiston plant makes frozen potato products including McDonald's french fries. A tour is available to anyone over the age of twelve which includes introductory slides and a trip through the plant. Lasting approximately 45 minutes it will give you a chance to see how the potatoes are processed. You will need to make advance reservations by calling 567-9733.

LAMB-WESTON, INC.

At Lamb-Weston, in Hermiston, raw potatoes are processed into frozen potatoe products. They offer viewing windows where anyone can see into their plant. A guide is on hand to answer questions and explain the process. Call 567-6476 to arrange for this tour.

MARLETTE HOMES, INC.

This mobile home factory will gladly give tours if you call ahead. Once there you will be guided through the factory and shown the many steps taken to produce a quality mobile home. Call 567-5546 to set up a tour time.

OREGON TRAIL

The old Oregon Trail crosses Butter Creek fourteen miles south of Hermiston. From there it makes it way west of the town of Cecil. Wagon ruts are still visible west of town. A stop at the Bureau of Land Management Interpretive Center in Cecil will give you a great deal of knowledge about the trail.

STANFIELD JULY 4th CELEBRATION

At nearby Stanfield's Fourth of July celebration you can watch a parade, fire department waterfight and fireworks.

IZEE

Izee is a ghost town located 29 miles west of Seneca. It was named for the IZ brand used by M. N. Bonham. The post office was officially established in 1889.

JOHN DAY

JOHN DAY FOSSIL BEDS

The John Day Fossil Beds are some of the most productive fossil deposits yet discovered. Remains of Mastodon, Oredon, small camels, various cat species, rodents, turtles and three different species of three-toed horses have all been unearthed here. Dates, figs, peanuts and Eucalyptus were also once abundant.

Since this is a national monument, information can be obtained from the U.S. Department of the Interior as well as the John Day Chamber of Commerce. The three major areas are found near Clarno off State 218, east of Mitchell off State 207 and northwest of Dayville along State 19. See Section III under Clarno for more information.

KAM WAH CHUNG & CO. MUSEUM

The Kam Wah Chung Museum is located near the John Day City Park. The building is listed in the National Register of Historic Places. There is a minimal charge to tour the inside (open May thru October only). This building has served as a general store, Chinese temple, herbal medicine store and home at various intervals since its 1866 construction. Until the early 1940's it served as a center for the Chinese community of Eastern Oregon.

JANORA
BAYOT.

SPRING CATTLE DRIVE

One of Grant County's most interesting links with the Old West is the annual Spring cattle drive which makes its way through the town of John Day. The Grant County Chamber of Commerce can furnish you with details and dates.

KIMBERLY

FOSSILS

Fossils have been found all around Kimberly. Watch for signs marking areas like Foree Fossil Beds, Monro Fossil Beds, Sheep Rock, Picture Gorge, Mascall Fossil Formations and Leaf Fossils. For more information see Clarno in Section III.

FOX

At the town of Fox, east of Kimberly, you will find an old weathered church dating somewhere between 1877 and 1883.

JOHNNY KIRK SPRINGS

This rest area offers picnic facilities. It is located at milepost 117, between Foree and Monro Fossils Beds. The place was named for an eccentric pioneer bachelor who came to the area around 1870. He built his winter cabin near here and spent the balance of the year prospecting in the Blue Mountains.

SUNKEN MOUNTAIN

Along State 402, 16 miles east of Kimberly, you can see the awesome Sunken Mountain. This freak of nature

greets your eye amid the fascinating rock formations that
run from Kimberly to Long Creek.

KINZUA

JULIA HENDERSON PIONEER PARK
& SHELTON WAYSIDE

These two parks are located outside Kinzua along State
19. Picnic facilities and a chance to stretch your legs are
the attraction.

ROWE CREEK RESERVOIR

This man-made lake is privately owned but jointly
maintained with the Oregon State Game Commission.

LAKEVIEW

ANNUAL EVENTS

Lakeview offers several annual events. One, the Lake
County Round-Up has been going on since 1920. It is
held Labor Day weekend and features a parade which
includes the Loyal Order of Muleskinners with their 1880
stagecoach. Other area events include the Junior Rodeo
in June, Crazy Days and the Christmas Valley Days.
Contact the Lakeview Chamber of Commerce for days
and a listing of free events held in conjunction with these
festivities.

HUNTER'S HOT SPRINGS GEYSER

Two miles north of Lakeview, at Hunter's Hot Springs,
you can watch a geyser known as "Old Perpetual" The

200° water spouts out at 20 second intervals and reaches a height of 60'. This man-made geyser was created when well drilling operations were going in 1924. It has blown continuously ever since. At one time Indians from northern California and Nevada used the hot springs for the internment of their dead.

LAKEVIEW NATURE TRAIL

You can obtain a brochure at the Lakeview Chamber of Commerce for this nature trail. It lists mammals, amphibians, reptiles, birds, insects and plants found along the route.

ROCKHOUNDING

Thunder eggs, agates, jasper and agatized wood are found east of town. Blue agates can be located near US 395 two to five miles south and agate-filled thunder eggs, at Crane Creek. Kelly Creek produces agate, jasper and thunder eggs and west of town, at Dry Creek, great quantities of agate are found.

MALHEUR CAVE

The Malheur Cave turnoff is fourteen miles southeast of Princeton. Head north on Indian Creek Road for three miles before turning left onto a dirt road beside a small reservoir. The cave is just ahead.

This cave now belongs to the Masonic Lodge in Burns and is used for their annual meeting. They have built bleachers inside. The cave entrance has also been modified. Years ago the cave was used by the Paiute Indians as shelter and in the early 1880's it was the site of a bloody battle between the Paiute and Bannock tribes.

Be sure to bring some high powered lanterns if you plan on exploring inside. The 3000' lava tube has a ceiling which ranges from 8-20'. At the lower end of the cave you will find an underground lake. The depth has been measured at 23'. Here ocassionally, someone will catch a freshwater fish but no one seems to know how the fish get in. Note the lava flow lines, floor, ceiling and wall linings as well as minor lava formations and secondary mineralization. You can easily trace the flow lines which indicate semi-trench origin of this Pleistocine age tube. It was formed during the Voltage Flow basalt. Inside temperature is 60°

When you get back to State 78 if you head southeast past Jordan Valley you can visit some exposed lava beds.

MALHEUR NATIONAL FOREST

The Malheur National Forest contains 1,460,000 acres and includes land in Grant, Harney, Baker and Malheur counties. Within the forest you will find over 4500 miles of roads leading to delightful picnic and camp spots. Woodlands, meadows rich with wildflowers and over 250 miles of trails entice hikers and horesmen from all over. The Strawberry Mountain Wilderness area is also found here.

You can obtain information and look at area maps at Forest Service offices in John Day, Burns and Prairie City. They can tell you about lookouts and viewing areas such as Dixie Butte, Crane Point, Fall Mountain, Dry Soda, Indian Rock and Flagtail as well as West Myrtle, Calamity, Sugarloaf Mountain, King Mountain and Antelope Mountain.

MALHEUR NATIONAL WILDLIFE REFUGE

The Malheur National Wildlife Refuge is one of the nation's largest refuges with approximately 181,000 acres. It was created in 1908 by President Teddy Roosevelt to halt the near extermination of great colonies of nesting birds which had once inhabited the area. Today over 240 species of birds can be found here.

The land consists of natural marsh, meadows and man-made ponds surrounded by sagebrush and juniper. Here Sandhill Cranes, Whistling and Trumpeter Swans, pelicans, cormorants, herons and Ibis share the breeding grounds with waterfowl, hawks, ground birds and warblers.

The refuge headquarters has a museum which is open daily from 6:00 a.m. to 9:00 p.m. It shelters an egg collection along with mounted specimens of local birds and mammals. Here you can obtain literature, maps, bird lists, an auto tour brochure and information about the area.

The self-guided auto route covers 42 miles and runs the length of the historical Blitzen Valley. It offers a number of outstanding historical, geological and biological features. It can also lead you through the Diamond Craters, out to visit Peter French's famous round barn, to Krumbo Reservoir, along Steens Mountain and past many fascinating viewing areas.

About 4 miles west of the refuge headquarters is the Malheur Field Station. From here you can take the South Coyote Butte Nature Trail for an excellent orientation to local plants and exposure to the high desert region. At the Sod House Ranch you will find what is left of a cattle empire. Started in 1862 remains include a barn, beef wheel, stone cellar and old rock stockade fences.

MITCHELL

CAMP WATSON

All that is left of Camp Watson is on a little stream about five miles west of Antone. The site was selected in 1864. A temporary camp was located 4 miles to the east. The main camp had a log stockade, several groups of cabins, a blacksmith shop and a stage station. The graves of young soldiers killed in an Indian massacre can be found east of Mitchell, along US 26.

FAIRVIEW PARK

Fairview Park is located right next to Bull Prairie Lake, fourteen miles north of Spray. It is operated by the U.S. Forest Service and serves as a nice place to picnic.

MILTON-FREEWATER

MARIE DORION PARK

The Marie Dorion Park is located on the Walla Walla River, southeast of the city. You will find a "Trail of the Pioneers" leading to the top of the hill. From there you will have a clear view of both the river and the surrounding land. This is a great spot for a picnic.

YANTIS PARK

At Yantis Park you can sit back and relax in the partially shaded surroundings or venture across the stream to investigate the steep trails. At the top you will be rewarded with some beautiful views. Picnic tables, playground equipment and drinking water are available.

PENDLETON

BLUE MOUNTAIN COMMUNITY COLLEGE MUSEUM

You can visit this interesting museum on weekdays between 8:00 a.m. and 11:00 a.m. Here you can view over 6000 photographs depicting the area's past. The towns of Pendleton, Umatilla and Weston during the 19th century, the Old Oregon Trail, citizens and early homes, famous Indians and period clothing are all covered. There is also a century old collection of Bibles and a human hair picture.

CITY PARKS

Pendleton offers fourteen parks and playgrounds. Some of the more prominent include Aldrich and Til Taylor where you will find children's wading pools; Pioneer and Roy Raley, offering picnic facilities and play equipment; and Stillman Park where you will find everything from tennis courts to horseshoe pits. Pendleton High School also has tennis courts.

DEADMAN'S PASS

Southeast of Pendleton, twenty miles along I-84, is the Deadman's Pass rest area. Picnic facilities, drinking water and restrooms are offered beside the old stagecoach road. The area was named for an ambush that took place here in 1878. Historical information is available at the Oregon Trail display located there.

EMIGRANT SPRINGS STATE PARK

Six miles past Deadman's Pass lies Emigrant Springs State Park. The Oregon Trail passed through about half a mile south of these springs. Many wagons came down the canyon to camp here. Hiking, nature study and beautiful scenery are reason enough to stop today but the park also offers picnic facilities, restrooms, a children's playground and numerous other recreational delights. This place is especially popular during winter months when visitors bring sleds, toboggans and saucers for exhilerating rides down the hillside.

INDIAN FAIR & ART SHOW

At the Umatilla Indian Reservation you can view art work and poetry done by Native American artists. This festival takes place in early May and includes tribal displays, music and performances. The reservation is located 8 miles east of Pendleton on Mission Highway. The Pendleton Chamber of Commerce should be able to provide you with the exact date.

INDUSTRIAL TOURS

Harris Pine Mills — 276-1421
2203 SW Court Place
Tours are given weekdays between 10:00 a.m. and 3:00 p.m. at the 70 acre home office site of Harris Pine Mills. Call ahead for reservations. The tour will show you the steps involved when processing trees from Oregon's forests into unfinished furniture.

Pendleton Grain Growers — 276-2287
McKennon Station
This processing plant is the biggest processor of seed grain in the entire Northwest. Tours are given by appointment only on weekdays between 8:00 a.m. and 4:00 p.m.

Pendleton Woolen Mills
1307 SE Court Place
Here you will see carding and spinning operations, dying, weaving, spooling, warp dressing and the Jacquard looms which weave the complicated blanket patterns. All in all, twelve different steps are observed. Tours are given hourly, weekdays between 8:15 a.m. and 3:00 p.m., excluding lunchtime.

McKAY CREEK NATIONAL WILDLIFE REFUGE

Five miles south of Pendleton you will find the McKay Creek National Wildlife Refuge. Open water, marsh and grasslands cover the 1,837 acres and provide a resting and feeding area for Canadian Geese and ducks during their annual migration. McKay Reservoir is located just south of the refuge.

PENDLETON ROUND-UP & HAPPY CANYON DAYS

For eight days during September all of Pendleton gets geared up for the annual Pendleton Round-Up. It starts out with a grand Dress-Up Parade through downtown Pendleton and includes numerous free events like the Junior Indian Beauty Pageant, American Indian Beauty Contest, Main Street Cowboy Show, Tribal Ceremonial Dancing Contest and displays. Six Northwest Indian tribes gather to share their customs and lifestyles through exhibits, pageants and races. There is a charge to attend the rodeo.

You won't want to miss the two hour Westward Ho Parade. No motorized vehicles are allowed. Indians marching in tribal dress, pack trains, stage coaches, ox teams and mule teams make it a camera buff's paradise.

Pendleton has some lesser known annual events too. They host the Invitational Swim Meet, Oregon Trail Appaloosa Regional Show and Pendleton Arts Festival. Contact the Pendleton Chamber of Commerce for information regarding these activities.

ROOT FESTIVAL

Indian festivals are a way of viewing cultures which are being left behind in today's fast paced world. This celebration honors the Indian New Year in late April and is a form of Thanksgiving. The event includes exhibition dancing and ceremonies and is well attended. There is a charge to take part in the traditional feasting.

VERT MEMORIAL MUSEUM

This museum is open to the public by appointment only. You can arrange for a tour by calling 276-6924. Once there, you will see what has been referred to as one of the finest displays of Native American culture in the state of Oregon. Beadwork, basketry, arrowheads and geological specimens mixed with artifacts of pioneer days help to paint a picture of early Eastern Oregon life. The museum is located at SW Fourth and Dorion Streets.

PILOT ROCK

HARVEST FESTIVAL

Each August Pilot Rock holds their annual Harvest Festival. It features a parade, produce, displays and logging and craft exhibits. Contact the Pendleton Chamber of Commerce for the exact date.

INDIAN LAKE RECREATION AREA

About fifteen miles southeast of Pilot Rock is the Indian Lake Recreation Area. There you will find Southeast Birch Creek and Humptepin Lake. Picnics, swimming, fishing and hiking can all be enjoyed there.

PINE GROVE

Take Birch Creek Road about ten miles south of Pilot Rock to Pine Grove. You will find the remains of a general store, boarding house, school and stamp mill.

U. S. GYPSUM COMPANY

At U. S. Gypsum raw wood chips are cooked, pressed into mat form, dried, cut and embossed. Children over the age of eleven will enjoy the one hour tour; but you must call ahead to make a reservation. The number is 443-2451.

PRAIRIE CITY

DEPOE PARK

Depoe Park, in Prairie City, has displays depicting the development of the lumber industry. This town was established some time before 1870.

STRAWBERRY CAMPGROUND TRAILS

This campground is situated at the very edge of the Strawberry Wilderness Area. From here hiking trails lead to five secluded lakes. These trails provide the only access and are limited to hikers and horses.

STEENS MOUNTAIN

This is an unusual mountain retreat in Oregon's high desert country. The mountain is a 30 mile long fault block which thrust its way a mile into the sky some 15 million years ago. Next, glaciers passed over the land leaving behind a rugged terrain containing valleys now known as Blitzen, Wildhorse, Kiger and Indian Creek. But the mountain has its gentle slopes as well.

You can get a spectacular view by taking Oregon's highest road, Loop Road, east from Frenchglen. Your reward will be views of mountains, plains, lakes and plenty of blue sky. The highest peak in the Steens is 9,773'.

All around vegetation ranges from desert plants to varieties of dwarf alpine flora. Deer, antelope, sage grouse, Chukar partridge, mourning dove and quail are all common.

You can obtain information and maps on the area at the Bureau of Land Management office in Burns.

STRAWBERRY MOUNTAIN WILDERNESS AREA

In July and August the meadows and hillsides here are bright with an array of color found only in blooming wildflowers and bushes. Trappers and fur traders were the first to visit this area; an old trapper's cabin can be found along the Strawberry Mountain Trail in Red Basin. Next came the miners; many abandoned mines can be found along the north side of the mountain. The Bannock, Paiute and Snake Indians fought back this invasion as best they could.

This wilderness area contains 33,000 acres in a very complex geological area dating from the Miocene period. Mule deer, Rocky Mountain elk, black bear, cougar and bighorn sheep live here along with coyotes, bobcats and badgers. Birds of prey and small fur bearing mammals are in abundance.

Trails through the area range in length from just over a half mile to nearly sixteen miles. They traverse meadows, cross creeks, travel up mountains, wind around lakes and cross some of the most beautiful high desert country you'll ever see. Stop at the Forest Service office in John Day or Prairie City for trail information and a chance to look at maps of the area.

UKIAH

BATTLE MOUNTAIN STATE PARK

You'll be rewarded with some gorgeous views when you visit Battle Mountain. This was the site of the last great battle involving the Bannock, Paiute and Snake Indians against the U. S. Army. The Indians were defeated by General Oliver Howard. Today the site harbors a state park complete with hiking trails, picnic facilities and restrooms. The park is located 9 miles north of Ukiah along US 395.

CAMAS CREEK STATE PARK

Two miles south of Ukiah via US 395, you will find this lovely little park nestled in the pines. The babbling creek, tables and fireplaces make it a tranquil place for a picnic.

45th PARALLEL

Pause for a moment as you take US 395 across the Umatilla/Grant County Line. At this point you are halfway between the equator and the North Pole as you cross the 45th parallel.

TOWER MOUNTAIN LOOKOUT

Tower Mountain Lookout will offer you a spectacular view of the Wallowa-Whitman National Forest. You can climb the tower for an even better view. To get there take Camas Creek Road 30 miles southeast of Ukiah.

UKIAH-DALE STATE PARK

Stream fishing and beautiful views are two big enticements at this park. Picnic facilities, drinking water, wood stoves and restrooms are available. To reach the park take US 395 3 miles southwest of Ukiah-Dale.

UMATILLA

4-H OPEN HORSE SHOW

On the last weekend in July, the Umatilla 4-H holds its annual horse show at the Umatilla County Fair Grounds giving area members a chance to exhibit both their animals and riding abilities. Contact the local Chamber of Commerce for details.

HAT ROCK STATE PARK

This large park offers nearly 180 picnic sites, drinking water, electric stoves, restrooms, bathhouse, boat ramp and hiking trails. It is located nine miles east of Umatilla and offers both lake and stream fishing.

LAKE WALLULA RECREATIONAL AREA

Lake Wallula offers beaches, parks, swimming, boating, water skiing, fishing, picnic tables, hiking trails and nature study. Several recreational and wildlife areas dot the land along the Oregon shore. The lake is part of the Columbia River, formed as a result of the McNary Dam construction.

At the McNary Wildlife Park you can enjoy nature trails, camera blinds, fishing ponds and some delightful sights as you watch the waterfowl. Umatilla Marina Park, McNary Park, Spillway Park, McNary Beach and Hat Rock State Park all give access to the water.

McNARY LOCK & DAM

Four viewing areas are located on the Oregon side of the dam. Here you can get information on the control room, fish counting sector, generator room and dam operation. You can watch as the fish make their way up the fish ladders and boats go through the navigational locks. At McNary Beach Park you can enjoy swimming, boating, fishing and water skiing. Picnic tables, restrooms and dressing areas are also found there.

UMATILLA MARINA PARK

This park includes a paved boat ramp, overnight moorage, restrooms, dressing rooms and picnic facilities. You can enjoy swimming, fishing and water sports here just off State 730.

UMATILLA NATIONAL FOREST

The Umatilla National Forest runs from the southeastern corner of Washington into northeastern Oregon. The land supports a variety of wildlife including one of the largest herds of Rocky Mountain Elk in the nation.

Information on the area, as well as an opportunity to pour over maps of the area with the Forest Service staff, can be had at offices in Dale, Heppner, Pendleton and Ukiah. Ask about the Wenaha-Tucannon Wilderness area, Clearwater Lookout, Sunset Point, Table Rock, Big Hole Viewpoint, Target Meadows, Umatilla Breaks Viewpoint, the Marcus Whitman Trail and Potamus Point. The Umatilla National Forest offers many spectacular views.

UMATILLA NATIONAL WILDLIFE REFUGE

Near Boardman, the Umatilla National Wildlife Refuge provides a nesting place for wintering waterfowl and ducks. Over 90,000 Canadian Geese winter here and practically any species of western duck can be found along with mule deer, coyote and various other mammals. The refuge waters harbor steelhead, salmon, sturgeon and bass.

WALLOWA-WHITMAN NATIONAL FOREST

Offices in Baker, Enterprise, Halfway, Joseph, La Grande, Union, Unity and Wallowa can provide you with information on the Wallowa-Whitman National Forest. Here you can pour over maps with the experts to pick hiking trails best suited to your wants and experience.

The Wallowa-Whitman National Forest ranges from the gentle Blue Mountains to the rugged Wallowas and the spectacular canyons of the Snake River.

WESTON

ATHENA CITY PARK

Athena is just east of Weston and offers a spacious, well-manicured park where picnic facilities, including two large barbecues are available. The nearby high school offers tennis courts.

The town was established as Centerville in 1878, but was renamed for the Greek goddess in 1889.

CALEDONIAN PICNIC

This also takes place in Athena. The festivities include Scottish dancing, bagpipe competition and a pole throwing contest. People come from all over to compete.

Kilt races, children's activities and Scottish displays are other free activities. There is a charge to attend the barbecue. Contact the Athena Chamber of Commerce for details on this July event.

ELLIOT'S MEMORIAL PARK

Elliot's Park, in Weston, makes a nice spot for a picnic. Tables, drinking water and children's playground equipment are all there for your enjoyment.

HISTORIC BUILDINGS

Weston is the second oldest town in Umatilla County. At one time the community supported four livery stables, and two hotels. The first area post office was established in 1867. The entire town is being considered for placement on the National Register of Historic Places. Buildings built between 1879 and 1910 of locally made bricks dot the streets. The Sailing House is already listed on the register. It was once the home of an influential pioneer family.

Tour the town. Look at the library, town hall and museum buildings. At the library you'll see old photographs and maps of the area. The town hall was once a bank and still contains the original vault and etched teller windows. The museum has old paintings, an antique buggy and fire fighting equipment. You'll have to enquire at City Hall for admission. This historic village is not a tourist attraction yet; it's streets are uncluttered. Stop by and get acquainted with the past.

JAWS OF MYSTERY MUSEUM

This tiny little museum located in Athena focuses on sharks. No regular hours are posted, but if you're already in Athena stop by and take your chances. It just may be worth the stop.

JUBILEE LAKE

East of Weston, north of Tollgate, is Jubilee Lake. Here you will find stream and lake fishing, swimming and hiking. In the winter visitors arrive carrying sleds and toboggans. Picnic facilities and restrooms are available.

PIONEER PICNIC

Weston's Pioneer Picnic is held on Memorial Day weekend. The Pioneer Parade includes both children and adults in full pioneer dress marching through this historic town. The queen who rules over it all is chosen from one of the area's real pioneer women. The two day function includes a number of free events. There is a charge for the barbecue.

POTATO SHOW & FAIR

This is another of Weston's annual events. Held in October, it features craft projects, cooking and 4-H items centered around fall produce. Who knows, if you're in the area, it could be fun!

SMITH FROZEN FOODS

At this plant you can enjoy an opportunity to watch as raw vegetables are processed into frozen foods. Major items include corn, carrots and peas. Tours can be arranged by calling 566-3515.

TARGET MEADOWS FOREST
SERVICE AREA

Near Tollgate, off State 204, is the Target Meadows recreational area. Hiking trails, stream fishing and picnicking can all be enjoyed here.

WOODWARD FOREST SERVICE
RECREATION AREA

Hiking trails, picnicking and stream fishing are all offered at Woodward. To find it take State 204 five miles west of Tollgate.

SECTION V
EAST TO THE IDAHO LINE

This last section runs east to the Idaho border. Along the upper portion of the state, that border is known as Hells Canyon, the deepest and most spectacular river canyon in the world. Wilderness hiking trails, glacial lakes and serenity all lie awaiting the exploration of the hardy traveller.

The area's not all wildlands either. Baker and La Grande are the two largest population centers with many smaller cities dotting the countryside. Each has its own special attraction.

The southern portion of Section V is relatively open and sparsely populated.

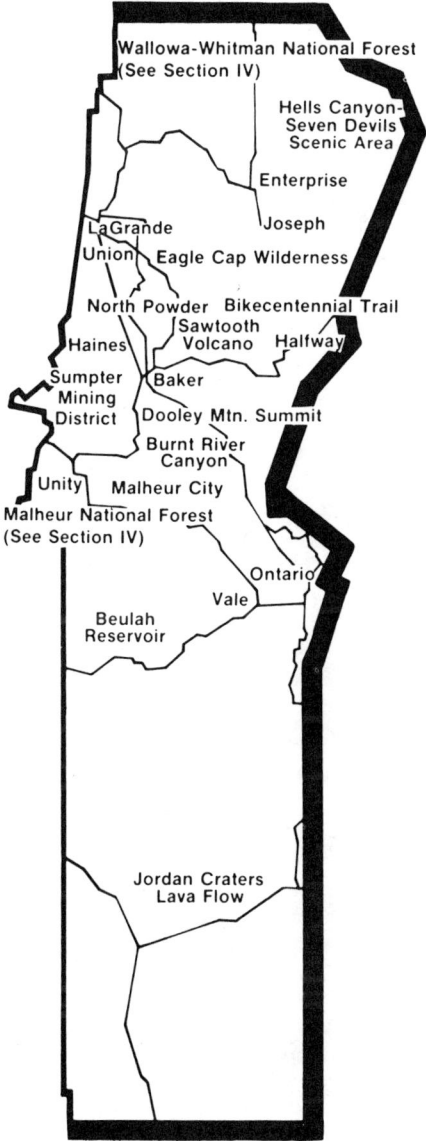

Wallowa-Whitman National Forest
(See Section IV)

Hells Canyon-
Seven Devils
Scenic Area

Enterprise

Joseph

LaGrande
Union
Eagle Cap Wilderness

North Powder   Bikecentennial Trail
Sawtooth
Volcano   Halfway
Haines
Sumpter   Baker
Mining
District   Dooley Mtn. Summit
Burnt River
Canyon
Unity   Malheur City
Malheur National Forest
(See Section IV)

Ontario
Vale

Beulah
Reservoir

Jordan Craters
Lava Flow

BAKER

AUBURN

Auburn is located fourteen miles southwest of Baker on Blue Canyon Creek. The town was laid out in 1862. It was a typical mining town and at one time one of the largest settlements in Eastern Oregon. Not much remains.

FOUR-WHEELER ROADS

The Baker area should seem like heaven to four-wheelers. There are a great number of roads here leading through some scenic countryside and historical gold mining areas. State 7, 86 and 203 all give access to these.

Hiking is also great around here. Dutch Flat Creek, Lost Lake, Summit Lake, Red Mountain Lake, Little Crater, Rock Creek Lake, Baldy Lake and Crawfish Lake Trails are just a few good routes.

GEISER-POLLMAN PARK

If you intend to spend the day in Baker and are looking for a place to spread a picnic lunch, try the Geiser-Pollman Park. It sits along the banks of the Powder River and offers picnic tables, horse shoe pits and relaxation.

GOLD NUGGET DISPLAY

The Gold Nugget Display at Baker's U. S. National Bank is open during normal banking hours. Many nuggets are on display including the famous "Armstrong" nugget weighing 80.4 ounces. It was found near here in 1913. The bank is located at 2000 Main.

HISTORIC BUILDINGS

You will find many fine century-old homes in Baker. One fine example is the Ison House. Built in 1887 it has been completely restored to its original appearance. It now houses the Benjamin Franklin Federal Savings and Loan office. They have added a custom-built 11' walnut counter, marble top table, love seat and period chairs as well as wallpaper and carpeting that has been matched for authenticity. The house is open to the public during normal banking hours.

The Baker County Courthouse was built in 1908 of native quarried tufti stone. It has been well maintained over the years and includes a pioneer courtroom. Another notable building is the Old Carnegie Library at 2nd and Auburn. It now houses an art gallery.

MARBLE CREEK

The Marble Creek area is located seven miles west of Baker. It sits in a thickly timbered area offering a delightful setting for a picnic. Restrooms, drinking water, wood stoves and picnic tables are available.

PHILLIPS LAKE

Phillips Lake was created by the building of Mason Dam. A great hiking trail leads to an overlook above the dam. An interpretative trail known as "Trees are Like People" can also be taken.

SALMON CREEK PLACER

The Salmon Creek placer is located seven miles west of Baker. Take Pocahontas Road to Salmon Creek Drive. Turn left and drive for about a mile. Trailings from the pit extend half a mile and are nearly 1200' wide. You can stand on the very brink of a gigantic hole that was created by a giant hydraulic nozzle as it pulled up more than $400,000 worth of gold. Several homes now sit atop the plateau created by the trailings.

A gold town called Pocahontas once stood near here at the base of the Blue Mountains. It was established around 1863 near Marble Creek. Like many gold rush towns all that remains is the name.

BEULAH RESERVOIR

Just northeast of Beulah Reservoir you can see the ruts left behind by pioneer wagon trains along the Oregon Trail. The reservoir also provides a great recreational area.

BIKECENTENNIAL TRAIL

You can get a pamphlet covering the Oregon portion of this well-known biking trail from the Oregon State Highway Department. It covers the trip which runs from Copperfield, at the Oxbow Dam, across 644 miles of some of the state's best countryside. The trail ends at Fort Stevens, west of Astoria.

BURNT RIVER CANYON

East of Bridgeport is the Burnt River Canyon. Here you will find some fantastic scenery and the 130 mile long Eldorado ditch which was hand dug by Chinese laborers.

DOOLEY MOUNTAIN

Heading south out of Baker along State 7 you can take a road leading to the summit of Dooley Mountain. It will provide some fantastic views of vast landscapes, deep canyons and breathtaking scenery.

EAGLE CAP
WILDERNESS

The Eagle Cap Wilderness offers 480 miles of hiking trails within an area of nearly 294,000 acres. Mountains range from 3600' to 9845'. High alpine lakes and meadows, bare granite peaks and ridges, U-shaped glaciated valleys and timber present awesome scenes. A total of 50 lakes can be found nestled at the foot of slopes and hidden in basins. The land is abundant with wildlife. Mountain goats, deer, elk, bear, coyotes, squirrels, chipmunks, skunks, porcupines, weasels, beavers, badgers, bobcats, grouse and jays are common.

Spring blankets the ground with wildflowers. Buttercup, Lupine, fleaband, fawnlily , pedicularis, monkeyflower, penstemon bilia, phacelia, aster, springbeauty, buck-wheat, heather, bluebells and phlox bring an array of colors to the slopes and meadows.

Stop at the Enterprise office of the Wallowa-Whitman National Forest for a look at a map showing trails within the area. The staff there can aid you in selecting a hike which is suitable to your experience and time. Ask them about the rare Wallowa gray-crowned rose finch which nests nowhere else in the world except the Wallowa Mountains.

ENTERPRISE

ANNUAL EVENTS

The Wallowa County Chamber of Commerce can fill you in on the details of the many annual events happening in and around Enterprise. Events include Wallowa's Old-Fashioned Fourth of July, The Wallowa Mountain Rendezvous' Sled Dog Races, Hells Canyon Mule Days, Wallowa County Arts Festival, Alpenfest, horse shows and Chief Joseph Days. Most of these festivals have free parades and activities.

CHESNIMNUS-BUCKHORN LOOP

You can take a day long auto tour heading east/southeast out of Enterprise that will reward you with views of the historic Wallowa high sheep country, elk meadows and across the Imnaha-Snake River canyons. Buckhorn Lookout and Billy Meadows Station are just two notable stops along the route.

FLORA

Flora is a living ghost town. Still bustling, it contains the original hotel, school and general store along with other buildings from its early days. The town was named for the first postmaster's daughter in 1890 and is located 35 miles north of Enterprise on State 3.

LOSTINE RIVER CANYON

Another scenic route favored by photographers and veteran backpackers leads high into Wallowa country. Easy walking, plenty of viewpoints and alpine lakes provide the lure. The major part of the canyon is west/southwest of Enterprise. It is named, however, for Lostine which is northwest of Enterprise.

WALLOWA LAKE STATE PARK

Wallowa Lake is a classic morraine-held glacial lake. It is also considered to be one of Oregon's geological marvels. Trails abound, for easy exploration, and it provides a delightful spot for swimming and other water sports. The lake is located ten miles south of Enterprise.

HAINES

EASTERN OREGON MUSEUM

The Haines museum is a must! It absolutely fills the old high school gym. What a collection. They have the complete Bourne Bar, a turn-of-the-century parlor, a complete kitchen which also serves as a place to get warm during cooler months; plus endless aisles of implements and relics from the old west. One section holds nothing but long forgotten toys where children can play.

Outside is an 1880's Union Pacific depot and lots of heavy equipment, both horse and steam powered. The museum is open daily from April 1 to October 31 between 9:00 a.m. and 5:00 p.m. It is open by appointment only the balance of the year.

HALFWAY

COPPERFIELD

Copperfield is on the west bank of the Snake River, northeast of Halfway approximately 17 miles. It was founded by prospectors and boasted 1000 inhabitants by 1910. Fire has made its way through the town three times leaving barely a trace of its past. There are some ruins and a land once dotted with working mines.

CORNUCOPIA

When early prospectors came to this area in 1885 they were certainly hoping for the "horn of plenty". Mines were given names like The Last Chance, Queen of the West, Red Jacket and Union-Companion. Buildings and equipment remain.

You can take the Sullivan Creek Trail from here down to East Eagle Creek. After coming to the grave of Whiskey Sullivan you can turn back, head up East Eagle Creek to catch a trail into the Eagle Cap Wilderness or turn off up a steep trail to Big Kettle Creek.

Cornucopia is eleven miles northwest of Halfway. The mines here were once considered to be in Oregon's most productive gold lode.

HOMESTEAD

Homestead is northeast of Halfway, past Copperfield. The town was established about 1900 by the owner of the Iron Dyke Mine. You will find some old copper mines in the area along with several old buildings.

PINE-VALLEY COMMUNITY MUSEUM

The Pine-Valley Community Museum is housed in a turn-of-the-century church. Inside you will find displays of farming equipment, reconstructed mining equipment and a replica of the interior of the old Halfway U. S. National Bank. It is open summer weekends from 10:00 a.m. to 4:00 p.m.

HEWITT PARK

Hewitt Park is southwest of Halfway on the Brownlee Reservoir. Boat ramps, playground equipment and picnic facilities make it a great place to stop. Brownlee Reservoir is part of the Snake River.

SANGER

Northwest of Halfway, on the gravel road between Sparta and Medical Springs, you will find an old hotel. This, along with several original buildings, marks the site of Sanger, a living ghost town. Early records show that the town existed prior to 1871. The Sanger mine was one of the largest producers in the area.

SPARTA

Sparta is a former mining town. Buildings still standing include the old post office and a stone store. The town was named in 1871 but settlers were in the area as early as 1863. The area is still sparsely inhabited. It is located almost due west of Halfway but must be reached in a round about way.

HELL'S CANYON

Hell's Canyon is the site of the world's deepest canyon. It was carved by the Snake River and is located between the Wallowas and the Seven Devil's Mountains. The gorge forms a natural border between Oregon and Idaho. It averages 5,000' in depth with peaks towering well over a mile above the river.

This was once the site of many Indian camps. Carvings, rock faces and paintings have been found throughout. The Nez Perce wintered here for 120 centuries. Deer, elk, bighorn sheep and bear provided them with meat.

The Hell's Canyon National Recreation Area contains 662,000 acres in northeast Oregon and western Idaho. This includes the 190,000 acre Hell's Canyon Wilderness and segments of two rivers included in the National Wild and Scenic River system. You can obtain information on hiking trails by contacting the National Forest Service office in Baker or Enterprise. They also have detailed maps.

This area has several magnificent viewpoints. Hat Point is probably the most fantastic. From Imnaha it's a two hour drive over gravel roads. The Wallowa-Whitman National Forest office can provide you with a scenic drive flyer that points out Indian caves, viewpoints, rock cairns, hiking trails and an early Indian grave. When you at last reach Hat Point, you will be rewarded with a view 5,700' down into the deepest canyon on the continent. You can see for an incredible distance both up and down the Snake River as well as across to Idaho's Seven Devil's Mountains. This trench is 1,000' deeper than the Grand Canyon.

JORDAN CRATERS LAVA FLOW

The Jordan Craters Lava flow is the largest in the United States. Geologists claim it was active as recently as 500 years ago. The flow is 4 miles wide and 30 miles long. Rockhounds love it since it yields great quantities of obsidian. Agate and petrified wood can also be found.

To the northeast is Leslie Gulch Canyon. This 7½ mile long area has been described as looking much like the Grand Canyon painted with the colors of Bryce Canyon. You will also find caves throughout the area, many of which have yielded artifacts up to 6,000 years old. The Painted Canyon is colored in orange, red and lavender and dotted with spires, castles and other rock formations. Moss agate and jasper can be found throughout the area.

West of here, along US 95, you will find the Rome Formation. It was so named because the rocks resemble Roman ruins. Along the south side of the highway roofless rock walls mark the remains of once promising homesteads.

JOSEPH

CHIEF JOSEPH DAYS

This was the ancestral home of a very famous band of Nez Perce Indians led by Old Chief Joseph. They lived here in relative luxury on the abundant game and plentiful fish. When white settlers came to the valley the tribe went to war.

Each year the town hosts a week long Chief Joseph Days near Wallowa Lake. Held in late July it honors both the cowboy and the Indian. Contact the Joseph Chamber of Commerce for information regarding this event. There is a charge for some activities but many others are free.

NATIONAL INDIAN CEMETERY

Along the county road leading to Wallowa Lake, south of Joseph, you will find the National Indian Cemetery. It has been used for many generations as a burial place for both Nez Perce and Umatilla Indians.

WALLOWA COUNTY MUSEUM

Settlers came to the Wallowa Lake area prior to the 1880's. Some of the original buildings still exist. The most prominent was built in 1888 and houses the Wallowa County Museum. It was completely renovated and hosts many thousands of visitors each summer. Inside you will find both Nez Perce and pioneer displays. They are open from May 14 through September 30 daily from 10:00 a.m. to 5:00 p.m.

LA GRANDE

CITY PARKS

Two lovely city parks offer picnic facilities and play-ground equipment here in La Grande. Pioneer Park is just off US 30 in the northwest part of town. Riverside Park is on the north side of the Grande Ronde River.

COVE

Cove is located east of La Grande. It sits at the edge of the Wallowas. The town was founded in 1863 and contains remnants of the bygone days. The century old Episcopalian Chapel is worth visiting. Its steep roof and spired steeple blend beautifully with the backdrop of the 7,132' Mt. Fanny.

EASTERN OREGON STATE COLLEGE

A tour of the Eastern Oregon State College campus includes a visit to the Hoke College Center Art Gallery. It's a chance to get acquainted with local art.

HILGARD STATE PARK

You will find Hilgard State Park located seven miles west of La Grande on Interstate 84. Hiking trails and picnic facilities make it a pleasant place to stop.

IMBLER

North of La Grande is the town of Imbler. It was settled prior to 1891 and some of the original buildings still remain. One old wooden structure housed the livery stable and the Brooks House was considered the showplace of the late 1890's.

At Elgin, eight miles further north, are more 1890's buildings. The most impressive is the city hall.

MORGAN LAKE

Morgan Lake is a beautiful spot three miles south of La Grande. This is a very popular place with local fishermen.

MT. EMILY

Mt. Emily offers a view that is unequalled. You can take a road to the very top of this 6,064' mountain for a view of the entire Grande Ronde Valley. To the west and south are the hazy Blue Mountains. To the east are the snowy peaks of the Wallowas. The view from this spot was spectacular enough to be mentioned in many pioneer diaries.

STEAMING LAKE

Just south of La Grande is a steaming lake. This phenomena is caused when the hot magma of the earth's interior is forced nearer the surface where water is contained within the rock. When the hot magma heats this rock the water expands to find its way up through a fault or crack to the surface. It makes an unusual sight.

MALHEUR CITY

TOWN PROPER

Malheur City is located eleven miles north of Ironside off US 26. Here you will find some old primitive living quarters and a cemetery left behind from gold rush days. This area provided a lot of excitement in the late 1860's when prospectors were having a heyday searching for the gold which proved so plentiful around here.

NORTH POWDER

ANTHONY LAKE RECREATION AREA

This recreation area is approximately twenty miles west of North Powder. Besides being a well known winter sport area it offers several delightful picnic sites. Stop by the Anthony Lakes Forest Service station for information on land use. Ask for their descriptive brochure on the interpretive trail that runs between Anthony and Hoffer Lakes. It is full of information on how glaciers affected the land. Another area trail leads to the summits of several mountain peaks which offer panoramic views of the Elkhorn and Wallowa Mountains as well as the Powder River Valley.

ELKHORN CREST TRAIL

This 25 mile route is a strenuous day's hike for even the most experienced hiker. Many choose to camp midway at Twin Lakes beneath 9000' mountain peaks. You can pick up the trail at Anthony Pass, above the lake, and take it all the way to Marble Creek Pass, west of Baker. On a clear day you will be treated to views of the Seven Devil's Mountains, Cornucopias, Lookout Mountain and Squaw Butte as well as the Cascades. You can obtain information on this hike from the staff at the Forest Service office in Baker.

WOLF CREEK RESERVOIR

Just barely out of North Powder is the Wolf Creek Reservoir. It provides a lovely place to picnic and enjoy the water.

ONTARIO

LAKE OWYHEE

This is Oregon's largest lake. It is 53 miles long and offers 310 miles of shoreline within the heart of the Owyhee Mountains. The scenery is specatacular with rainbow colored cliffs towering along the water's edge.

OBON FESTIVALL

Each year the Idaho-Oregon Buddhist Temple holds their Obon Festival in Ontario. It happens in July and includes a Sanctuary Open House along with other festivities. It provides an opportunity to view Japanese displays and become acquainted with the Buddhist religion. This, the Obon Festival, is a festival of joy. The Ontario Chamber of Commerce can supply the date.

ROCKHOUNDING

The area surrounding **Ontario** offers thunder eggs, jaspers, petrified woods, black dendrites, green moss agates and golden plume agates. Succor Creek, Rockville and Adrian are all good areas.

SAWTOOTH VOLCANO

The Sawtooth Volcano is considered a unique phenomenon for this part of Oregon. It was created 15 million years ago but spread out over a low profile rather than rising into a cone. It covers more than 20,000 acres. The crater is about 5,000' wide with a rim of 19,000' extending from 100-400' above the volcano floor. In the center is a cone about 400' high. You can drive right into the Sawtooth Crater. The area provides some nice hiking trails.

SUMPTER MINING DISTRICT

AUSTIN

The town of Austin established their post office in 1888. Today only a few of the old buildings remain. The town got its name from two early settlers who operated a small store and hotel here.

BONANZA

Bonanza is marked by some decayed buildings and defunct hardrock mines. To reach it, take County Road 1030 off State 7, southwest of Sumpter.

BOURNE

Bourne lies seven miles off State 7. It was originally named Cracker in the 1870's. A flash flood in 1937 wiped out most of the older buildings, but a few remain on higher ground along with some of the old equipment and mines. This was one of the major gold producing centers at one time. The burned hulk of #2 dredge lies a half mile north of the junction of State 7 and Cracker Creek Road. Bourne is also the site of what was one of the longest continuous gold veins in the world.

ELKHORN MOUNTAIN OVERLOOK

Northwest of Sumpter, along State 7, is the Elkhorn Mountain Overlook. It provides a view of the Elkhorns and the upper Sumpter Valley. This mountain range is the result of volcanic eruptions, glacier and stream erosion.

The Granite Mountain Summit, less than 1½ miles from here, provides a view from 5,864'. Past this spot you can see the remains of what was once a stop, during gold mining days, for horse drawn stages that ran between Sumpter and Granite. It is known as the Gold Center Village. Walk a few hundred feet up the canyon for a first hand view. This dense stand of lodgepole pine has grown back, for the early miners burned off the forest to make prospecting easier.

There are many trails for hiking, biking, 4-wheeling and horseback riding in the Sumpter Valley area. Most are on land regulated by the U.S. Forest Service.

GRANITE

Granite was founded in the late 1860's and known as Independence. The name was changed about 1878. Reminders of the olden days include a schoolhouse, market, drug store, nickelodeon and cemetery. The Red Boy Mine, located between Granite and Olive Lake was one of the largest producing gold mines in the country during the early 1900's. At Olive Lake you can enjoy picnic facilities, drinking water, wood stoves and restrooms courtesy of the U.S. Forest Service.

The population here was once nearly 5,000. It's not totally uninhabited today and some of the old mines are currently being worked. Deteriorated buildings line main street where once a drugstore, freight office and Mercantile generated business. Later the Mercantile building became a combination saloon, boardinghouse, community hall with a dance floor occupying the entire upper level.

North of Granite you can see rock walls in the stream bottom. These were made by the Chinese miners as they moved the larger boulders so they could work up the finer gravel and sand underneath. This was approximately 100 years ago.

GREENHORN

At Greenhorn you can see the remains of the old jail and a few early cabins. The town was established in the

1890's although miners were here before that time. The population once reached 500 with nearly 2000 miners in the surrounding countryside.

Another small town, Robinsonville, stood nearby. It was a typical gold rush town with 26 saloons. Fire swept through town at the end of the 19th century leaving little behind.

Many mines once dotted the area. At the Lazy Man Mine the miner actually built his cabin directly over the mine shaft.

SUMPTER

Sumpter was settled during Civil War days and at one time had three newspapers, a school system, an opera house, stores and 15 saloons and brothels. The town's population was more than 3,000 in 1896, however a fire destroyed most of the buildings in 1917.

On the east edge of town you can see the remains of an old dredge that once ripped open the earth and pulled out over $15 million in gold. It once floated on its own lake and dug out the Sumpter Valley floor to a depth of 20'. There is a charge to tour the museum.

WHITNEY

Not much remains of Whitney although a few of its buildings still reflect its days as the primary station on the narrow gauge Sumpter Valley Railroad. A vivid imagination might easily conjure up ghosts of Wells-Fargo drivers, Japanese track layers, miners and lumbermen strolling about. The town was almost totally deserted in 1918 when the sawmill located here burned. Remains of the mill can be seen at the log pond.

UNION

BUFFALO BLUFF

Just one mile southeast of Union is a sheer cliff known as Buffalo Bluff. This interesting site got its name because area Indians often drove the wild buffalo across its edge, butchering them on the valley floor below. It also provides a view of the surrounding area.

CATHERINE CREEK

Catherine Creek offers 20 miles of good stream fishing. A state park is located 8 miles southeast of Union along State 203 to provide public access. Nearly 60 picnic tables, drinking water, wood stoves and public restrooms make it a convenient stop. Ice caves can be found in the nearby rock hillside.

HISTORICAL BUILDINGS

The town of Union has some delightful Victorian homes and buildings. They are privately owned and not open to the public but a walking tour will allow you to view them from the outside.

Miller House (1882)
101 East Bryan
The home is Gothic with trim inspired by designs from the Italian Renaissance Revival period. The Octagonal west tower and front porch were later additions. This is perhaps the grandest old home still standing in the Grande Ronde Valley. The interior has been restored to an almost original state.

Wright House (1882)
429 North Bellwood
This large Italianate Villa originally had two small porches. The present verandas were built about 1890. Note the original water tower and gazebo. The interior includes an imported marble fireplace and silver door handles.

Townley House (1894)
782 North 5th

This Queen Anne style home has a large stained glass window in the stairwell and huge Tudor chimneys.

Rustic House (1882)
612 South Main

This simple cottage sports some beautiful trim. The gable trim is Gothic while the one on the window casings is Rustic in style. The porch was added during the 1890's.

Octagonal Tower (1873)
475 North Main

This is another simple cottage. It is known for its ornate tower and porches of Renaissance style.

Cemetery (established in 1875)
East Fulton Street — at end of road.

This classic Victorian cemetery has many ornate head stones. The small tool shed is still in use. Note the pyramid roof and wide eaves. Notable stones include one sculptured from marble and shipped here from Italy and a monument to two men killed by the Indians in 1878 during the Bannock Indian uprising. The oldest section is located in the northest part with the earliest marker dated 1863. Here you will also find the grave of Kelsey Porter. He was the only man ever hung in Union County.

Old Jail
Union High School

The old Union jail currently houses the heating plant for Union High School. It is located on the northwest corner of the campus.

Sacred Heart Catholic Church (1873)
South Main

This church was originally built by the Methodists and used as their service building. In 1904 it was sold to the Catholic Church.

PONDOSA

Pondosa is located twenty miles south of Union. Here you will find the ruins of the mill which was an important part of this one time logging town.

UNION COUNTY MUSEUM

The Union County Museum has a collection which includes hundred year old quilts, jackplanes, oral history transcriptions, photographs and many other items ranging from farm equipment to Chinese artifacts. It also features a completely furnished Victorian room. The museum is open from May 15 through October 15 from 1:00 p.m. to 5:00 p.m., Thursday through Monday.

While there, ask for the brochure outlining a mini-tour of historical sites in the Grande Ronde Area.

UNITY

SOUTH FORK RECREATION AREA

The South Fork area is located seven miles west of Unity, off US 26. Here you will find a few good picnic sites, wood stoves and restrooms along the water.

UNITY LAKE STATE PARK

This state park is five miles north of Unity on Unity Reservoir. Facilities include picnic tables, drinking water, restrooms and a boat launch. This is a great area for water sports. There are some unique rock formations located around here.

VALE

BULLY CREEK RESERVOIR

The Bully Creek Reservoir is located eight miles northwest of Vale. This is a great water sports area and offers picnic facilities and a boat launch.

CENTRAL VALE DISTRICT

The Central Vale District is located in the southeastern corner of Oregon. It is managed by the Bureau of Land Management and includes picturesque stretches of the Owyhee River, volcanic formations in Leslie Gulch, Succor Creek and miles of rolling rangeland. A map listing recreational sites, hiking trails and other features can be obtained at the BLM's Vale office.

OREGON TRAIL

On Lytle Boulevard, six miles south of Vale, you will find a tribute to the pioneers of the famous Oregon Trail. Built in 1976, it marks the old wagon tracks with an interpretive historical display.

ROCKHOUNDING

Some of the better known areas around Vale include the following:

Hope Butte — cinnabar and petrified wood.

Jamieson Bog — agate with limbs embedded in it. Take US 26 to Jamieson then head northeast.

Juntura — agates containing dendrites. Take US 20 to Juntura then head south for about 8 miles.

Red Beds — apache tears. South of Harper, off US 20, 25 miles on Crowley Road to the gravel pit.

Graveyard Point — plume agate, yellow-red and blue. Located south of Homedale off US 95.

Obsidian — silver, gold sheen, rainbow and double flow. Take US 20 west to milepost 76 then turn south for 3 miles.

IMPORTANT ADDRESSES

Albany Convention & Visitors
Commission
435 W. First Avenue
Albany, Oregon 97321

Ashland Visitors & Convention
Bureau
110 E. Main
Ashland, Oregon 97520

Astoria Area Chamber of
Commerce
Port of Astoria Building
Astoria, Oregon 97103

Athena Chamber of Commerce
Athena, Oregon 97813

Baker County Chamber of
Commerce
490 Campbell Street
Baker, Oregon 97814

Bandon Chamber of Commerce
350 S. 2nd Street
Bandon, Oregon 97411

Beaverton Chamber of Commerce
12055 SW 1st
Beaverton, Oregon 97005

Bend Visitors & Convention
Bureau
164 NW Hawthorne Avenue
Bend, Oregon 97701

Brookings-Harbor Chamber of
Commerce
P.O. Box 940
Brookings, Oregon 97415

Bureau of Land Management
900 NE Multnomah
Portland, Oregon 97208

Bureau of Land Management
74 South Alvord Street
Burns, Oregon 97720

Bureau of Land Management
365 A Street West
Vale, Oregon 97918

Canby Chamber of Commerce
232 NW 2nd
Canby, Oregon 97013

Cannon Beach Chamber of Commerce
201 East Second Street
Cannon Beach, Oregon 97110

Cave Junction Chamber of Commerce
P.O. Box 312
Cave Junction, Oregon 97523

Central Oregon Recreation
Association
P.O. Box 230
Bend, Oregon 97709

Clatskanie Chamber of Commerce
95 S. Nehalem
Clatskanie, Oregon 97016

Coos Bay Chamber of Commerce
P.O. Box 210
Coos Bay, Oregon 97420

Coquille Chamber of Commerce
119 N. Birch Street
Coquille, Oregon 97423

Corvallis Convention &
Visitors Bureau
350 SW Jefferson
Corvallis, Oregon 97333

Cottage Grove Chamber
of Commerce
P.O. Box 587
Cottage Grove, Oregon 97424

Dallas Chamber of Commerce
P.O. Box 377
Dallas, Oregon 97338

Depoe Bay Chamber of
Commerce
P.O. Box 21
Depoe Bay, Oregon 97341

Deschutes National Forest
211 NE Revere Street
Bend, Oregon 97701

Detroit Chamber of Commerce
150 Detroit Avenue
Detroit, Oregon 97342

Eugene-Springfield Convention
& Visitors Bureau
305 W. 7th
Eugene, Oregon 97401

Estacada Chamber of Commerce
P.O. Box 296
Estacada, Oregon 97023

Florence Chamber of Commerce
P.O. Box 712
Florence, Oregon 97439

Forest Grove Chamber of
Commerce
2417 Pacific Avenue
Forest Grove, Oregon 97116

Fremont National Forest
34 North D Street
Lakeview, Oregon 97630

Gold Beach Chamber of
Commerce
P.O. Box 55
Gold Beach, Oregon 97444

Grant County Chamber of
Commerce
710 S. Canyon Blvd.
John Day, Oregon 97845

Grants Pass Visitors &
Convention Bureau
P.O. Box 970
Grants Pass, Oregon 97526

Gresham Chamber of Commerce
P.O. Box 696
Gresham, Oregon 97030

Harney County Chamber of
Commerce
18 West "D" Street
Burns, Oregon 97720

Hermiston Chamber of Commerce
540 S. US Highway 395
Hermiston, Oregon 97838

Hillsboro Chamber of Commerce
334 SE 5th Avenue — Suite A
Hillsboro, Oregon 97123

Hood River Chamber of
Commerce
Port Marina Park
Hood River, Oregon 97031

Jacksonville Chamber of
Commerce
185 N. Oregon Street
Jacksonville, Oregon 97530

Joseph Chamber of Commerce
P.O. Box 13
Joseph, Oregon 97846

Junction City Chamber of
Commerce
516 Greenwood Street
Junction City, Oregon 97448

Klamath Falls Chamber of
Commerce
125 N. Eighth Street
Klamath Falls, Oregon 97601

La Grande Chamber of Commerce
101 Depot Street
La Grande, Oregon 97850

Lake County Chamber of
Commerce
Lakeview Court House
Lakeview, Oregon 97630

Lake Oswego Chamber of
Commerce
500 SW Fourth Street
Lake Oswego, Oregon 97034

Lebanon Chamber of Commerce
1040 Park Street
Lebanon, Oregon 97355

Lincoln City Chamber of
Commerce
3939 NW US Highway 101
Lincoln City, Oregon 97367

Lowell Chamber of Commerce
107 E. Third
Lowell, Oregon 97452

Lower Umpqua Chamber of
Commerce
P.O. Box 11
Reedsport, Oregon 97467

Madras-Jefferson County
Chamber of Commerce
P.O. Box 770
Madras, Oregon 97441

Malheur National Forest
139 NE Dayton Street
John Day, Oregon 97845

McMinnville Chamber of Commerce
417 N. Adams
McMinnville, Oregon 97128

Medford Chamber of Commerce
304 S. Central
Medford, Oregon 97501

Mehama Chamber of Commerce
P.O. Box 995
Mehama, Oregon 97384

Milton-Freewater Chamber
of Commerce
P.O. Box 49
Milton-Freewater, Oregon 97862

Monmouth/Independence
Chamber of Commerce
189 S. Pacific
Monmouth, Oregon 97361

Mount Angel Chamber
of Commerce
345 N. Main Street
Mount Angel, Oregon 97362

Mt. Hood National Forest
19559 SE Division
Gresham, Oregon 97030

Mt. Hood Recreation Association
Zig Zag, Oregon 97073

Myrtle Point Chamber of
Commerce
212 Spruce Street
Myrtle Point, Oregon 97458

Newberg Chamber of Commerce
809 E. First
Newberg, Oregon 97132

Newport Chamber of Commerce
555 SW Coast Highway
Newport, Oregon 97365

North Clackamas County
Chamber of Commerce
15010 SW McLoughlin Blvd.
Milwaukie, Oregon 97222

Nyssa Chamber of Commerce
507 Main Street
Nyssa, Oregon 97913

Ochoco National Forest
Federal Building
Prineville, Oregon 97754

Ontario Chamber of Commerce
173 SW 1st Street
Ontario, Oregon 97914

Oregon Tri-City Chamber of
Commerce
719 Center
Oregon City, Oregon 97045

Oregon Coast Association
P.O. Box 670
Newport, Oregon 97365

Oregon Department of Fish
& Wildlife
506 SW Mill Street
Portland, Oregon 97208

Oregon Economic Development
Department
Tourism Division
595 Cottage St., NE
Salem, Oregon 97310

Pendleton Chamber of
Commerce
25 Dorion
Pendleton, Oregon 97801

Philomath Chamber of Commerce
1604 Main Street
Philomath, Oregon 97370

Port Orford Chamber of
Commerce
P.O. Box 637
Port Orford, Oregon 97465

Portland Convention &
Visitors Association
26 SW Salmon
Portland, Oregon 97204

Portland Parks and Recreation
1107 SW 4th Avenue
Portland, Oregon 97204

Prineville Chamber of
Commerce
390 N. Fairview
Prineville, Oregon 97754

Redmond Chamber of Commerce
427 SW 7th
Redmond, Oregon 97756

Rogue River National Forest
333 W. 8th Street
Medford, Oregon 97501

Roseburg Chamber of Commerce
410 SE Spruce Street
Roseburg, Oregon 97470

St. Helens Chamber of
Commerce
174 S. Columbia River Highway
St. Helens, Oregon 97051

Salem Area Convention
& Visitors Bureau
220 Cottage Street NE
Salem, Oregon 97308

Sandy Chamber of Commerce
P.O. Box 536
Sandy, Oregon 97055

Scappoose Chamber of
Commerce
P.O. Box 605
Scappoose, Oregon 97056

Seaside Chamber of Commerce
7 North Roosevelt
Seaside, Oregon 97138

Silverton Chamber of Commerce
216 Oak Street
Silverton, Oregon 97381

Siskiyou National Forest
1504 NW Sixth Street
Grants Pass, Oregon 97526

Sisters Chamber of Commerce
P.O. Box 476
Sisters, Oregon 97759

Siuslaw National Forest
545 SW 2nd
Corvallis, Oregon 97330

Springfield Chamber of
Commerce
223-H North A Street
Springfield, Oregon 97477

Sweet Home Chamber
of Commerce
1218 Main Street
Sweet Home, Oregon 97386

The Dalles Chamber of Commerce
404 W. Second Street
P.O. Box 460
The Dalles, Oregon 97058

Tillamook Chamber of Commerce
3705 Highway 101 North
Tillamook, Oregon 97141

Toledo Chamber of Commerce
311 NE 1st Street
Toledo, Oregon 97391

Umatilla National Forest
2517 SW Hailey Avenue
Pendleton, Oregon 97801

Umpqua National Forest
2900 NW Steward Parkway
Roseburg, Oregon 97470

Union Chamber of Commerce
P.O. Box 400
Union, Oregon 97883

Waldport Chamber of Commerce
P.O. Box 419
Waldport, Oregon 97394

Wallowa County Chamber
of Commerce
P.O. Box 427
Enterprise, Oregon 97828

Wallowa-Whitman National
Forest
Federal Office Building
Baker, Oregon 97814

Wemme Chamber of Commerce
P.O. Box 158
Wemme, Oregon 97067

Willamette National Forest
211 East Seventh Avenue
Eugene, Oregon 97401

Wilsonville Chamber of
Commerce
P.O. Box 111
Wilsonville, Oregon 97070

Winema National Forest
Post Office Building
Klamath Falls, Oregon 97601

Winston Chamber of Commerce
P.O. Box 68
Winston, Oregon 97496

Woodburn Chamber of Commerce
230 W. Hayes
Woodburn, Oregon 97071

Yachats Chamber of Commerce
P.O. Box 174
Yachats, Oregon 97498

INDEX

G

H

342

M

N

O

XYZ

Please send me the following books —

_____ copies of WASHINGTON FREE @ $9.95 each

_____ copies of OREGON FREE @ $9.95 each

_____ copies of FREE CAMPGROUNDS OF WASHINGTON &
OREGON @ $5.95 each

I have enclosed a check for $ _____. (Please add $1.00 per book
to cover shipping costs.)

If VISA/MasterCard include:

Card # _____ Exp. Date _____

Signature _____

Name _____

Address _____

City/State/Zip _____

Send this order form to: Ki² Enterprises
P.O. Box 13322
Portland, Oregon 97213

Please send me the following books —

_____ copies of WASHINGTON FREE @ $9.95 each

_____ copies of OREGON FREE @ $9.95 each

_____ copies of FREE CAMPGROUNDS OF WASHINGTON &
OREGON @ $5.95 each

I have enclosed a check for $ _____. (Please add $1.00 per book
to cover shipping costs.)

If VISA/MasterCard include:

Card # _____ Exp. Date _____

Signature _____

Name _____

Address _____

City/State/Zip _____

Send this order form to: Ki² Enterprises
P.O. Box 13322
Portland, Oregon 97213

Please send me the following books —

_____ copies of WASHINGTON FREE @ $9.95 each

_____ copies of OREGON FREE @ $9.95 each

_____ copies of FREE CAMPGROUNDS OF WASHINGTON &
        OREGON @ $5.95 each

I have enclosed a check for $ _____. (Please add $1.00 per book
to cover shipping costs.)

If VISA/MasterCard include:

Card # _____ Exp. Date _____

Signature _____

Name _____

Address _____

City/State/Zip _____

Send this order form to: Ki² Enterprises
              P.O. Box 13322
              Portland, Oregon 97213

- -

Please send me the following books —

_____ copies of WASHINGTON FREE @ $9.95 each

_____ copies of OREGON FREE @ $9.95 each

_____ copies of FREE CAMPGROUNDS OF WASHINGTON &
        OREGON @ $5.95 each

I have enclosed a check for $ _____. (Please add $1.00 per book
to cover shipping costs.)

If VISA/MasterCard include:

Card # _____ Exp. Date _____

Signature _____

Name _____

Address _____

City/State/Zip _____

Send this order form to: Ki² Enterprises
              P.O. Box 13322
              Portland, Oregon 97213